Contents

CW00740893

Unitarian Women
A Legacy of Dissent

Edited by Ann Peart

The Lindsey Press
London

Published by the Lindsey Press
on behalf of the General Assembly of Unitarian
and Free Christian Churches
Essex Hall, 1–6 Essex Street, London WC2R 3HY, UK

© General Assembly of Unitarian and Free Christian Churches 2019

ISBN 978-0-85319-092-9

Designed and typeset by Garth Stewart, London

Preface

My interest in the history of Unitarian women began long before this book was envisaged. For some years I have seen it as my 'calling' to work towards redressing the gender imbalance and injustice that are evident in most studies of Unitarianism, especially in works on its history. The late Revd Dr Len Smith (Principal of Unitarian College Manchester) and the Revd Dr Peter Godfrey encouraged me to begin a PhD on Unitarian women, which I eventually completed in 2006. I am particularly grateful to Dr Ruth Watts for her early encouragement of my interest in the subject, and for her many writings in which she made explicit the connections between Unitarian thought, its potential for gender equality, and the importance of education in bringing about greater gender justice. This book has been informed by those insights.

I thank the Lindsey Press Panel of the General Assembly of Unitarian and Free Christian Churches for inviting me to produce the book. It is designed both for Unitarians (and those interested in Unitarian history) and for others with a concern for women's and feminist studies and history. I hope that it will become a resource for a variety of users.

I am grateful to those who have contributed chapters on specific women or topics: Andrew Hill on Catharine Cappe and Hannah Lindsey; Alan Ruston for his chapters on Helen Allingham and Dorothy Tarrant, and for his contributions to the chapters about the Langham Place Group, about women in Unitarian administration, and about the Unitarian Women's League; Derek McAuley on Unitarian women in Ireland, and Rory Castle Jones on Unitarian women in Wales. In addition, Alan has given me long-term support and encouragement, and Andrew was a very supportive sounding board and consultant on historical matters. David Dawson has been extremely helpful in abridging two of Alan's articles and giving general encouragement. Susan Killoran, the Librarian of Harris Manchester College, Oxford, has responded remarkably promptly to my frequent requests for scans of obituaries from the Unitarian journals. Above all, I thank Catherine Robinson for the enormous amount of work involved in copy editing, proof reading, and preparing the volume for the press.

After my initial appeal for information many people offered ideas, and for these I am grateful; if all the suggestions had been taken up, at least one more volume would be needed. It would be good if other women took up the challenge to discover and write about the rich heritage of Unitarian women's stories.

Ann Peart
Manchester, January 2019

Introduction
Ann Peart

As in most other denominations, there are usually more women than men in Unitarian congregations; yet the story of the movement is often told through men's experiences and writing. We know little of the thoughts, beliefs, and experiences of women Unitarians before the twenty-first century. For most of the time that Unitarianism has existed as a movement in the UK and Ireland, women's experiences of social situation, expectations, education, employment, and so on have differed from those of men, and so they have experienced the world, including their religion, from a different perspective. This book is an attempt to explore the ways in which Unitarian women have experienced their faith, and how it has influenced them in their activities in the wider world.

The women portrayed here are not necessarily typical of many in Unitarian congregations. Our brief from the Lindsey Press Panel was to write about Unitarian women who made a difference to their world. This means that to qualify for inclusion the women for the most part have had to be pioneers, to push boundaries, and go beyond what most women did. Therefore by definition they stand out from the majority of women in Unitarian congregations.

If anyone is in doubt about the maleness of the image of Unitarianism presented by our historians, a glance at the indexes of any standard text, such as works by Len Smith and Earl Morse Wilbur, will show that Unitarian women are almost entirely absent from them. The compilation of works by Alan Ruston, *On the Side of Liberty: A Unitarian Historical Miscellany*, published by the Lindsey Press in 2016, still gives an overwhelmingly male picture. However, Alan has written several chapters for this book (and has indeed produced other work on Unitarian women).

The male bias in our history creates a partial and limited picture. For example, those literate men who dominate our history were usually educated in academic theology and biblical studies, and they generally felt it necessary to define, promote, and develop Unitarianism primarily as a system of belief.

Women, on the other hand, have until comparatively recently been excluded from formal theological education and have generally shown less interest in the niceties of doctrine. Instead, they have been much more interested in praxis – the action element of the reflection/action process – and in religious practices and communities. The way in which allegiance to a Unitarian community had an impact on everyday life and social relations often differed according to gender. For example, it has been noted by feminist historians that, in particular for middle-class women, church-related activities provided one of the few ways in which it was acceptable to exert an agency that transcended the public/private division in Victorian society. The roles that women were able to play within Unitarian communities were historically very different from those taken by men. The ministers, committee members, officers, and decision makers were male, while women taught the children, visited the sick, and made the tea. This gave women a different perspective on their faith, and on their opportunities to make a public impact.

One of the dilemmas in planning this book was having to decide whom to include and whom to exclude. There are generally two distinct understandings of what it means to be a Unitarian. One is based on belief, traditionally in God as unity rather than God as trinity, but more importantly on the duty of individuals to think for themselves and trust their own conscience, and a belief in the inherent worth of every human being. The second concept is based on community, and a consideration that belonging to a congregation (or other Unitarian group) is the most important criterion. Never at any point in their history have the Unitarian communities in the UK and Ireland consisted only of people with strictly Unitarian beliefs. Conversely there are people who have had Unitarian beliefs but did not join any Unitarian community. I have opted for the community definition, and so I have included, for example, **Frances Power Cobbe**, who defined herself theologically as a Theist rather than as a Unitarian, but was a member of several congregations and very active in Unitarian circles. I have omitted Jane Marcet and Mary Somerville, who had views compatible with Unitarianism but do not seem to have belonged to a congregation.

There are also historical complications when trying to define Unitarians. A considerable number of congregations now identifying themselves as Unitarian date from the 1662 expulsions of clergy following the reform of the Church of England, so were founded before Unitarian theology was developed in the UK. Until 1813 it was illegal to deny the Christian doctrine of the Trinity, so the term 'Unitarian' was not often used. The congregations that became Unitarian were often called independent, or Presbyterian, or may have been linked to another denomination. I have therefore included **Anna Laetitia Barbauld**, a rational dissenter of the eighteenth century, whose theology was Arian rather than Unitarian, because she was extremely important both in her own day and for the later development of the Unitarian movement. A further complication arises from the fact that Unitarianism was extremely unpopular at various times in its history, including being associated with sedition in the 1790s and considered heretical for much of its existence. So sometimes Unitarians kept quiet about their affiliation or belief, in order to achieve their goals or gain social acceptance. **Elizabeth Reid** did not use the word 'Unitarian' when founding Bedford College, and **Margaret Gillies** kept her Unitarianism hidden in order to gain acceptance as an artist.

It is sometimes very difficult to identify particular Unitarian women. Friendship networks extended beyond sectarian boundaries, and this sometimes blurs the distinction of who counts as a Unitarian. I have included some women who did not call themselves Unitarian, or who rejected their family upbringing as Unitarian, but who had sufficient connections with the movement and influence on it to have played a significant role in the story of Unitarian women. **Mary Wollstonecraft**, **Harriet Martineau**, **Barbara Leigh Smith Bodichon**, and **Bessie Rayner Parkes** fall into this category. I hope that a picture of Unitarians emerges that is different from that presented in traditional history books: a picture grounded in interaction with everyday people, rather than with theological or theoretical ideas. One thing that stands out is the importance of the Unitarian beliefs that no one is damned and that everyone can be helped to achieve a better life and overcome adversity, especially through education.

It must be emphasised that this book does not attempt to be a history of Unitarian women – that would be a much larger and more systematic work. Rather, by telling the stories of some women representative of different times and spheres of interest, giving an idea of their achievements, I and my fellow contributors have tried to show how their faith context related to their public actions. Many more women would have fitted these criteria but have had to be omitted because of limitations of space: **Mary Dendy**, who worked with children with special needs ... **Lady Byron**, who helped the social reformer **Mary Carpenter** ... **Anna Swanwick**, the classical scholar ... **Mary Ann Evans**, better known as George Eliot the novelist ... **Margaret Gaskell** (daughter of Elizabeth), active in philanthropic, educational, and cultural concerns ... **Helen Watts**, the suffragette ... **Kitty Wilkinson** of Liverpool, active in the field of public health ... and **Beatrix Potter**, the creator of Peter Rabbit, are among those who could have been included, together with a larger selection of women ministers.

The book is divided into five parts and is arranged in an approximately chronological order, except for Part Five, which is geographically based. It begins with the rational dissenters of the eighteenth century and ends about 1970, beyond which it is difficult to have a sense of perspective. Each part has an introduction written by me, giving the background and context, followed by chapters on individual women or groups of women. Friendships and networks of family ties or other links have always been important to women. It is rarely possible to explore these in retrospect, but in contrast to the rest of the book the chapter by Andrew Hill offers one such example.

PART ONE
'Double Dissenters'

Introduction to Part One
Ann Peart

It was during the second half of the eighteenth century that the Unitarian movement began to form in Britain. Its main characteristic was an insistence on applying reason to the interpretation of the Christian faith, and on pressing for 'civil and religious liberty' so that the dictates of reason could be applied. There was a considerable variety of beliefs about Jesus. Some leading figures, like Joseph Priestley and Theophilus Lindsey, who considered that Jesus was essentially human, identified their theology as Unitarian; others, such as Richard Price, who still thought of Jesus as in some sense divine, though with a lesser status than God the Father, were often called Arians. The term that described them all was 'rational dissenters'.[1]

Through much of the eighteenth century there was increasing toleration of religious dissenters, and a broadening of beliefs and practices within the Church of England. Attempts to obtain the repeal of the Test and Corporation Acts, which barred dissenters from entering certain professions and limited their civil rights, gained increasing support until the 1790s. However, reaction to the violence associated with the French Revolution, whose ideals the rational dissenters supported, generated suspicion of anyone who regularly drank toasts 'to civil and religious liberty'. Twice the Habeas Corpus Act was suspended. In 1795 the Treason Act was strengthened to include challenging the authority of the King in speech or in writing, and in the same year the Seditious Meetings Act was passed.[2] All these created a climate of repression and fear among dissenters, and several, including Gilbert Wakefield and Joseph Johnson the publisher, were imprisoned, while some Scottish men (including the Unitarian Thomas Fyshe Palmer) were transported to Australia. Although this political climate affected dissenting women only indirectly, it had all sorts of impacts on their lives. Anna Laetitia Barbauld, for example, went beyond the bounds of what was then socially acceptable in order to defend civil and religious liberties in her writings, and incurred some disapproval in doing so.[3] Gilbert Wakefield's daughter Anne went to live with Unitarian friends while her father was in prison, and in Lancashire she renewed her acquaintance with Anna Laetitia's adopted son and nephew, Charles, developing a friendship which resulted in their marriage.[4] Other social causes involved women more directly; for example, in support of the campaign against the slave trade some households, including that of the young Lucy Aikin, gave up using sugar from American slave plantations.[5]

Those late-eighteenth-century women whose public writings and actions became well known have been described by scholars such as Marlon Ross and William Keach as 'double dissenters'.[6] Originally this description referred to the fact that women were denied their civil rights twice over: once as dissenters, and again as women; but it can also be applied more broadly. Not only did they, usually with their families, dissent from the Established Church of England: they also dissented from the prevailing cultural restrictions on what respectable middle-class ladies might do or write. The experience of exclusion from formal education and from public and political platforms led to their marginalisation, and what has more recently been described by many feminist writers as the 'epistemological privilege (or preference)' of knowing not only the men's acknowledged public language, but also women's domestic lives and language – an area of which men were generally ignorant. So women who had both a public presence and a domestic life had a greater range of experience on which to draw.[7] This is not to say that men did not have domestic, private lives, but their experience of their households did not include many of the details that only women shared.

Although they were denied public agency, women played significant roles in the developing Unitarian movement. In the following chapters of Part One, Anna Laetitia Barbauld, Catharine Cappe, and Hannah Lindsey are given particular prominence, and a further chapter concerns Mary Wollstonecraft, Mary Hays, and Lucy Aikin. Andrew Hill's chapter on Cappe and Lindsey gives a rare insight into the development of their personal relationship. Usually it is not possible to explore such a friendship in detail, but this chapter enables us to observe the support that the two women gave each other for their more public works, details of which can be found in other publications. The other chapters can only hint at the friendships that enhanced the lives of women activists.

All of these individuals were part of significant networks of rational dissenting women (and men). Each one made an important contribution to Unitarianism, and most of them influenced broader society too. **Anna Laetitia Barbauld** was well known as a poet in her day; she also pioneered new techniques for teaching reading to young children, and for developing a liberal school curriculum. She wrote material for the education of young women and families, and contributed to the public expression of rational dissent on freedom and religion, as well as introducing a more holistic element into Unitarian thought. **Catharine Cappe** contributed to Unitarian thought and the defence of the new movement, at first as an interpreter and developer of her late husband's works, and later as an established author in her own right. Her situation in York allowed her considerable influence on Manchester College (for whose students 'no test, or confesssion of faith' was required) and its many visitors while it was based there from 1803. In York generally she mixed with women from other denominations to lead the reform of several charities and schools. Her writings led to her recognition nationally as a Unitarian philanthropist, writer, and advocate of women's involvement in public life.[8] **Hannah Lindsey** is just beginning to be recognised as an essential member of the team who enabled the first avowedly Unitarian congregation in England to become established. Her drive, her organising skills, and her fundraising work were essential not solely for that one congregation, but for the development of a national network of Unitarians, for which Essex Street Chapel in London was often the communications hub.[9] Without her work, many Unitarian publications would not have appeared, and important documents would have been lost.

Mary Wollstonecraft was never a Unitarian, but she was helped and profoundly influenced by the rational dissenting congregation of Newington Green and its minister, Richard Price. In return, her feminist writings influenced generations of British liberals, including many Unitarians. **Mary Hays** found her way from more orthodox dissent into Unitarianism, and she was a member of the Essex Street Chapel congregation during the time of Hannah Lindsey. She was able to take advantage of the liberal atmosphere within rational dissent to begin publishing her views, and she went on to enlarge the possibilities for life writing and history from women's experience. **Lucy Aikin**, Barbauld's niece, also became a historian and pioneered what might be called social history, investigating the daily lives of real people. She was also a formidable exponent of British Unitarianism, as her correspondence with the American William Ellery Channing reveals. Her long life provides a link from the early stages of Unitarianism in England to the mid-nineteenth century, when it grew significantly.

None of these women wrote in isolation. They each had a large network of women friends, and of Unitarian connections of both sexes. Perhaps because they were denied public roles, their friendship groups were particularly important in helping them to find more public ways of acting, and to sustain them in their work. The three main subjects in Part One of this book all knew each other. Andrew Hill reveals the long and close friendship of Catharine Cappe and Hannah Lindsey; Anna Laetitia Barbauld knew them both, having first met Cappe in 1774, and then Lindsey, whom she encountered in the same dissenting circles after they both moved to the London area. The only one of the three to be born into a rational dissenting family, Anna Laetitia (*née* Aikin), had links, either by blood ties or by marriage, to many of the leading dissenting families such as the Kinders, Kenricks, Belshams, Wakefields, and Wellbeloveds. During her lifetime she also developed friendships with the families of the boys who attended her school in East Anglia and of the girls and young women whom she tutored privately. Catharine Cappe was the centre of a network of women in York and beyond, including the Anglican Faith Grey, with whom she started a spinning school, reformed the Grey Coat School, and established a girls' friendly society. Naturally all this involved a great number of their friends, from a variety of denominations. Cappe's close friendship with Charles Wellbeloved, minister of St Saviourgate (Unitarian) Chapel and head of Manchester College, enabled her to support and influence the college in numerous ways. Her social gatherings were likened to a 'blue-stocking coterie' and attracted a wide range of visitors.[10] Hannah Lindsey's circle at Essex Street in London was more Unitarian in outlook. It included her half-sister **Jane**, who had married the future co-minister, John Disney; **Elizabeth Rayner**, who was a benefactor of both Essex Street Chapel and Joseph Priestley; **Elizabeth and Sophia Chambers**, who often provided hospitality for free thinkers; and **Ann Jebb**, who had supported her husband's work for university reform, writing under the pseudonym of Priscilla, and after his death in 1786 had remained an active Unitarian and social reformer.[11] More distant friends included **Mary Lee**, wife of the Member of Parliament John Lee, who was a chapel trustee, and the poet **Mary Scott**. One important network for early Unitarians was centred on the rational dissenting publisher, Joseph Johnson, who, as well as publishing their works, liked to entertain a variety of radical writers and thinkers.[12] His circle included Anna Laetitia Barbauld, Mary Wollstonecraft, and Mary Hays, among many others, and he published the early works of Lucy Aikin.

Even though women were denied access to formal education in dissenting academies, all the subjects of Part One had some access to the social life and informal education generated by the dissenting academies in Warrington, York, or London (Hackney), and so they developed connections and friendships with many ministers and their families.The importance of these networks in strengthening the new Unitarian community and supporting the women's work will become apparent during the course of the following three chapters.

Endnotes

1   Ann Peart, 'Forgotten Prophets: The Lives of Unitarian Women 1760–1904' (unpublished doctoral thesis, University of Newcastle, 2006), pp.29–32: https://theses.ncl.ac.uk/dspace/bitstream/10443/245/1/peart05.pdf.

2   Wikipedia, *Seditious Meetings Act 1795,* accessed 31 October 2018: https://en.wikipedia.org/wiki/Seditious_sMeetings_Act_1795.

3   Peart, op. cit., pp. 30–2.

4   Betsy Rodgers, *Georgian Chronicle: Mrs Barbauld and her Family* (London, Methuen & Co, 1958), p.165.

5   Ibid., p.112.

6   Marlon B. Ross, 'Configurations of feminine reform: the woman writer and the tradition of dissent', in *Revisioning Romanticism: British Women Writers 1776–1837*, edited by Carol Shiner Wilson and Joel Haefner (Philadelphia, University of Pennsylvania Press, 1994), pp.91–110; William Keach, 'Barbauld, romanticism and the survival of dissent' in *Romanticism and Gender* (Cambridge, D.S. Brewer, 1998), pp.44–61.

7   Liz Stanley and Sue Wise, *Breaking Out Again: Feminist Ontology and Epistemology* (London, Routledge, 1993), pp.188–9, 227–8.

8   Helen Plant, *Unitarianism, Philanthropy and Feminism in York, 1782–1821: The Career of Catharine Cappe* (York, Borthwick Institute of Historical Research, University of York, Borthwick Paper no 103, 2003); Camilla Leach and Joyce Goodman, 'Catharine Cappe (1744–1822), Unitarian education and women's lives', *Faith and Freedom* vol. 51 part 2, no 147, 1998, pp.117–28.

9   G.M. Ditchfield, 'Hannah Lindsey and her circle: the female element in early British Unitarianism', *Enlightenment and Dissent*, no. 26, 2010, pp.54–79.

10 Plant, op. cit., p.19.

11 Ditchfield, op. cit., pp.59–60; John Gascoigne, *Oxford Dictionary of National Biography*, 'Jebb, John (1736–1786)', www.oxforddnb.com, accessed June 2018.

12 Gerald P. Tyson, *Joseph Johnson: A Liberal Publisher* (Iowa City, University of Iowa Press, 1979).

1 Anna Laetitia Barbauld (1743–1825)

Ann Peart

'In the last quarter of the eighteenth century a shy, intellectual young woman from rural England became a famous British writer. The work she did during a forty-year career changed English speaking culture on both shores of the Atlantic; at her death in 1825 her name was predicted to last as long as the English language.'[1]

This is how William McCarthy introduces Anna Laetitia Barbauld in his authoritative biography (2008). Anna Laetitia is one of the four women named in *The English Presbyterians* by Gordon Bolam and others (one of the most comprehensive histories of British Unitarianism[2]), and she is said to have done more for women's rights than her better-known contemporary and acquaintance, Mary Wollstonecraft.[3] Anna Laetitia left sufficient written work to enable us to consider the way she put her rational dissenting faith into practice, and also to explore the strategies that she used to make her voice heard in an age when middle-class ladies did not preach, make public speeches, or even write about theology.

Born in 1743 at Kibworth Harcourt in Leicestershire, where her father, the Revd John Aikin, ran a small school for boys, Anna Laetitia (known as Nancy in the family) was denied the formal education given to boys and young men, but she picked up more knowledge than most young women, and was clearly very intelligent. Taught by her mother, Jane (*née* Jennings), she could read at the tender age of two, and she persuaded her father to teach her Greek and Latin. Throughout her time in the family home, pupils joined the family at meal times, and Anna Laetitia could share the educational discussions that took place. Her horizons expanded in 1758, when her father became a tutor at the dissenting academy in Warrington. Here she could join in the stimulating social life that included both pupils and tutors. She formed lifelong friendships with Joseph Priestley (one of the tutors) and his wife Mary (*née* Wilkinson), and she developed a circle of young women friends.[4] Lucy Aikin, Anna Laetitia's niece, described the atmosphere at Warrington in these words:

> *The most cordial intimacy subsisted among the tutors and their families, with whom the elder students associated on terms of easy and affectionate intercourse; and while the various branches of human knowledge occupied their graver hours, the moments of recreation were animated by sports of wit and ingenuity well adapted to nerve the wing of youthful genius.*[5]

Anna Laetitia looked back on those times as possibly the happiest in her long life. Surrounded by dissenters and lively-minded companions, she began to write poetry. Her first known poem, addressed to her brother John when he went off to medical school in Edinburgh in 1764, is lost, but her poem addressed to the Priestleys, lamenting their loss when they left Warrington in 1767, survives.[6] From the outset Anna Laetitia used poetry to express personal feelings of grief, friendship, and admiration, but she went beyond this to explore religious, theological, and political issues, often from a domestic starting point. One poem that later became popular was *The Mouse's Petition*, written when she was staying with the Priestleys in Leeds and found a mouse in a cage waiting to be used in an experiment on gases. Writing as the mouse, she questioned the killing of animals for scientific purposes, and made allusions to the struggle for civil liberty for humans too.[7]

Her first public venture was an appeal in verse (circulated privately) on behalf of the independence movement in Corsica. This was inspired by the dissenters' concern for civil liberties and was influenced by her reading of contemporary writers such as Francis Hutcheson and James Thompson; but what made it groundbreaking was that no woman had written such political polemic in blank verse before.[8] When her brother John returned to Warrington in 1771, he encouraged her to contribute six songs to a work on song writing which he published (anonymously). In the same year, 1772, William Enfield's collection of hymns included five by Anna Laetitia, again anonymously.[9] Her brother also encouraged her to publish a volume of poems under her own name. This was printed in Warrington in December 1772, but published in London by Joseph Johnson, a leading dissenter.

It was immediately a great success, with three more editions printed in 1773, followed by a further two in England and one in America. William McCarthy considers that by 1800 'Barbauld may well have been the most eminent living poet, male or female, in Britain'.[10] The book of poems was followed by a joint enterprise with John, a collection of essays on a variety of topics, which was also well received. However, their budding publishing business was interrupted by Anna's marriage and subsequent removal from Warrington. Her husband, six years her junior, was Rochemont Barbauld, a student at the Warrington Academy from 1767 to 1772. He was a colourful character of French Huguenot descent who had spent his early years in Germany. Originally destined for the Anglican priesthood (his father was a rector in London and also served as one of the King's French preachers in the friary at St James's Palace), he converted to rational dissent. After some opposition from her family, possibly on the grounds of Rochemont's tendency to mental instability, they married in a service conducted in the Warrington parish church by Rochemont's father in 1774, when Anna Laetitia was 31 years old.[11]

The Barbaulds set up home in Palgrave, a village near the county town of Diss, in Norfolk, where Rochemont was appointed as minister to the dissenting congregation and provided with a house big enough to accommodate a boarding school for boys, which would be run jointly by the couple. In spite of her considerable duties in looking after the domestic side of the school, keeping the accounts, and teaching the younger boys, Anna Laetitia found time to publish (in 1775) *Devotional Pieces, Compiled from the Psalms and the Book of Job*. Its preface is the most significant element: a long essay entitled 'Thoughts on Devotional Taste, on Sects, and on Establishments'.[12] An original and controversial philosophical enquiry and sociological description of religion as it was currently practised, it was aimed at improving the devotional imagination and was a forerunner of James Martineau's work in the following century. In it she turned from the usual promotion of rational dissent as emphasising reason and eschewing 'enthusiasm' to the need for religious practice to appeal also to the emotions and aesthetic senses: as she put it, 'an affair of sentiment and feelings, in the sense it is properly called devotion'.[13] This essay was criticised by her friend the highly rational Joseph Priestley, and the two engaged in some prolonged discussions. Anna Laetitia, in common with many women of her time and since, disliked doctrinal controversies; she considered that the habit of disputing on religious subjects was detrimental to the 'operation of religious impressions', a view which was echoed by many, including John Gooch Robberds and William Gaskell much later in the nineteenth century. She summed up her position in a letter to Nicholas Clayton, writing:

> *Are Philosophy and Devotion then inconsistent? No they are different views of the same subject, they require to be corrected by each other. The devotion of a mere philosopher will be cold, the religion of a mere pietist will be superstitious. But is it not owing to our imperfect natures that these two voices do not coalesce? I believe that it is & that in another world Philosophy and Devotion will be entirely the same thing.*

This contrasts with Priestley's view that religious controversy is necessary to the defence of religious truth, 'which is indeed the necessary foundation of all religious practice'.[14]

The Barbaulds remained childless, but in 1777 they adopted John's third son, Charles Rochemont Aikin. Parenthood provided the stimulus for Anna Laetitia's next publications, *Lessons for Children from Two to Three Years Old* (1778), *Lessons for Children of Three Years Old* (1778), and *Lessons for Children from Three to Four Years Old* (1779). These provided a new standard for early reading books, with large type, wide margins, good-quality paper, and short sentences with simple subject matter which related directly to the experience of small children but included imaginative stimulation, with animals given voices, and an introduction to more poetic forms of speech with similes, analogies, metaphors, and literary allusions, and inculcating a reverence for the Earth and all its inhabitants.[15] The curriculum in the school was a broad one, with Anna Laetitia teaching history, geography, and literature through public speaking. She developed her methodology of teaching from a basis of childhood and domestic experiences, then expanding these to the local area, and then to the nation and beyond, a technique that she was to use with devastating effect in her later political writings. The Barbaulds' aim was to produce responsible enlightened citizens who could relate their daily lives to national and international events. The school was extremely successful, both financially (with as many as 41 pupils a year) and educationally; several former pupils had successful careers and retained fond memories of their schooldays.[16] The most influential book that Anna Laetitia produced during her time at Palgrave was her *Hymns in Prose for Children*, published in 1781. In the preface she laid out her philosophy of religious education:

> *The peculiar design of this publication is to impress devotional feelings as early as possible on the infant mind: fully convinced, as the Author is, that they cannot be impressed too soon, and that a child, to feel the full force of the idea of God, ought never to remember the time when he had no idea – to impress them, by connecting religion with a variety of sensible objects, with all that he sees, all that he hears, all that affects his young mind with wonder and delight; and thus by deep, strong and permanent associations, to lay the best foundations for practical devotion in future life.*

As the hymns were reprinted regularly up to the early twentieth century and were in common use in middle-class homes and Unitarian Sunday Schools for over a hundred years, and were learned by heart by a high proportion of their readers, their influence cannot be over-estimated. In the nineteenth century many Unitarian writers referred to them. Their inculcation of trust in a benevolent God, mediated through family and the natural world, did much to bring warmth and 'sensibility' into the cold rationality of Priestleyan Unitarianism.[17] In the mid nineteenth century the novelist Charlotte Yonge surveyed children's literature and considered that three quarters of the gentry of the last three generations had learned to read from Barbauld's books. [18]

Despite the engagement of two additional teachers, the popularity of the school, with well over the planned limit of thirty boys, resulted in exhaustion for the Barbaulds, and in the summer of 1785, after eleven years, they gave it up. After one year spent travelling on the continent and another exploring various possibilities in London, they eventually settled in Hampstead, then a village four miles from the centre of London, where Rochemont was engaged as minister to the small dissenting congregation.[19]

For some years Anna Laetitia contented herself with teaching individual pupils, including her nephew Arthur, John's eldest son, and a variety of young women and girls, but she was eventually roused into action by the events of the French Revolution and the English reaction to it, together with agitation for the repeal of the Test and Corporation Acts (which made the holding of public office, and also attendance at Oxford and Cambridge universities, conditional on being a practising member of the Church of England and swearing an oath of allegiance to the Crown).

Of course in the later part of the eighteenth century it was not considered acceptable for a respectable middle-class lady to conduct worship, preach, make speeches in public, or even write political articles. Part of Anna Laetitia's genius is that she managed for the most part to stay on the socially approved side of the boundary of lady-like decorum, while expanding her influence into preserves that were traditionally male. Middle-class ladies were expected to confine themselves to the domestic sphere – although it was assumed that they would teach young children and girls.

Earlier Anna Laetitia had used verse as a medium for expressing both religious and political views. Her poem supporting the uprising in Corsica is an early example of one that was considered acceptable by polite society. However, she now wrote a prose polemical piece, but published it anonymously, as from a (male) dissenter. Her *Address to the Opposers of the Repeal of the Corporation and Test Acts* was published within a month of the failure of the motion to repeal the acts; it was an immediate success, with four editions produced by the end of the year, 1790. Reckoned to be the only known article written by a woman in this public debate, it is a very elegant and passionate piece advocating the civil rights of dissenters, and although its arguments are not original, they had not been used so effectively before. In common with other literature from the rational dissenters, it included praise of the democratic ethos of the French Revolution, a view which was to cause problems in the following years. The connection between religious freedom and civil rights, already expressed in traditional after-dinner speeches and the toast 'to civil and religious liberty', led many people to fear the religious radicals as a possible source of revolutionary fervour within Britain, as they were to be in Ireland also.[20]

This suspicion of rational dissenters greatly affected Anna Laetitia, her family, and friends, as demonstrated in a letter to her adopted son, Charles, in which she wrote that her husband and two other men were the only ones not to have joined the 'loyal associators' in Hampstead; they suffered a good deal of unpleasantness, including anonymous letters, while Joseph Priestley received threats and abuse on a daily basis, and Norwich friends were regarded as dangerous. In 1791 Priestley's home and meetinghouse in Birmingham were destroyed, as were other dissenters' meeting houses and chapels, in the so-called 'Church and King Riots'. These attacks and the use of anti-sedition legislation to persecute dissidents intensified their insecurities. Joseph Johnson, who published many dissenting works, including those of Anna Laetitia, was among those who were imprisoned for a time.[21]

When the female identity of the author of the *Address* became known, many commentators were horrified, and Anna Laetitia was vilified as a virago, a fishwife, an 'unsexed female', and generally unwomanly. This lasted for a couple of years, until Mary Wollstonecraft's publication of her *Vindication of the Rights of Woman* in 1792 attracted even more unwelcome attention. Up to this point Anna Laetitia's networks had included both dissenters and members of the establishment, such as the Bluestocking Circle, an informal but influential women's literary discussion group. But from this time onwards tensions between dissenters, who were seen as unpatriotic and potentially treasonous, and the political and religious establishment became intensified, and Anna Laetitia was more distanced from her Anglican friends.[22] This did not deter her from further engagement in the struggle, in spite of more personal worries such as a reduction in the couple's finances, necessitating a move to a smaller house in Hampstead, and the increasing instability of her husband's mental state, probably a manic-depressive disorder, resulting in both reckless spending and erratic behaviour towards his wife.[23]

Anna Laetitia's next foray into public debate was a reply to Gilbert Wakefield's tract denouncing public worship as unscriptural and unnecessary. Her *Remarks on Mr Gilbert Wakefield's "Enquiry into the Expediency and Propriety of Public or Social Worship"* (1792) were first published anonymously, but her authorship was soon acknowledged. She gave a well-argued defence of the importance of communal worship, insisting that it met a human need, and was part of normal social behaviour. She recognised its broader impact, stating: 'Every time Social Worship is celebrated, it includes a virtual declaration of the rights of man'.[24] The following year (1793), when the government announced a public day of fasting and humiliation, on which all places of worship were ordered to pray for divine aid in the war against France, she published a discourse, or sermon, entitled *Sins of Government, Sins of the Nation; or a Discourse for the Fast, Appointed on April 19 1793*. It was an immediate success, running into four editions, and although it was originally published anonymously, as from 'a volunteer', her authorship soon became known. This is possibly the only such fast-day sermon written by a woman, although of course it was never preached, at least by the author. In it she employed the same technique that she had used in her children's books, working from the experienced domestic scale up to that of national policies. Anna Laetitia applied the sort of moral judgement made in family life to national politics, for example in terms of living within one's means, avoiding pride and cruelty, and cultivating good relationships with one's neighbours; the effect was that of questioning the morality of the war but without overtly contravening the treason laws. Similar techniques were used in her two *Civic Sermons to the People*, published as anonymous tracts by Joseph Johnson in 1792, addressed to the common working people of England. The first, entitled *Nay, Why Even of Yourselves, Judge Ye Not What Is Right*, made a plea for more general education and the dissemination of proper information, and explained why good government is the concern of everyone, in that it affected

> *how much of your wages and hard earnings are taken from you in taxes*
> *– how much of your corn you may put into your own barns, and how*
> *much you must put into the barns of other people – for what things you*
> *may be put in prison, and for what things your life may be taken away –*
> *by what means you may obtain redress if you have suffered wrong from*
> *anyone – to which of your children your little property will go after you*
> *are dead, or whether to any of them? – on what occasions you may be*
> *obliged to go into other countries to fight and kill people whom you have*
> *never quarrelled with, or perhaps be killed yourselves.*[25]

Anna Laetitia went on to discuss the new sedition laws (which created problems for dissenters in claiming their right to freedom of conscience). By referring to the new laws, and the ignorance of them which allowed so-called 'Friends of the Government' to mistake 'the matter so far as to think that pulling down of houses was promoting the peace and prosperity of the kingdom', she drew attention indirectly to the riots that had destroyed several dissenting meetinghouses and ministers' homes, including Priestley's. She claimed that the invitation to study government did not apply to the 'dissolute, idle, intemperate':

> But you, in whatever rank of life you are, who are sober, industrious, and thoughtful; you who respect the property and rights of your neighbour, and therefore demand that your own rights and property should be respected; you who have a home, and therefore have a country; you who have a provident care for your families; who are accustomed to say to yourselves, I will not buy strong drink to-day, because my children will have no bread tomorrow – you are worthy to consider the affairs of a community, which, tho' more complicated, are not materially different.

The second civic sermon, *From Mutual Wants Springs Mindful Happiness*, asked why some men are set over others to govern them; it begins its reply by asking 'of what use Government is, for nothing that is useless can be worth supporting at all'. It argued from the necessity of trade in order to acquire the means of existence, and from the experience of men in local clubs, and continued:

> If your child wants to know what a State is, take him between your knees and say to him, "My child, when you were very little, our small cottage, and its spot of garden-ground, was all that you were acquainted with of the wide world. Your mother nourished you at her breast; I carried you in my arms; your brothers and sisters played with and caressed you... This first society is called a Family. It is the root of Society. It is the beginning of order, and kind affections, and mutual helpfulness and provident regulations. If this spring be pure; what proceeds from it will be pure."

Anna Laetitia proceeded by expanding the circle to society and to the state; she explained the need for laws, law enforcement, taxes, and democracy by working from the domestic scale upwards. These civic sermons are elegant, powerful critiques of the political state of the nation at that time, and are remarkably insightful for the twenty-first century too.[26]

Other important writings by Anna Laetitia include several sermons, particularly ones intended to mark fast days, when the government ordered everyone to attend church and pray for particular causes or events. Of course the sermons were not actually preached by Anna Laetitia, but were published anonymously by Joseph Johnson. They were particularly effective anti-war pamphlets and went so far as to recommend 'honourable delinquency', which today would be called civil disobedience. It seems that these are the only existing examples of such sermons written by a woman.[27]

During the 1790s Anna Laetitia resumed writing a variety of pieces which were either circulated privately or published in various journals or anthologies, and she was increasingly recognised as an authority on literature. In 1802 she moved to Stoke Newington, four miles to the east of Hampstead, when Rochemont was engaged as morning preacher at the Newington Green dissenting chapel. As this provided a lower stipend, Anna Laetitia's writings on literary matters became increasingly important as a source of income. In addition to various reviews in the style of Samuel Johnson, she wrote a biography of the author Samuel Richardson and edited six volumes of his letters, and then over the following years up to 1810 edited forty volumes of British novelists, ensuring that women writers were well represented.[28]

Unfortunately Rochemont's mental condition deteriorated, and he became increasingly violent towards his wife, which led to a temporary separation in 1808, followed by his death by drowning later that year.[29] Naturally Anna Laetitia found Rochemont's illness and probable suicide extremely distressing, but she persevered with her literary work and added to the number of journals for which she wrote reviews. The continuing war with France, which escalated into a conflict involving most of Europe, and America and parts of Asia too, had devastating effects on both the British economy and the rights of its citizens. The rational dissenters' belief in the progress of humankind was hard to maintain. Anna Laetitia responded to this by publishing a 334-line poem, *Eighteen Hundred and Eleven,* in which she took a gloomy view of the current situation, condemned the use of war, and foresaw the decline of England as a significant power. The future hope was in America, she prophesied, and England would become a subject of ancient history, as the Greek and Roman empires had become. Her poem also promoted a pacifist anti-war stance. This critique of English government and society aroused much hostility, some of it misogynist, much accusing her of being unpatriotic, and branding the poem as wicked and dangerous. This reaction shook Anna Letitia, who was already prone to depression, and she published very little after this, apart from some work on modern history and some literary reviews.[30] She continued to take in individual pupils, mainly young women; this teaching was probably her main source of income in her later years. Some pupils merely visited and/or engaged in correspondence with her; others stayed with her for years; many became her friends. Probably nearly forty women came under her direct influence. One, Eliza Hamond, was her pupil and then companion from 1809 to 1822. Although only one of her published works was designed specifically for women (*The Female Speaker,* 1811, an anthology designed to be recited aloud which modelled the way in which an inquiring mind investigates topics), Anna Laetitia's influence lived on throughout the nineteenth century in women such as Harriet Martineau, Sarah Austin, Lucy Aikin, Julia Smith, even perhaps Florence Nightingale, and Barbara Bodichon.[31] She died in 1825 at the age of eighty-one.

Anna Laetitia could be said to have had four different careers: as poet, educationalist, political and religious writer, and literary critic and editor. Of course these overlapped; one of the reasons why she was so influential was that she first made her name as a poet, working in a genre that was acceptable for respectable women to publish. Her pioneering work in educational methods has now been acknowledged, thanks to the work of Ruth Watts, but her significant influence on the development of Unitarianism is still largely unrecognised. Yet her influence can be traced in the thought of significant figures such as James Martineau, and her appeal for a holistic peace-loving faith is still relevant in the twenty-first century.

Endnotes

1 William McCarthy, *Anna Letitia Barbauld: Voice of the Enlightenment* (Baltimore, John Hopkins University Press, 2008), p. ix.

2 C. G. Bolam, J. Goring, H.L. Short, and R. Thomas, *The English Presbyterians: From Elizabethan Puritanism to Modern Unitarianism* (London, George Allen & Unwin, 1968).

3 Ann Peart, 'Forgotten Prophets: The Lives of Unitarian Women 1760–1904' (unpublished doctoral thesis, University of Newcastle, 2006), <https://theses.ncl.ac.uk/dspace/bitstream/10443/245/1/peart05.pdf>.

4 McCarthy, op.cit., pp.17–80.

5 Padraig O'Brien, *Warrington Academy 1757–86, Its Predecessors and Successors* (Wigan, Owl Books, 1989), p.93.

6 McCarthy, op cit., p.73.

7 Peart, op.cit., p.68.

8 McCarthy, op.cit., pp.100–4.

9 Ibid., pp.105–7.

10 William McCarthy and Elizabeth Kraft (eds.), *The Poems of Anna Letitia Barbauld* (Athens, USA and London: University of Georgia Press, 1994), p. xxxiii.

11 McCarthy, op.cit., pp.124–41.

12 Ibid., pp.159–65.

13 Anna Laetitia Barbauld, *The Works of Anna Laetitia Barbauld with a Memoir by Lucy Aikin*, 2 vols. (London: Longman, Hurst Rees, Orme, Brown and Green, 1826), Vol 2, p.232.

14 Peart, op. cit., pp.60–6.

15 Ibid., pp.51–2.

16 McCarthy, op.cit., pp.165–89.

17 Peart, op.cit., p.53.

18 McCarthy, op.cit., p.217.

19 Ibid., pp.239, 240–60.

20 Peart, op.cit., pp.70–5; McCarthy, op.cit., pp.268ff.

21 Peart, op.cit., pp.31–2.

22 McCarthy, op. cit., pp.280–1.

23 Ibid., pp.289–90, 361–2.

24 Peart, op.cit., p.59; McCarthy, op.cit., pp.313–9.

25 Peart, op.cit., p.75.

26 Ibid., pp.75–6.

27 Ibid., pp.50–60.

28 McCarthy, op.cit., pp.405ff, 423–30.

29 Ibid., pp.436–40.

30 Ibid., pp.469–81; Peart, op.cit., pp.82–3.

31 McCarthy, op.cit., pp.509–11.

2 Hannah Lindsey and Catharine Cappe: a feminine friendship[1]

Andrew Hill

Early acquaintance

Hannah Lindsey (1740–1812) was born in north Yorkshire, the daughter of Joshua Elsworth, who died in 1742 when she was just two years old. Her mother re-married, making Hannah the step-daughter of Francis Blackburne, the Anglican Archdeacon of Cleveland. Catharine Cappe (1744–1821) was born five miles away, the daughter of Jeremiah Harrison,[2] from 1748 to 1763 the latitudinarian (liberal) Vicar of Catterick, and of Sarah Winn, a relation of the aristocratic family of the same name from Nostell Priory near Wakefield. As a child Catharine had overheard a conversation in her father's study which she said 'settled her creed for many years': 'There can be no doubt', her father had said, 'that our Saviour Christ was that great personage who existed with God before all ages' – in other words, that actually he was not God.[3]

Many years later, Catharine wrote in her *Memoirs*: 'With Mrs. Lindsey, I had been very early acquainted. She was the only one among my young associates, from whom I could possibly gain any improvement; but as she was four years older than myself, I was hardly competent to be a companion to her.'[4] However, as they grew, the age difference between the two women would become less significant, while their association matured into a relationship of significant friendship. From Catharine's viewpoint this friendship may be traced retrospectively through her published *Memoirs* (1822) and her 'Memoir of Mrs. Lindsey by Mrs. Cappe' (1812) in the *Monthly Repository* soon after Hannah's death; and from Hannah's viewpoint – rather more contemporaneously – through her husband's now published correspondence.[5] In terms of dates and other details, the latter is more reliable, while the former depends rather more upon Catharine's long-term memory.

As well as being daughters of clergymen, both women would also marry clergymen. Hannah would marry Theophilus Lindsey, 17 years her senior, another staunch latitudinarian who would resign his living and become a pioneering Unitarian minister. For a while he was Rector of Kirby Wiske in Yorkshire's North Riding, and from 1755 Vicar of Piddletown (also known as Puddletown) in Dorset. Catharine credited her mother, Sarah Harrison, for having mentioned at an accidental meeting with Theophilus that Mrs. Blackburne had 'a daughter by a former marriage of uncommon talents'. The memory of this encounter had remained with Theophilus and was revived later by a letter from Revd Daniel Watson. He had written about

> *a visit he had lately made at Richmond and happened to mention Miss Elsworth as possessing uncommon talents; and this little circumstance confirming the prejudice in her favour made upon his mind by the accidental conversation already mentioned some years before, he wrote immediately to inquire of Mr. Watson (who was at that time the tutor of my brother), if he knew whether the young lady was disengaged, and in consequence of Mr. Watson's reply, Mr. Lindsey came to Richmond; and on a second visit, in the latter end of the summer, on 29th of September, 1760, the marriage took place, Mrs. L. having just completed her 20th year.[6]*

Three years later, in 1763, Theophilus and Hannah returned together to Yorkshire when, following the death of Catharine's father, Theophilus was appointed to be his successor as Vicar of Catterick. However, it would be another 25 years before Catharine would marry.

A Catterick friendship

In 1763, following the Lindseys' return to north Yorkshire, Hannah and Catharine, now aged 19, were able to resume their childhood acquaintance, which would then develop into life-long friendship sustained by regular and personal correspondence. Meanwhile Catharine and her mother had removed from the Catterick vicarage, first to a house in Long Preston and then to Bedale, five and a half miles from Catterick.[7]

Initially, Hannah expressed some nervousness about resuming the friendship with Catharine, lest 'some distance/strangeness might have developed between them during the intervening years'. She probably had in mind the fact that following her father's recent death Catharine had spent some time with her mother's wealthy Winn relatives at Nostell Priory.[8] However, Theophilus had set Hannah right by remarking: 'Is it not more probable, from what we know of her [Catharine's] character, that we may be greatly over rated by her, than that she should be disingenuous and insincere?'[9]

Years later, following Hannah's death, Catharine would recall being invited by her old friend to spend a few days of 1765 with the Lindseys at Catterick. She wrote about it in her 'Memoir of Mrs. Lindsey':

> *At Catterick in the following year, I had the happiness of being first introduced to Mr. Lindsey. Residing with my mother at that time in the neighbourhood, I was invited by my old friend to spend a few days with them, and never can I forget the impressions made upon my mind, by their conversation, their plan of life, the habits of self-denial it included, the great objects they had constantly in view and the admirable means they adopted to secure the attainment of them.*[10]

From Catharine we learn that Hannah was

> *usefully employed in domestic occupations, in which she excelled: in visiting the sick, studying the case, if any difficulty occurred, (for she had a good medical library, and great acuteness in the discrimination of diseases), and in prescribing and making up medicines. She was careful always to obtain the best drugs from Apothecary's Hall, and generally administered them in person; and such was her knowledge, her care, and her assiduity, that if the disease was not absolutely incurable, she generally succeeded.*[11]

In addition she 'carried into effect, [their intention] of inoculating at their own expense, for the small-pox, then very fatal, all the poor children of Catterick and its vicinity'.[12]As it happened, Hannah's uncle on her mother's side owned an apothecary's shop near Richmond,[13] and two of her step-brothers, Thomas and William Blackburne, were both medical doctors.[14] 'To the poor', noted Catharine, Hannah 'was a skilful physician, not only supplying and preparing medicines for their relief, but generally administering them in person.'[15]

Catharine also noted that Hannah spent some of her leisure time gardening. The garden, the lane, the church-yard, and the little surrounding shrubbery were all kept with such extreme neatness as to wear 'an appearance of great comfort, if not of elegance'.[16] This pleased Catharine, since she noted that her father 'had previously planted the garden with ornamental trees . . . woodbines, laburnums, roses and jesamines'.[17] She also observed that the Lindseys saved very little of their income and were constantly giving away books and medicines, and sometimes money, to the sick and needy in the parish.[18]

Theophilus and Hannah Lindsey leave Catterick

Theophilus' discomfort concerning the Anglican Church's Thirty-Nine Articles of Religion, and the required regular use of parts of the Anglican liturgy with which he was uncomfortable, led eventually to his resignation, a decision to which Hannah gave her wholehearted support. He delivered his farewell sermon as Vicar of Catterick on Sunday 28 November 1773. On the following Sunday evening, 5 December, Hannah wrote to Catharine, then living with her mother eight miles away at Bedale:

> *This day is over, and my husband's presence made me as happy as I can be among this sorrowing people. . . . John's [their servant's] grief was native . . . I am persuaded he will often be your visitor to enquire about us. . . . Two days more will accomplish this painful removal and send us into the wide world again; but if the great Governor do but go with us, we shall have nothing to fear.*[19]

So 'on that evening [Thursday], Dec. 8', records Catharine, Hannah and Theophilus 'came to Bedale, where they slept', and 'the next morning, I accompanied them as far as Wakefield, in their journey southward'[20] to London, where Theophilus would establish the first-ever Unitarian chapel in Essex Street off the Strand, using a modified Anglican liturgy. Catharine later wrote:

> *It was not till I saw them drive away in the chaise which was to convey them on the doubtful pilgrimage that I felt the full pressure of the loss I was about to suffer. In vain did I look around for comfort; friends and companions like these were nowhere to be found; and the world appeared to my afflicted spirit like one vast dreary wilderness.*[21]

Catharine visits Nostell Priory and Boynton

Since, at Wakefield, Catharine was close by Nostell, she took the opportunity of spending a few days at her mother's brother's nearby stately home, the Priory, where her aunt Mary and her children made her most welcome. However, Sir Thomas Winn Bt. was not at home:

> *for when he returned, and was told that I [Catharine Harrison] had been there, after having accompanied Mr. and Mrs. Lindsey as far as Wakefield, together with the occasion of their leaving Catterick, he became exceedingly angry and gave strict orders that I should never be permitted to enter his house any more.*[22]

Catharine then spent some time at Boynton in the East Riding with the current Sir George and Lady Strickland,[23] who, she was pleased to learn, 'sincerely honoured Mr. Lindsey's integrity' and at whose home she read a pleasing article in *The York Chronicle* extremely supportive of Theophilus. It was written by someone writing under the pseudonym 'Lover of All Good Men'. He was Newcome Cappe, a dissenting clergyman from York, a widower with four children. He would later become Catharine's husband. Not only was he a known dissenting sympathiser of the latitudinarian cause, but he was also a friend and colleague of both Joseph Priestley and Theophilus Lindsey. The three of them together would make a significant Yorkshire contribution to the Unitarian tradition. On occasion Theophilus would be impatient with Newcome's reticence and reluctance to publish his radical religious views, and on other occasions he would be anxious that Newcome should moderate Priestley's enthusiasms.[24]

Catharine visits London

Catharine had other Winn relatives, living at Little Warley in Essex. Sir George Allanson-Winn (1725–1798), a barrister and a 'baron of the exchequer' for Scotland, was a great-grandson of Sir Rowland Winn, 1st Baronet of Nostell.[25] When Sir George was away on business, Catharine was welcome company for his pregnant wife and their daughter Georgina at their London home. But the baby was still-born, and Lady Winn died in childbirth.[26] However, in May 1774, these visits gave Catharine an opportunity to visit Mr and Mrs Lindsey in their new London home:

> *I found them [she wrote] in a small lodging, upon the ground-floor of a house in Featherstone Buildings, Holborn, the first floor was occupied by more affluent lodgers, and I had an apartment up two pair of stairs, in the pilgrim style. Mr. Lindsey had no place for the remnant of his library, but a small closet through the bed-chamber, which served at once for his study, and for their store-room and cellar. The books were piled upon each other, and as there was no room for a chair or table, were so contrived, as that part of them should serve as a seat, and another part as a writing-desk. Under all these circumstances, Mr. L. was cheerful.[27]*

On another occasion when Sir George was away in Scotland, Catharine 'had the consolation of regularly attending Essex chapel on the Sunday, and of seeing Mr. and Mrs. Lindsey at other times, yet the distance from Albemarle-street, was so considerable, that this indulgence could not be frequent, especially, as I had promised to leave my little charge [Georgina Winn] as seldom as possible.'[28]

Catharine soon realised that visiting the Lindseys in London was a very different experience from visiting with them at Catterick. Not only were London visits expensive, but the Lindseys were also considerably busier: 'surrounded as they were by persons of the first talents, and attainments in literature.[29] ... my society could add nothing to them; but was on the contrary, as I have already remarked, rather an incumbrance than an assistance.'[30]

Nevertheless, Catharine did spend Christmas 1775, summer 1776, and spring 1778 with the London Winns, partly for 'the purpose, principally, of spending some time near Mr. and Mrs. Lindsey', but also to investigate the financial implications of possibly setting up her own school in York. However, her two Winn aunts 'very earnestly desired me to desist from my project', which in their estimation would remove her from the rank of a gentlewoman. Other considerations that they raised were 'the sum of money too, that would be required for taking and furnishing a large house . . . and added to this, my having seceded from the Established Church'.[31]

About the same time (1782), Catharine received a letter from Sir George Allanson Winn to say that Georgina was ill and would Catharine visit them immediately.

> *I did not hesitate [wrote Catharine] to comply with the request, according to the promise formerly made, and joined them in Brook-street, the beginning of December. She was in transports of joy on my arrival. "Will you promise me," she said, as she flew into my arms, "that you will not go away again, until I am quite grown up?" "I will promise you, my love, that I will not leave you, until you are perfectly recovered." Alas! of her recovery, there was little probability; she was dreadfully emaciated, and seemed declining very rapidly in a sort of atrophy; and although she had still considerable remains of muscular strength, and her physicians gave some hope, yet her altered voice, and pale, ghastly countenance, were but too certain indications of the termination to be expected.[32]*

Catharine and her mother move to York

Not surprisingly, the friendship between Catharine and Hannah was acquiring a different perspective. Gradually, it seems, the nature of their relationship was developing from one of frequent physical proximity and face-to-face encounter into one of intimate correspondence. In 1794 Catharine wrote that 'one great relief to my mind, during these years of anxiety and apprehension, was the regular correspondence of my friend Mrs. Lindsey'.[33] Most of the correspondence was deeply personal and is unavailable to the historian, since Hannah requested that after her death Catharine should destroy her letters; and Catharine rightly complied with the spirit of her request.[34] She did, however, in her 'Memoir of Mrs. Lindsey' (1812) provide three extracts 'by way of example': about a mutual friend with apoplexy, about Joseph Priestley on his final Sunday in London before leaving for America, and an extract from a Priestley letter once he had settled.[35]

Meanwhile, in 1777, Catharine and her mother removed from Bedale, first to Barwick-in-Elmet, a few miles east of Leeds, where her wayward brother had taken up farming, and then to York, where her two Winn aunts lived and where Catharine began pursuing her own philanthropic and welfare interests, focusing on the education of girls and the financial welfare of women. She most definitely rejected the notion that public life was an all-male affair.[36] It was at this time that her personal relationship with Newcome Cappe, the minister of the dissenting chapel in St. Saviourgate, began to develop. They would marry in 1778, making Catharine step-mother to four young adult children and the principal carer of an increasingly handicapped husband.

The Lindseys' visits to Yorkshire

As Catharine became less free to visit London, it happened that the Lindseys began making regular return trips to north Yorkshire in order to visit Hannah's mother and step-father in Richmond. The journey took four days by coach from London to York, so it was convenient to break the journey, and to meet and stay with York friends on the way. Theophilus and Hannah stopped over in York in 1783;[37] in 1785, when Theophilus 'preached for Mr. Cappe, and was truly grieved that so eminent a Teacher, scholar and excellent person should be destined to speak to so few and those of such inferior note';[38] and again in 1787, but just too late to see Hannah's step-father, Archdeacon Francis Blackburne, before he died.[39] The Lindseys came again in August 1791, when Theophilus met up with the Yorkshire political reformer Christopher Wyvill, a Unitarian sympathiser who had supported the Feathers Tavern petition (a petition to Parliament to relieve Anglican clergy of the requirement to subscribe to the Thirty-Nine Articles, replacing the qualification by a simple declaration of belief in the Bible),[40] and also in 1793, when they visited both the Cappes and the Wellbeloveds in York.[41]

In 1795 'we were ten days at York with our friends', wrote Theophilus to Russell Scott on 30 December 1795;[42] and to John Rowe in 1798 Theophilus wrote 'at York we passed ten days with our friends Mr and Mrs Cappe, most eminent Christians both'.[43] They visited Yorkshire again in 1799, on the way to see Hannah's mother, Hannah Elsworth, before she died. However, they were summoned away on the sixth day of their visit.[44] On 13 August Theophilus wrote to Thomas Belsham (then the Unitarian minister of the New Gravel Pit congregation in Hackney): 'My wife's respectable good mother still continues too enfeebled to leave her room or sit up more than an hour . . . and desirous of being released from it if it might be the will of heaven';[45] and to John Rowe on 5 October 1799: 'We left London on June 20 upon receiving a letter from Richmond in Yorkshire that my wife's aged parent was extremely ill and desirous to see her before she died'.[46]

In the event Hannah's mother died at Richmond, aged 85 or 86, on 23 August 1799.[47] Hannah wrote to Catharine from Richmond, and Catharine included a rare direct extract from the letter in her *Memoirs*:

> *My mother died yesterday at six o'clock, without a wish unaccomplished, and without a struggle; far beyond my expectation, for she had passed a very suffering day. She was perfectly sensible, and quite herself. We had all prayed by her in the afternoon, a prayer Mr. Lindsey had composed and used, suited to her case, and her attention suspended all complaint*

at the time, as also during family prayer at night, which was always in her room. She took leave of us, knowing us distinctly, so that nothing could be more satisfactory. . . Now that my exertions are over, my poor system is much shattered, and although I did all I could to relieve and comfort such an excellent parent, and she felt it, yet such is my diseased state, that I cannot but rejoice and be thankful for this additional favour, added to innumerable others, which the Giver of nothing but good, has bestowed upon me. I shall however, seek to turn to other duties, and trust the same support will be afforded, whilst any work remains to be done.

Hannah then added: 'We hope in our return, to pass a little time with you, to take a personal leave of our dearest friends in the north, whither we shall never return again.'[48] The warning was prophetic, for Hannah and Theophilus were beginning to feel their age and never did visit Yorkshire again.

Theophilus's later years

In 1797 Hannah wrote to Catharine reflectively:

You have a thousand pleasant visions and gratifications belonging to your temper, of which I am quite incapable, from my irritable frame, sadly increased by early impressions, in which pleasure was not an ingredient: duty and necessity have made me do some right things; nobody would love me if they knew me as I know myself, and therefore I never thought they did it much, and did not wonder at it. I have been more of a useful than loveable creature, from meaning well and taking pains to do what was allotted to me. This is not a good picture of your friend's mind, but it is a true one. My chief happiness has arisen from an union with one of the best, gentlest and most indulgent of human beings, and being employed in doing the rough work in the important station to which he was called, and which kept me from the world and its temptations, which ought to have made me better: but I have not caught his spirit, owing to the discordant particles of which I am composed, – I wish they may end this corruptible body.[49]

Then, late in December 1800, Catharine's husband Newcome Cappe died, aged 68 years, after a series of strokes. The following June, Hannah and Catharine were in correspondence about Theophilus's ill health. He had written to Christopher Wyvill, at Burton Hall near Bedale, that 'we are too old for such long Yorkshire journies';[50] but also they had been to their country retreat 22 miles away from London at Morden and had to return home early.[51]

In September 1802, Hannah – who was by now scribing most of Theophilus's letters – wrote to Thomas Belsham: 'I have heard no more of Dr. [Robert] Cappe or his journey, & fear my poor friend his [step] Mother [i.e. Catharine Cappe] is not well, as she is a most punctual correspondent.'[52] More likely Catharine was too busy to write. Her step-son Robert Cappe, an Edinburgh medical graduate and briefly a medical officer at The Retreat, York, had suffered much ill health and died at sea while on a health voyage to Italy.

Hannah wrote again to Thomas Belsham on 23 July 1803. By this time she had heard from Catharine: 'By a letter from Mrs. Cappe we learn that Mrs. Wellbeloved [wife of Charles Wellbeloved, Newcome Cappe's successor at St. Saviourgate Chapel] is safe in bed of her third pair of twins . . . It is hoped the Mother will continue to do well.'[53]

Catharine's final London visits

In 1803/1804 Catharine was determined to gratify a wish that she had long entertained: to visit London in company with her daughters and have the pleasure once more of seeing her excellent old friends Mr. and Mrs. Lindsey.[54] She engaged lodgings and they stayed in London about six weeks, no doubt spending time with the Lindseys (although no record is known).

She managed to organise London visits again in 1807 and in 1808. By 1808, however, Theophilus could no longer concentrate on any book which was read to him other than the New Testament, and it was evident to Catharine that the life of 'her aged friend' was drawing to its close. 'It was extremely painful to me', she wrote, to leave him like that, since he had always enjoyed her company and friendship. 'I charge you,' Mrs. Lindsey had told her servants, 'do not tell your master that Mrs. Cappe is going away'. But Catharine had been ill herself and felt that it was necessary to leave 'a close lodging in Essex-street'. To remain in London any longer would be extremely expensive. Also, she wrote, 'I could be of no real service to one who was surrounded by so many affectionate friends, and I was greatly wanted at home'.[55]

On 20 August 1808 Theophilus and Hannah wrote to Thomas Belsham, conveying thanks from Catharine for information regarding Thomas Madge, a ministry student at Manchester College at York,[56] and expressed her hopes that 'he will cease to incur debts he cannot pay'. Then they continued:

> We have not one of our usual kind visiting friends left in town, & should be quite solitary but for Mrs Cappe, and Dr Blackburne[57] when he is at leisure to eat our dinner, now at 3 o'clock as Mr Lindsey grows very languid for want of food by that hour, & if he eats anything before it spoils his best meal.[58]

Catharine last saw Hannah during the month of September.[59] Theophilus lived for another six weeks and died on 3 November 1808. Four days later, in York, on 7 November Catharine received a letter from Hannah:

> I write to give you the satisfaction of knowing, that by the mercy of God, my dear departed saint fell asleep in perfect serenity, and knew me almost to the last, said in his own sweet tone, and plainly, 'my love;' a word he had repeated when awake, and able, both day and night. When I said to him on the afternoon of Thursday, 'My dearest love, you and I shall live together for ever,' he replied in an audible voice, 'aye.' His countenance now dead, is so exactly expressive of his constant benignity, that it conveys satisfaction to all who behold it, and solaces me to contemplate.[60]

By the same post, she also received this account of Theophilus's death from Hannah's step-brother, Dr William Blackburne:

> I feel a degree of complacency, unusual on such occasions, in announcing to you, the easy transit of our excellent and venerable friend to the realms of peace. Mr. Lindsey, expired at ten minutes past six yesterday evening,

without a sigh, or the least change in the placidity of his aspect. He had been confined about six days to his bed, the oppression on the brain gradually increasing each day, till the final happy and gentle extinction of life.[61]

Hannah would live for another four years. Catharine recorded:

The last letter I received from her, seven weeks ago, was dated on, the 18th of Dec. [1811] and it has obtained with me a kind of sanctity as being her last letter. It is short, but written in her usual manner, containing many affectionate expressions of esteem and regard. "You I know" she says, "will be kind to me, whether I wrote or not." [62]

On Monday 13 January a group of friends drank tea with Hannah. A week later she had a paralytic seizure which deprived her of speech, and on Saturday 18 January 1812 she quietly died.[63] In Hannah's will Catharine was bequeathed £50 as a measure of the significance of their friendship.

The contribution of Hannah and Catharine to the development of Unitarianism

Grayson Ditchfield has highlighted the significance of Hannah Lindsey and of other women supporters of rational dissent such as Catharine Cappe in challenging 'the male dominance of its main organizational bodies'.[64] Not only was Hannah Theophilus's 'right-hand woman', she also played a leading part in the design and layout of the chapel in Essex Street, 'daily superintending the various workmen employed in the building, and contriving how to make the most of the small allotted space'.[65] Also she was responsible for most of the business side of her husband's London ministry – a role that she was reluctant to lay down even after Theophilus's death. In addition, as at Catterick, she continued with her practice of giving medical help and assistance to those living in the narrow streets and alleys round and about Essex Street. Hannah Lindsey 'can be regarded without exaggeration', writes Professor Ditchfield, 'as the co-founder of Essex Street chapel, and thus of the modern Unitarian denomination'. [66]

Catharine lived for another ten years after the death of Hannah, during which time she reformed the York Spinning School and Greycoat School and organised a local women's friendly society. When told that women were not permitted to visit women in the York County Hospital, she found 50 female subscribers and thereby ended the all-male dominance of its management.[67] At the same time she involved herself with Unitarian concerns – not just editing, interpreting, and publishing Newcome's sermons and other papers, but also showing a direct interest in the welfare of the staff and students of Manchester College after its removal to York in 1803 under the supervision of Charles Wellbeloved, Newcome Cappe's assistant and successor at St. Saviourgate.[68] Also towards the end of her life Catharine was engaged in correspondence with American Unitarian ministers, including William Ellery Channing.[69] She was, thereby, one of the first British recipients of the texts of his Dudleian lectures and of his 1819 Baltimore sermon 'Unitarian Christianity', and she thus constituted a significant channel by which the newer and gentler 'Channing Unitarianism' first seeped into Britain.[70]

Conclusion

Neither Catharine nor Hannah had children of their own, although Catharine was the step-mother of four young adults – the youngest, Robert, being 16 years old when Catharine married his father. Instead, both women might be considered 'midwives' who assisted at the birth of two related streams springing from Richmondshire in north Yorkshire which, over time, flowed and merged into the modern British Unitarian river. Hannah's stream would flow through Essex Street, London, attempting to conserve something of the order and dignity of a liturgical tradition of worship; while Catharine's flowed into and through the puritan and rational dissenting tradition of worship in York and elsewhere which she had adopted when she married Newcome Cappe.

Endnotes

1   I am especially grateful to Professor
    Grayson Ditchfield and to Dr Ann
    Peart for reading this chapter and
    making helpful suggestions; and to
    York Unitarian Claire Lee for the loan
    of her personal copy of Catharine
    Cappe's *Memoirs of the Life of the Late
    Mrs. Catharine Cappe Written by Herself*
    (London, 1822).

2   *Church of England Database Person ID*
    118631. He was also 'preacher' at Long
    Preston, 1731–1763.

3   Catharine Cappe, *Memoirs* 3 (op.cit.,
    1822), pp.31–2.

4   Ibid., p.78.

5   G.M. Ditchfield, ed., *The Letters of
    Theophilus Lindsey (1723–1808)*, 1.
    1747–1778, 2. 1789–1808 (The Boydell
    Press, 2007, 2012), hereafter cited as
    Lindsey Letters 1 and *Lindsey Letters* 2.
    I am grateful to Dr Ditchfield for my
    copies of these two volumes.

6   Catharine Cappe, 'Memoir of Mrs.
    Lindsey', *Monthly Repository* 7, 1812,
    pp.109–18.

7   Ibid.

8   Ibid., pp.111–18.

9   Cappe, *Memoirs* 14, p.109.

10 Cappe, 'Memoir of Mrs. Lindsey',
    op.cit.

11 Cappe, *Memoirs* 14, pp.111–12.

12 Cappe, *Memoirs* 18, p.151.

13 Grayson Ditchfield, 'Hannah Lindsey
    and her circle: the female element
    in early English Unitarianism',
    Enlightenment and Dissent 26 (2010),
    p.65.

14 *Lindsey Letters* 1:105 and note 17:
    Thomas Blackburne d.1782; 1: 347 and
    note 2: William Blackburne.

15 Cappe, 'Memoir of Mrs. Lindsey',
    op.cit., p.111. Grayson Ditchfield rather
    more cautiously describes Hannah as
    'a self-taught but uncertified physician'
    (Ditchfield, op.cit., 2010, p. 66).

16 Cappe, *Memoirs* 14, p.112.

17 Cappe, 'Memoir of Mrs. Lindsey',
    op.cit., p.112a. At a later date, 1816, on
    a return visit to Catterick Catharine
    was disappointed because 'the
    interesting view of the church yard,
    planted with trees, and adorned by a
    shrubbery . . . is now entirely shut out
    in the approach from the village, by
    a high wall which has usurped their
    place' (*Memoirs* Appendix (1822),
    pp.423–4).

18 Cappe, *Memoirs* 18, p.151.

19 Cappe, *Memoirs* 20, pp.164–5.

20 Ibid., p.165.

21 Cappe, 'Memoir of Mrs. Lindsey',
    op.cit., p.113.

22 Cappe, *Memoirs* 20, p.166.

23 Sir George Strickland (5th baronet) had
    married Elizabeth Letitia Winn (1730–
    1813), a kinswoman of Catharine's
    mother Sarah Winn. Their son William
    (1753–1834, 6th baronet) was a student
    at Warrington Academy, from which
    he was expelled for rioting (*Dissenting
    Academies Online*; Felicity James, Ian
    Inkster (eds.), *Religious Dissent and
    the Aikin–Barbauld Circle, 1740–1860*
    (Cambridge University Press, 2011),
    p.146 note 8).

24 Andrew M. Hill, 'Newcome Cappe at York', *Transactions of the Unitarian Historical Society* 25:3 (April 2013), p.162.

25 https://en.wikipedia.org/wiki/George_Allanson-Winn,_1st_Baron_Headley.

26 Theophilus Lindsey to William Turner of Wakefield 6 October and 3 November 1774 (*Lindsey Letters* 1: 137 and 139).

27 Cappe, *Memoirs* 21, pp.175–6.

28 Ibid., p.183.

29 Catharine mentions 'the Priestleys', who were then living at Bowood in Wiltshire; 'the Franklins', except that Benjamin Franklin's wife never came to Europe; 'the Jebbs': John (d.1786), another lapsed latitudinarian Anglican, and his writer-wife Ann (d.1812), both regular worshippers at Essex Street (see Anthony Page 'The Enlightenment and a second reformation: the religion and philosophy of John Jebb (1736–86)', *Enlightenment and Dissent* 17 (1998) pp.48–82); 'the Lees': John, the attorney-general, and Mary, both from Yorkshire and associated with Mill Hill Chapel, Leeds; 'the Prices': Richard, the Dissenting minister at Newington Green London, and his wife Sarah; and 'the Sargents': John and Rosamund, with whom the Lindseys occasionally stayed in Kent (Cappe, *Memoirs* 22, p.161.)

30 Ibid., pp.185–6.

31 Cappe, *Memoirs* 24, pp.197–8.

32 Cappe, *Memoirs* 28, pp.220–21.

33 Cappe, *Memoirs* 33, p.263.

34 Hannah Lindsey's letters to her brother Francis Blackburne are extant (see Grayson Ditchfield, op. cit., 2010).

35 Cappe, 'Memoir of Mrs. Lindsey', op.cit., p.115.

36 See Andrew M. Hill, 'A pattern of York feminism: Catharine Cappe as spinster, wife and widow', *Transactions of the Unitarian Historical Society*, forthcoming; Helen Plant, *Unitarianism, Philanthropy and Feminism in York, 1782–1821: The Career of Catharine Cappe*, University of York Borthwick Paper 103 (2003).

37 G.M. Ditchfield (ed.), *Lindsey Letters* 1, p.lxxiv.

38 Ibid., p.319: Lindsey to William Tayleur, 23 July 1785.

39 Ibid., p.352: Lindsey to William Tayleur, 1 September 1787.

40 *Lindsey Letters* 2, p.472: Lindsey to William Tayleur, 12 September 1791.

41 Ibid., p.607: Lindsey to William Tayleur, 25 May 1795, note 7.

42 Ibid., p.621.

43 Ibid., p.674: Lindsey to Thomas Belsham, 10 September 1798, and p.675 to John Rowe, 15 October 1798.

44 Cappe, *Memoirs* 36, p.301.

45 *Lindsey Letters* 2, p.683: Lindsey to Thomas Belsham, 13 August 1799.

46 Ibid., p.684: Lindsey to John Rowe, 5 October 1799.

47 Ibid., p.684, footnote 1.

48 Cappe, *Memoirs* 36, pp. 299–300.

49 Cappe, 'Memoir of Mrs. Lindsey', op.cit., p.116.

50 *Lindsey Letters* 2, p.724: Lindsey to Christopher Wyvill, 16 June 1801.

51 Catharine Cappe, *Memoirs* 38, pp.315–16. Morden is historically part of Surrey.

52 *Lindsey Letters* 2, p.741: Lindsey to Thomas Belsham, 27 September 1802 and note 16.

53 Ibid., p.751: Lindsey to Thomas Belsham, 23 July 1803.

54 Cappe, *Memoirs* 41, pp.338–40. Catharine refers to her step-daughters as her daughters.

55 Cappe, *Memoirs* 45, pp.362–4.

56 Thomas Madge was minister at Norwich 1811–1825 and at Essex Street, London 1825–1859.

57 Dr William Blackburne, Hannah Lindsey's brother.

58 *Lindsey Letters* 2, p.782: Theophilus & Hannah Lindsey to Thomas Belsham, 20 August 1808.

59 Cappe, 'Memoir of Mrs. Lindsey', op.cit., p.116.

60 Cappe, *Memoirs* 45, pp.364–5.

61 Ibid., p.364: Dr. Francis Blackburne to Catharine Cappe.

62 Cappe, 'Memoir of Mrs. Lindsey', op.cit., p.117.

63 Ibid.

64 Grayson Ditchfield, op.cit., 2010, p.58.

65 Cappe, 'Memoir of Mrs. Lindsey', op.cit., p. 114.

66 Ditchfield, op. cit., 2010, p.68.

67 Andrew M. Hill, 'A pattern of York feminism: Catharine Cappe as spinster, wife and widow', *Transactions of the Unitarian Historical Society*, forthcoming.

68 Cappe, *Memoirs* 47, pp.380–91; V.D. Davis, *A History of Manchester College from its Foundation in Manchester to its Establishment in Oxford* (1932), chapter 6, 'Manchester College, York'; David Wykes, 'Dissenting academy or Unitarian seminary? Manchester College at York (1803–1840)', *Transactions of the Unitarian Historical Society* 19:2 (1988), pp.113–29.

69 The Harvard Divinity School library copy of the 1822 edition of Catharine Cappe's *Memoirs* is autographed 'W.E. Channing' on the title page.

70 Andrew M. Hill, 'Channing and British Unitarianism: sowing the seeds', *Transactions of the Unitarian Historical Society* 19:2 (1988), pp.74–5.

3 Mary Wollstonecraft, Mary Hays, and Lucy Aikin

Ann Peart

Mary Wollstonecraft (1759–1797)

Mary Wollstonecraft is often credited with being the mother of the feminist movement in England, having been 'rediscovered' by feminist writers in the twentieth century. She was a contemporary of Anna Barbauld (see Chapter 1), and the two had considerable influence on each other, in various ways. Wollstonecraft's first significant contact with rational dissenters probably began when she moved to north London in 1784, in order to set up a girls' school.[1] A difficult family situation obliged her to assume the burden of supporting various relations and friends, including two of her sisters; running a school was one of the few ways in which women in the late eighteenth century could become financially independent. After a brief stay in Islington, she was encouraged to move to Newington Green, where the congregation of the dissenting meeting house proved very helpful. In particular, **Hannah Burgh** (also known as Sarah), the widow of a schoolmaster, James Burgh, in the four years before her death in 1788 developed a very close friendship with Mary, treating her as if she had been her own daughter. She almost certainly lent her money to rent a large house and helped her to set up the new boarding school, which quickly attracted pupils, including two sons of Mrs Disney (presumably **Jane Disney**, the wife of the assistant minister of Essex Street Chapel).[2] Mary ran the school on progressive lines, with a care for the children's physical welfare as well as encouraging them to develop the power of independent thinking.

While at Newington Green Mary got to know the minister of the chapel, Richard Price, and he became a major influence on her own thinking, introducing her to other rational dissenters and their promotion of a reasoned approach to religion and education. However, although she attended services

Mary Wollstonecraft: portrait by John Opie, c. 1790
(© Tate Gallery, London)

at the dissenters' meeting house at Newington Green to hear Price's political sermons, she never left the Church of England, although her views on the afterlife seem to concur with the assurance of mercy (rather than damnation) that characterised the faith of rational dissenters.[3]

The school at Newington Green failed to thrive, suffering particularly during Mary's absence to support a dying friend in Portugal. It closed in 1786, when she moved to Ireland as a governess (a position found with the help of Richard Price and Hannah Burgh). But the two years of close contact with rational dissenters in London had transformed her thinking and started her career as a writer. In the summer of 1786 she produced *Thoughts on the Education of Daughters*, in which she argued that girls should be taught to think for themselves from an early age. The Revd John Hewlett, a radical Anglican clergyman and friend of Hannah Burgh, introduced Mary to Joseph Johnson, the Unitarian radical publisher, thus initiating a lifelong association and an entrée into his social circle.

The outlines of Mary Wollstonecraft's life are well known. Her unhappy spell as a governess lasted only one year, after which she returned to London and made her living as a professional writer, starting with various educational works before turning to responses to Edmund Burke's reflections on the French Revolution. *A Vindication of the Rights of Men,* first published anonymously in 1790 and then revised in her own name, was followed by *A Vindication of the Rights of Woman* (1792). She then began an affair with the American journalist Gilbert Imlay, moving to France with him and bearing his child before returning to London without him in 1795. After two suicide attempts, and a trip to Sweden, she became the lover of William Godwin, a radical philosopher and former rational dissenting minister; they married just before the birth of her second daughter, but Mary died a few days later in September 1797. Throughout these years she had maintained a stream of publications, including work on the French Revolution, two novels, travel writing, translations, reviews, and essays.

Nowadays she is best known for her *Vindication of the Rights of Woman,* which was a hastily written polemic decrying the social status of women in that they were denied access to proper education and were thus unable to fulfil their potential and become independent and equal citizens. After this publication, and her return from France with an illegitimate child, her reputation became such that women like **Anna Laetitia Barbauld**, who depended on their social respectability for their audience, treated Mary Wollstonecraft with some caution. The two probably met at the home of their publisher, Joseph Johnson, and it seems that Mary was a great admirer of Barbauld, including some of her writings in her educational anthologies. There was some misunderstanding about one of Barbauld's early poems, but William McCarthy is convinced that there was much agreement and mutual respect between the two, in spite of Wollstonecraft's critique of 'sensibility', a culture of introspection and feeling esteemed by Barbauld.[4]

Mary Wollstonecraft's reputation was further damaged by the publication of a biography by William Godwin within a year of her death in which he made it clear that her first daughter was born out of wedlock, and suggested (erroneously) that she had abandoned all religious belief. Anna Laetitia Barbauld was well aware of the conflict between dissent and cultural conformity when in 1804 she wrote to Maria and Richard

Edgeworth, who were considering a publication of women's writing: 'Mrs Hannah More [a respected writer and philanthropist who was a member of the Bluestocking Circle] would not write along with you or me, and we should probably hesitate at joining Miss Hays, or, if she were living, Mrs Godwin'. So although many of Wollstonecraft's writings had some initial success, they were later not considered suitable reading for polite society. Nevertheless, particularly in Unitarian circles, she was read widely. When William Turner, minister at Hanover Square, Newcastle on Tyne, wrote to his daughter **Mary Turner** in 1812, shortly before her marriage to John Gooch Robberds, minister at Cross Street Chapel Manchester, giving her some advice about the married state, he assumed that she had 'perused the strong and often coarse, though too often well-founded strictures of Mary Wollstonecraft'.[5] The radical Unitarians centred on W. J. Fox's ministry in London promoted Wollstonecraft's ideas, and they are considered in Part Two of this book.

Mary Hays (1759–1843)

Mary Hays, a friend of **Mary Wollstonecraft** and acquaintance of **Hannah Lindsey**, was strongly influenced by **Anna Laetitia Barbauld** (although there seems to be no record of their having met) and was clearly a rational dissenter, being for a time a member of the Essex Street Chapel.[6] She has recently been recognised as a woman who developed gendered critiques of male Enlightenment thought and pioneered a way of doing women's history. She was an early exponent of the feminist claim (as voiced in the late twentieth century) that 'the personal is political'.

Born in Southwark, she was raised as a Baptist and suffered the death of her father when she was about fifteen; this seems to have left her with a need to find male mentors in her adult life.[7] John Eccles, with whom she developed a passionate relationship, mainly by letter, died just after their families had agreed that they could marry, and this too influenced her future reliance on male mentors, but it gave her a sort of honorary widow status, which allowed her to develop both informal educational activities and, subsequently, a literary career. She came under the influence of the liberal Baptist Robert Robinson, and through him she met several leading rational dissenters, including staff of the dissenting academy in Hackney, where she may even have attended some lectures. Men such as William Frend, George Dyer, Joseph Priestley, and John Disney influenced her considerably, and she found that the dissenting emphasis on rational discussion, with respect for differing views, gave her a model for developing her own ideas.[8]

Her first venture into publishing, in 1792, using the name 'Eusebia', was a reply to Gilbert Wakefield's *Enquiry into the Expediency and Propriety of Public Worship*. Mary drew on Anna Laetitia Barbauld's work on the importance of forming early habits or associations, and although she referred to herself as 'a woman, young, unlearned, unacquainted with any language but her own', her work was well received, being further refined in a second edition.[9] This success gave her access to the radical circle of Joseph Johnson, the publisher, including William Godwin, who later became a close friend and mentor. It also enabled her to publish her first full-length book, *Letters and Essays, Moral, and Miscellaneous* (1793), which was dedicated to John Disney, minister at Essex Street Chapel, 'as an unaffected tribute of esteem, for distinguished worth and genuine liberality of mind'.[10] This wide-ranging collection of pieces shows the breadth of Mary Hays' reading and contributed to the debates in dissenting circles on topics such as materialism and necessity, 'pulpit elocution', civil liberty, and the 'influence of Authority and Custom on the Female Mind and Manners'.[11] This last topic was particularly important for Mary, as she developed a concept of female improvement enabling individual choice within a framework of morality and virtue. Like Barbauld, she stressed the importance of 'sensibility', or reflection upon feelings and taste, but in later works she developed this further, particularly in those of her novels that acknowledged the reality of female sexual desire.

Her next book, *Memoirs of Emma Courtney* (1796), brought her both fame and notoriety.[12] In stressing the importance of 'candour', or honesty, and claiming a role for women's moral agency, this semi-autobiographical novel revealed her passionate feelings for William Frend and scandalised respectable society. The following year she was distressed by the death of her friend, Mary Wollstonecraft, and was the first to write a sympathetic obituary (published anonymously), running to 49 pages and defending Wollstonecraft's life and writings. Also unsigned was her *Appeal to the Men of Great Britain in Behalf of Women*, stressing the importance of education for women and claiming that the character of women is culturally and socially constructed, rather than inherently inferior. This was published in 1798, when after Wollstonecraft's death feminist concerns had taken a reverse and were deemed no longer respectable; but apparently it had been written earlier, before the publication of Wollstonecraft's *Vindication*.[13] It was reviewed favourably by the radicals, but, in common with the work of most other rational dissenters, ridiculed by the right-wing press.[14]

Mary Hays' second novel, *The Victim of Prejudice* (1799), influenced greatly by William Godwin, continued the practice of drawing on her own life events, and according to her 'Advertisement' delineates 'the mischiefs that have ensued from the too great stress laid on the reputation for chastity in women'.[15] This was the last of her overtly feminist writings addressing the limitations imposed on women during her time. She was lampooned in the press, notably as the ugly Bridgetina Botherim in Elizabeth Hamilton's popular novel, *Memoirs of Modern Philosophers* (1800).[16] From this time she became more isolated and less involved with most Unitarians and rational dissenters, but with an increasing awareness of the importance of commemorating and celebrating women's lives. This she did with a groundbreaking multi-volume work of women's biography. The Unitarian publisher Richard Phillips, who had featured Mary Hays' work in his liberal *Monthly Magazine*, published six volumes of her *Female Biography: or, Memoirs of Illustrious and Celebrated Women, of All Ages and Countries* in 1802. Consisting of more than three hundred entries, its scope included a wider variety of women than in previous works, from Wollstonecraft and the republican historian Catharine Macaulay back through teachers, scientists, preachers, actors, poets, spies, and queens to prehistory.[17] This development of women's life writing into a historical context was a continuation of her work to promote the interests of women and their access to learning. It was groundbreaking in that it did not exclude women who were not models of decorum or virtue, and it emphasised a tradition of learned women. The work was so successful that it enabled Mary to buy a small house in Camberwell and employ a servant, although she also spent time working as a governess and teaching in a school.[18] She continued to write, producing further novels and articles, most notably *Memoirs of Queens* in 1821, arguing that women made at least as good rulers as men. Recently the Female Biography Project based at Chawton House has produced a new edition of her biographical works and is helping to establish her originality and importance as an Enlightenment scholar (and early feminist).[19] Even in her later years Mary Hays maintained some links with other women, including the new generation of Unitarian women who were active in the public sphere, such as **Harriet Martineau** and **Elizabeth Gaskell**, to whom she bequeathed a letter from Mary Wollstonecraft.[20] According to the memoir written by Unitarian minister Edmund Kell soon after her death, Mary Hays retained her Unitarian faith to the end, and died trusting in a benevolent God.[21]

Lucy Aikin (1781–1864)

Lucy Aikin, niece of **Anna Laetitia Barbauld**, represents a transition between the rational dissenting women of the long eighteenth century and the Victorian Unitarians. She has recently received attention from feminist historians who have highlighted the interplay between her private, family situation and her more public writings, and also her largely unrecognised contribution to historical method in relation to women.[22] Lucy was born in Warrington, where her grandfather was the divinity tutor at the dissenting academy, and her father, John Aikin (brother of Anna Laetitia), was a medical doctor, with an interest in writing. She was brought up in a rational dissenting environment where children of both sexes were encouraged to participate in rational discussion and to read widely. The family moved to London in 1792 and then to Stoke Newington in 1797, where she was close to Anna Laetitia.

She was educated at home, and her aunt's educational writings, including *Hymns in Prose for Children*, made a great impression on her. She appears to have been a lively, talkative child, and on one occasion that she recalled in later life, when she argued with her father about a perceived injustice, he replied, 'Why Lucy, you are quite eloquent!', and Lucy wrote

'O! never-to-be forgotten praise! Had I been a boy, it might have made me an orator; as it was, it incited me to exert to the utmost, by tongue and by pen, all the power of words I possessed or could ever acquire – I had learned where my strength lay.'[23]

Lucy's first published writings appeared when she was just sixteen, and a variety of articles and reviews followed in various journals.[24] Her first whole book was a poetry anthology published by Joseph Johnson in 1801, and her first major original work, *Epistles on Women, Exemplifying Their Character and Conditions in Various Ages and Nations*, in 1810, was also published by Johnson.[25] This 'bold and confident tribute to female power', written in verse, gives a history of humankind from the Garden of Eden to 1750, using the four-stage theory (hunting and gathering, pasturage, agriculture, industry and commerce) developed by Scottish Enlightenment thinkers, to show how social progress is linked to the treatment of women.[26] Interestingly, Lucy does not claim equality for women, but emphasises the domestic and maternal virtues that women have developed.[27] She does, however, stress girls' and women's need for access to a good education. Recent research has re-evaluated her *Epistles* as an important intermediary work, forming a link between the thinking of the Enlightenment anthropologists and the later feminists of the 1830s and 1840s.[28]

During her lifetime Lucy produced a large amount of published material, including original works, translations, family memoirs, collections of work by family members, including her father, John Aikin, and her aunt Anna Laetitia Barbauld, works for children (some under the pen name of Mary Godolphin), biography, and fiction, but she is most remembered for her historical output.[29] Her *Memoirs of the Court of Queen Elizabeth* (1818), *Memoirs of the Court of James the First* (1822), and *Memoirs of the Court of Charles the First* (1833) break new ground in their emphasis on the details of individual lives and the domestic history of the court, blended with a consideration of cultural and religious developments. This was a unique form of what has come to be known as social history, with both an in-depth investigation of a small segment of time and social situation and a larger study of the cultural trends of the time.[30] She used an impressive array of sources, manuscript as well as printed, but paid little attention to armed conflict (because she regarded war and violence as unethical), preferring to turn political questions into ethical ones. Unusually, she included a considerable amount of biographical detail, as this allowed her readers to discern the principles behind the actions of the protagonists.[31] Thus the *Memoirs* were at once both serious history and entertaining reading. This made them very popular, but it did not enhance her reputation as a historian.

Lucy never married; she remained in the parental home, helping her mother to nurse her ailing father until his death in 1822, when mother and daughter moved to Hampstead. After her mother's death in 1830, she remained in Hampstead for the rest of her life, apart from six years spent in south-west London with her niece Anna Letitia, who was married to Philip Hemery Le Breton; she moved back with them to Hampstead, where she died in 1864, aged 82.[32]

Lucy Aikin was always conscious of being part of a family that was prominent in the community of rational dissent and the burgeoning Unitarian movement. She attended her local chapel and promoted the values of rational inquiry, justice, and candour. Lately she has been criticised for 'sanitising' her memoirs of her father, John Aikin, and her aunt, Anna Laetitia Barbauld, making them appear less radical and more respectable to nineteenth-century readers.[33] Her wide range of friends and contacts within the movement extended throughout England and beyond, and her extensive letter writing and her friendships with many of the leading families did much to foster the sense of community in the growing denomination. Some of her correspondence with the prominent American Unitarian William Ellery Channing has been published; it shows her wide grasp of both the British Unitarian movement and the wider culture beyond Unitarianism.[34] Her emphasis on family and domesticity veiled the impact of her groundbreaking publications, but nevertheless many of the female Unitarian activists knew Lucy Aikin and read her work.

Endnotes

1 Lyndall Gordon, *Mary Wollstonecraft: A New Genus* (London, Little, Brown, 2005), pp.40–79.

2 Ibid., p.41.

3 Ibid., p.371; Janet Todd, *Mary Wollstonecraft: A Revolutionary Life* (London, Weidenfeld & Nicolson, 2000), pp.59–60.

4 William McCarthy, *Anna Letitia Barbauld: Voice of the Enlightenment* (Baltimore, John Hopkins University Press, 2008), pp.62, 351–5.

5 Jenny Uglow, *Elizabeth Gaskell: A Habit of Stories* (London, Faber and Faber, 1993), p.32.

6 Gina Luria Walker, *Mary Hays (1759–1843) The Growth of a Woman's Mind* (London, Routledge, 2018 (first published in 2006 by Ashgate), p.116.

7 Walker, op.cit., 2018; Marilyn L. Brooks, 'Mary Hays: finding a "voice" in dissent', *Enlightenment and Dissent*, 1 (1995), pp.3–4; Marilyn L Brooks, 'Mary Hays', in *Oxford Dictionary of National Biography* (2009), www.oxforddnb.com, accessed June 2018.

8 Brooks, op.cit., 1995, p.13.

9 Ibid., p.15.

10 Ibid., p.18.

11 Ibid., p.19.

12 Marilyn L. Brooks, ed., *Memoirs of Emma Courtney* by Mary Hays (Ontario, Broadview Press, 2000).

13 Walker, op.cit., 2018, pp.195–7.

14 Ibid., p.198.

15 Brooks, op.cit., 2009.

16 Walker, op.cit., 2018, pp.202–4.

17 Ibid., pp.222–9.

18 Brooks, op.cit., 2000, pp.31–3.

19 Gina Luria Walker, 'The invention of female biography', *Enlightenment and Dissent* 29, 2014, pp.79–121.

20 Walker, op. cit., 2018, p. 236.

21 E Kell, 'Memoir of Mary Hays: with some unpublished letters addressed to her by Robert Robinson, of Cambridge, and others', *Christian Reformer* 129 (1844), pp.813–14.

22 Felicity James, 'Lucy Aikin and the legacies of dissent' in *Religious Dissent and the Aikin–Barbauld Circle 1740–1860*, ed. by Felicity James and Ian Inkster (Cambridge, Cambridge University Press, 2012), pp.183–204; Michelle Levy, '"The different genius of woman": Lucy Aikin's historiography' in James and Inkster, pp.156–82.

23 Philip Hemery Le Breton, 'Memoir of Miss Aikin', in *Memoirs, Miscellanies and Letters of the Late Lucy Aikin*, ed. by Philip Hemery le Breton (London, Longman, Green, Longman, Roberts & Green, 1864), p.x.

24 Ibid., p. xix.

25 Lucy Aikin, *Epistles on Women, Exemplifying Their Character and Conditions in Various Ages and Nations* (London, Joseph Johnson, 1810).

26 James, op. cit., pp.190–93.

27 Ibid., p.193.

28 Kathryn Gleadle, *The Early Feminists. Radical Unitarians and the Emergence of the Women's Rights Movement, 1831–51* (London, Martin's Press, 1995), pp.67–8; James, op.cit., pp.190–91.

29 Le Breton, op. cit., xix–xxvii.

30 Levy, op. cit., pp.158–60.

31 Ibid., p.161.

32 Le Breton, op.cit., pp. xii–xxvii; James, op.cit., pp.185–7; Geri Walton, *English*

Author Lucy Aikin (Mary Godolphin), www.geriwalton.com/english-suthor-lucy-aikin-mary-godolphin, accessed 4 August 2018.

33 McCarthy, op.cit., pp.141–2; James, op.cit., pp. 98–201.

34 Anna Letitia Le Breton, editor, *Correspondence of William Ellery Channing, D.D. and Lucy Aikin, from 1826 to 1842* (London, Williams and Norgate, 1874).

PART TWO
Widening Circles

Introduction to Part Two

Ann Peart

During the first half of the nineteenth century Unitarianism developed and changed considerably. The law that made denial of the doctrine of the Trinity illegal was repealed in 1813. The Dissenters' Chapels Act of 1844 permitted congregations that had been Unitarian for more than 25 years to keep their buildings and trust funds. By 1850 many of the old Presbyterian, General Baptist, and other rational dissenting congregations had declared themselves to be Unitarian. From 1836 nonconformists in England and Wales had the right to be married in their own place of worship, rather than in an Anglican parish church.[1]

The wider acceptance of diversity of belief was reflected in the broader movements for reform, leading to the repeal of the Test and Corporation Acts (which barred non-Anglicans from public office) in 1828, followed by the Catholic Emancipation Act a year later. The Reform Act of 1832, for which many Unitarians had campaigned, brought greater democracy to the political system and helped to foster interest in campaigns for other reforms, such as universal suffrage.[2]

In 1825 the formation of the British and Foreign Unitarian Association brought together several of the national bodies created in the 1790s onwards. It helped to support and co-ordinate missionary work, and provided a focus for Unitarian identity. The range of Unitarian beliefs widened, with James Martineau and others beginning to promote a faith based on internal conscience rather than the authority of scripture.[3]

The Unitarian women featured in this section were for the most part involved in the social and educational campaigns of the time. The one exception is **Elizabeth Gaskell**, who is perhaps more representative of most middle-class Unitarian women of that time, being concerned for people on an individual basis, but avoiding overt involvement in politics. Some women, such as **Margaret Gillies**, in the field of art, and **Elizabeth Jesser Reid**, in the sphere of education, are known for their contributions to a single area of society. Many of the more 'radical unitarians'[4] who found the mainstream Unitarians too restrictive were active in various causes, especially those concerned with women's rights, and found that their radicalism took them out of the Unitarian mainstream, although they retained its principles. Included in this group are **Harriet Martineau, Harriet Taylor (Mill), Eliza Flower,** and **Sarah Flower Adams.** These women, and their associates, are significant in that they helped to keep alive the aspirations of **Mary Wollstonecraft** and other feminists of the late eighteenth century.

Endnotes

1   Leonard Smith, *The Unitarians: A Short History* (Arnside, Lensden Publishing, 2006), pp. 82–3, 88–9; C. Gordon Bolam, Jeremy Goring, H. L. Short, Roger Thomas, *The English Presbyterians: From Elizabethan Puritanism to Modern Unitarianism* (London, George Allen & Unwin, 1968), p.244.

2   Smith, op.cit., p. 82; Raymond Holt, *The Unitarian Contribution to Social Progress in England* (London, Lindsey Press, 1938), pp.129–32.

3   Smith, op.cit., pp.82–3, 95–7.

4   Kathryn Gleadle, *The Early Feminists. Radical Unitarians and the Emergence of the Women's Rights Movement,* 1831–51 (London, Palgrave Macmillan, 1995), pp.5-6.

4 Harriet Martineau (1802–1878)

Ann Peart

Most Unitarians know something of James Martineau, influential minister, educator, and writer, but to the rest of the Western world it is his older sister Harriet (1802–1878) who has the claim to fame as a writer, journalist, and pioneer sociologist. Although she left the Unitarian movement in her early forties, she retained many of her Unitarian connections and never forsook the values of her Unitarian upbringing.

Harriet was the sixth of eight children born to **Elizabeth (*née* Rankin)** and Thomas Martineau, a textile manufacturer of Huguenot origin. The family lived in Norwich, an important centre of Unitarianism, and were very active in the Unitarian congregation at the Octagon Chapel, and also well connected with the wider movement. Like many middle-class girls, Harriet was first educated at home by her older siblings, but, unlike many, she then went to school, attending first a local school run by a Unitarian minister where four girls joined the boys' classes, and then a girls' school in Bristol run by her Aunt Kentish, with religious education by Lant Carpenter, the Unitarian minister who influenced her greatly.[1] In her autobiography Harriet describes herself as 'indolent', but from the age of eight she developed habits of self-discipline and daily reflection on her own conduct. From the age of about twelve she began to lose her senses of taste and hearing, and in later life she often used an ear trumpet.[2] Clearly a very bright young woman, she developed the habit of studying before breakfast, sometimes as early as five in the morning: translating Latin works and studying the Bible and works of philosophy such as David Hartley's theory of necessarianism, to which she remained faithful even when she eventually renounced Unitarianism.[3]

In her early twenties Harriet suffered several losses which altered the course of her life irrevocably. Her oldest brother, Thomas, to whom she was particularly attached, died in 1824; the following year the family

Harriet Martineau (after a portrait by George Richmond), signed 'C.F.1864'
(Courtesy of the Armitt Museum and Library, Ambleside)

business began to collapse, and her father died. The business failed completely four years later. Meanwhile Harriet was discreetly engaged to be married to John Hugh Worthington, junior minister at Cross Street Chapel, Manchester, but when he fell seriously ill with a brain condition she withdrew from the engagement, because he would not be able to give her the useful role of minister's wife. John Hugh died in the summer of 1827.[4] Harriet reacted to these bereavements with stoicism, refusing to surrender to emotional outbursts or expressions of self-pity. It seems that she took the advice that she had given to Helen, her widowed sister-in-law: that the best way to deal with grief was to engage in a strict discipline of study, coupled with public engagements. For Helen, this involved charitable works; for Harriet, it was a commitment to writing and being published.[5]

All this left Harriet with the need to earn money. Her increasing deafness ruled out the traditional role of governess, but she was very good at needlework. And since the age of nineteen she had been writing articles on religious subjects for the Unitarian periodical the *Monthly Repository*, starting with a piece on **Anna Laetitia Barbauld** and the writer and social reformer Hannah More, and going on to a variety of religious and philosophical topics, at first without payment, but after 1829 for an annual fee of £15.[6] Then Harriet expanded her writings into other areas, most notably political economy. She was inspired by the didactic principles in Jane Marcet's *Conversations on Political Economy* (1816), in which a girl converses with her (female) tutor. Jane Marcet (1769–1858) later became a friend of Harriet and was known for her books explaining science to women and children. While Jane held Unitarian views, there seems to be no evidence that she belonged to the Unitarian movement.[7] Harriet's monthly series of short stories illustrating the basic principles of economics ran for two years from 1832 and proved very successful. They made her name as a writer, and brought her to the attention of a wider public.[8]

During this time Harriet moved to London and set up house with her widowed mother. This gave her an opportunity to mix with other writers and like-minded people, notably those connected with W.J. Fox and his Unitarian congregation at South Place. Thus she became involved with women's rights activists such as **Barbara Leigh Smith (later Bodichon)** and the 'radical unitarians' described by Kathryn Gleadle, who are the subject of a later section in this book.[9]

After the publication of her *Illustrations of Political Economy* in 1832, Harriet's literary and financial future was assured. In 1834 she set off to tour the United States of America and study its society, accompanied for the first year by a young Unitarian woman, **Louisa Jeffrey**. Unitarian connections and introductions aided Harriet's travel, although her increasing support for the anti-slavery campaign did not receive universal approval. On her return to England in 1836 she used her acute powers of observation and analysis to produce *Society in America*, which soon became a classic; it was followed by *Retrospect of Western Travel*, a more conventional travel book. She followed this with a small book entitled *How to Observe Morals and Manners*; this guide to the principles of social observation has been described as the first book on sociology. Although Harriet claimed to be a populariser rather than an original thinker, she is regarded by many as a pioneer in social research and social analysis.[10] Her 'methodical self consciousness',[11] combined with an extensive knowledge of history and literature, undergirded by her commitment to a morality imbued with the values of her Unitarian upbringing, including her belief in cause and effect as shown in necessarian philosophy, was directed towards a goal of improving society.

During this period of her life, Harriet's literary output was large and various, including two novels, *Deerbrook* and *The Hour and the Man,* as well as short stories and many articles for journals and in support of social campaigns, especially those opposed to slavery and supportive of women's legal and financial rights. Some of these articles were collected later in *Household Education* (1849).[12] But in 1838 Harriet's health gave way, and she collapsed while visiting Venice. Returning to England, she moved north and rented rooms in Tynemouth in order to be near her doctor, her brother-in-law Thomas Greenhow. For some years she led the restricted life of an invalid. It is probable that an ovarian cyst had caused a prolapsed uterus, and for some years she was confined to a sofa. The symptoms did not stop her writing; she completed some of the fiction that she had started while in London, and published *Life in the Sickroom.* She ascribed her recovery in 1844 to her undergoing courses of mesmerism, but was understandably upset when Greenhow published a different account which described her condition in detail. In consequence of this invasion of her privacy she severed her relations with the Greenhows.[13] Her interest in the practice of mesmerism led to a friendship with Henry George Atkinson, phrenologist, free thinker, and proponent of the priority of natural laws over religious beliefs.

The improvement in her health enabled Harriet to travel again. She set off on a tour of Egypt and the Near East in 1846–7 with three companions from Liverpool: the Unitarians Mr and **Mrs Richard Yates** (who paid for the trip) and William Ewart, the Member of Parliament for Liverpool. Studies of the religions of Egypt, Sinai, Palestine, and Syria convinced Harriet that there was a pattern in religious development, and that 'all ideas are the common heritage of all men' – the Old Testament figure of Moses being key to this revelation. R.K. Webb has interpreted Harriet's reading of Moses as embodying 'the dissenter's rejection of a priesthood, the Hartleyan or phrenological doctrine of conditioning, the liberal's faith in education;

... a necessarian'. Visiting the places where Jesus of Nazareth had lived convinced her of his essential humanity.[14] The subsequent publication in 1847 of *Eastern Life, Present and Past*, in which detailed observation and interpretation implied a rejection of Christianity as the one true faith, aroused great controversy. The publication of her *Letters on the Laws of Man's Nature and Development* (1851), which gave a platform for Atkinson's ideas, made Harriet's departure from Unitarian beliefs evident. This was the main cause of a break with her brother James, who had been a very close friend since childhood and a literary adviser in her early adulthood. He wrote a critical review of the Atkinson book; she attempted to prevent him from being appointed to a post at Manchester New College in 1857 and to the chair of philosophy at the new University College London in 1866. They never met again. James initially resisted her demand for the return of all her letters but eventually complied, but not before making summaries of them.[15] Harriet rejected religion, as she considered that it failed to address scientific questions, but she never lost her faith in a moral universe, and what might be called 'scientific humanism'. In Auguste Comte's *Positive Philosophy*, which she translated and condensed, she found a coherent philosophy of evolutionary progress that spoke to her, although she rejected many aspects of it, including its theocratic structure and its views of women.[16]

Settling into her new house and smallholding near Ambleside in the Lake District, with two maids to help with the daily work, Harriet continued to write – notably *A History of England during the Thirty Years' Peace* – and to support good causes. Locally she gave lectures to working-class audiences and established a building society to provide housing in Ambleside. She began writing leader articles for the *Daily News*, a liberal counterpart to *The Times*. Between 1852 and 1866 she regularly contributed at least two and sometimes up to six leaders a week, except for a three-month break in 1855 to work on her autobiography. The advent of the rail service to Windermere, together with a good postal system, meant that she could receive news by the 7.30 evening post and dispatch a responsive article to the London office by the following afternoon, although after her illness in 1855 she usually restricted her writing to the mornings.[17] Her leading articles covered an enormous range of topics, which she treated with her customary analysis and sometimes dogmatic logic, thus enhancing her influence on Victorian society. Fortunately she could write quickly and accurately. A constant stream of visitors and correspondence added to the demands on her time.

The symptoms that Harriet had experienced in 1855 were probably due to the enlargement of her ovarian cyst, but she was convinced that she had a heart problem, and that this would prove fatal in the near future, so she abandoned her other writing for a time and produced her Autobiography, with instructions that it should not be published until after her death. Her niece Maria, daughter of her brother Robert, now a prominent Birmingham citizen, became her companion, secretary, and general aide. The two women seem to have admired each other, and got on well. From this time Harriet did not travel far, but continued to write for publication for another fifteen years. After Maria's death from typhoid in 1864, another niece, Jenny, took over until 1873, when she was replaced by a paid companion, Miss Goodwin.

Harriet died in 1876. She had achieved her aspiration of becoming financially self-sufficient through her writing (rejecting several offers of a state pension and gifts or loans from friends in years when her health had rendered her less able to write), and she had successfully run a household and smallholding on very sustainable principles. She retained the industrious habits and directness of speech of her Unitarian upbringing, as well as friendship networks and an ingrained disposition to dissent. Not without reason has she been called 'Mrs Barbauld's Daughter'.[18] Although she had rejected religion, her commitment to the moral life was absolute. Many worthy causes benefitted from her generosity; she frequently gave away one third of her income.[19] All her writing was directed towards improving society, and the people in it. Her necessarian views were not always popular, and her logic sometimes led her to over-simplify issues. Her own moral outlook sometimes clouded her analysis, but she remained at heart a reformer. At one time she was considered to be the leading British feminist of the 1830s, and from then onwards she campaigned for women to have more control over their lives.[20] But she insisted that women had to be worthy, better educated, more able to earn their own living, and morally strong. She campaigned for better, healthier working conditions and equal pay, and greater access to education, supporting the foundation of both Queen's College and **Elizabeth Reid's** Bedford College in London, as well as the first professional school of nursing and women's medical education.[21] Although she agreed with much of Mary Wollstonecraft's work on the rights of women, she condemned Mary's erratic love life and attempted suicide, describing her as a 'poor victim of passion, with no control over her own peace'.[22] Similarly, she disapproved of the extra-marital relationship between **Mary Ann Evans** (the novelist **George Eliot**) and George Lewes, and the close friendship of the married John Stuart Mill and **Harriet Taylor**, but she supported their work. Her early role models had been Anna Laetitia Barbauld and to some extent Hannah More, and although she formed friendships with many women, especially those working to improve society, she often found them to be too 'epicurean' in their susceptibility to emotion and lack of self-discipline.

Unitarian and literary networks came into play for a variety of campaigns. With **Florence Nightingale** (who was born into a Unitarian family, but was closer to the Anglican church in later life), she exposed the inefficiencies and disasters of the Crimean War. Through her vast correspondence she kept in touch with activists in both England and America, signing John Stuart Mill's petition for women's suffrage in 1866, and at the end of her life supporting the campaign to repeal the Contagious Diseases Acts (which permitted the police to detain and inspect any woman – but no man – suspected of venereal infection). She was one of the first people to make a link between the treatment of slaves in America and the treatment of women in England, and she devoted much energy to the anti-slavery campaigns in both countries.[23] Although Harriet eventually abandoned her allegiance to Unitarianism, its values and early training were the force behind her remarkable achievements and her significant life.

Endnotes

1   Harriet Martineau, *Autobiography* (originally published 1877) (Virago, 1983), Vol. I, pp.53ff; R.K. Webb, 'Martineau, Harriet', *Oxford Dictionary of National Biography*, www.oxforddnb.com (accessed 9 August 2018).

2   Webb, ODNB, op.cit.

3   Webb, ODNB, op. cit.; Martineau, *Autobiography*, pp.104ff.

4   Ann Peart, 'Forgotten Prophets: The Lives of Unitarian Women 1760–1904' (unpublished doctoral thesis, University of Newcastle, 2006) <https://theses.ncl.ac.uk/dspace/bitstream/10443/245/1/peart05.pdf>, pp.142ff

5   Ibid., p.130.

6   R.K. Webb, *Harriet Martineau: A Radical Victorian* (London, Heinemann, 1960), pp.97ff.

7   Ruth Watts, *Women in Science; A Social and Political History* (London, Routledge, 2007), pp.91–8; Vera Wheatley, *The Life and Work of Harriet Martineau* (London, Secker and Warburg, 1957), pp.105–6.

8   Webb, ODNB, op.cit.

9   Kathryn Gleadle, *The Early Feminists. Radical Unitarians and the Emergence of the Women's Rights Movement, 1831–51* (London, St Martin's Press, 1995).

10 Susan Hoecker-Drysdale, 'HM and the rise of sociology', *A Harriet Martineau Miscellany* (The Martineau Society, 2002), pp.163–9.

11 Harriet Martineau, *Society in America,* ed. Seymour Martin Lipset (New York, Anchor Books, Doubleday, 1962), p.7.

12 Webb, ODNB, op.cit.

13 Ibid.

14 Webb, 1960, op.cit., p.291.

15 Valerie Sanders, 'James and Harriet: brother and sister', *Transactions of the Unitarian Historical Society,* Vol. 22 No. 4 (2002), pp.321–8.

16 Webb, ODNB, op.cit.

17 Webb, 1960, op.cit., pp.313–15.

18 William McCarthy, *Anna Letitia Barbauld: Voice of the Enlightenment* (Baltimore, John Hopkins University Press, 2008), p.510.

19 Webb, 1960, op.cit., pp.312–14.

20 Gayle Graham Yates (ed.), *Harriet Martineau on Women* (New Brunswick, Rutgers University Press, 1985), pp.19–21.

21 Ibid., p.21.

22 Harriet Martineau, *Autobiography,* p.400.

23 Yates, op.cit., p.18.

5 Elizabeth Jesser Reid (1789–1866)

Ann Peart

Elizabeth Reid (1789–1866) is best known as the founder of Bedford College in London, the first higher-education institution for women in the United Kingdom. She was steeped in Unitarianism and remained faithful to the movement all her life – with a fervent belief in a benevolent God, the ethical teachings of Jesus, and trust in an afterlife in which all would meet again in a better state – in spite of the difficulties that it caused her.[1] Her father, William Sturch, was a prosperous ironmonger who had left his original General Baptist connections to become one of the first members of the Essex Street Unitarian Chapel.[2] Not much is known of Elizabeth's early life, but her rather casual approach to English grammar and her lack of knowledge of French suggest that she may have had little formal education. Henry Crabb Robinson described her as a 'slight figure of a woman who with a delicate woman's nature combines a great portion of both moral and religious zeal – a very generous person ... a most amiable woman, with a quick perception of all sorts of excellence'.[3] Her enthusiasms were sometimes carried to excess, and she often upset people, though she was quick to forgive others. **Julia Smith** (aunt of **Barbara Bodichon** and **Florence Nightingale**) said that 'her failures are better than other people's successes; they are worthier, and they sometimes produce more visible good effects, though not exactly the effects she looked for and worked for'.[4]

One of her closest friends was **Harriet Martineau**; unlike most of Harriet's friendships, the closeness between them lasted many years, until Elizabeth's death in 1866, and they often visited each other. Harriet's scheme for building homes for working-class people in Ambleside was largely funded by Elizabeth.[5] The two were in many ways opposites, their temperaments and gifts differed, but they shared a devotion to causes such as the anti-slavery campaign and women's education. In 1822 Elizabeth married John Reid, a medical practitioner, a childless widower thirteen

Elizabeth Jesser Reid
(Courtesy of Camden Local Studies and Archives Centre)

years her senior, but he died when they had been married just over a year, leaving her very well off. She enjoyed entertaining and had a wide circle of friends, many of whom, like her, were engaged in reform movements and charitable societies.[6]

Elizabeth was an ardent supporter of anti-slavery campaigns. The World Anti-Slavery Convention held in London in 1840, organised by the British and Foreign Anti-Slavery Society, roused the feelings of many women when the American women delegates were denied their place on the all-male ground floor of the meeting hall and relegated to the gallery, as was the usual practice in England at this time.[7] The more radical anti-slavery campaigners, often influenced by the American William Garrison, had included women's rights and other issues in their work, whereas the Evangelical Christians had not. Elizabeth entertained American abolitionists from both sides of the debate, but she sided with the more radical Garrisonian wing. Her hospitality to all campaigners continued, especially towards visiting American women.

Harriet Beecher Stowe stayed with her in 1853, when she came to speak to private groups of women about slavery,[8] and Sarah Remond, the first African-American woman to undertake a public speaking tour of Britain and Ireland, during 1859–1861, boarded with Elizabeth when she became a student at Bedford College.[9] By this time Elizabeth had become a committee member of the Garrisonian London Emancipation Committee.[10]

The cause to which Elizabeth devoted her money, and most of the last twenty years of her life, was the founding of a college of higher education for women, run largely by women, on non-denominational lines. These last two qualities were in contrast to the Anglican Queen's College, founded in March 1848 and governed mainly by clergymen. Elizabeth found supporters for her venture among her Unitarian friends, both women and men, but the unpopularity of Unitarianism led to the word being omitted in all documentation. Men were essential to the project, for both legal and social reasons: because married women could not own property, the trustees had to be male; most women were not familiar with committee work, and as few women were educated to a sufficient standard, most of the teaching had to be done by men.[11] At first the novelty of having both women and men on the various committees proved problematic, but the women soon learned committee procedures. The question of religious studies also posed a problem: Elizabeth did not want the college to appear 'Godless', so she wished biblical studies to have a place on the curriculum. Arrangements were made to offer the subject on a non-creedal basis, but this aspiration proved very difficult to fulfil, and the subject was dropped after nine years.[12] In spite of these difficulties, a house was found in Bedford Square, and the college opened in October 1849, with many of the 68 students being Elizabeth's Unitarian friends. They included **Anna Swanwick**, with her mother and sister; **Fanny Wedgwood** (wife of the barrister and academic Hensleigh Wedgwood, and friend of Harriet Martineau); four women in the Martineau family; **Julia Smith with her nieces Bertha, Blanche, and Barbara** (who became Madame Bodichon and left the college a substantial legacy); **Margaret Howitt**, daughter of William and Mary; **Laura Herford**; and **Mary Ann Evans** (George Eliot), who studied Latin for one term.[13] The wide age range of the students, from girls as young as twelve or thirteen, brought by their governesses, to mature women, made it difficult to create a close-knit community of learning. Most of the students attended on a part-time basis, with some attending only a single lecture.

At first the college faced considerable difficulties. Its association with nonconformity, and Unitarians in particular, proved a disadvantage in attracting both funding and students, but Elizabeth persevered with her original vision, in spite of having to compromise on matters such as governance. The lower age limit was twelve, and it was soon found necessary to establish a separate school to teach the younger girls and bring others up to a standard at which higher education could begin. This school was established in January 1853, open to pupils between the ages of nine and fifteen; it gained a good reputation, but failed to produce a supply of students to the college and was eventually closed.

Francis Newman, then professor of Latin at University College and the first principal of University Hall, was a keen supporter and teacher at the college, but his heterodoxy meant that he departed even from the Unitarians, and his involvement was a mixed blessing.[14] Bedford College, as it became known from 1859, began submitting women for London University degrees when this was first permitted in 1878, and eventually it became a constituent college of the University.[15] From the beginning women took an active role in teaching and running the college; its original constitution included a group of 'Lady Visitors', represented on the governing body, whose duties included providing chaperones when male professors were in the building. Apparently this practice lasted until 1893.[16] **Catherine Aikin** (great-niece of Anna Laetitia Barbauld, niece of Lucy Aikin) acted as the secretary for the visitors for the whole of this time.[17]

Although Elizabeth was 59 years old when the college opened, and in poor health, she played a significant role in its activities until 1860, when she created a trust for its future management, with (for legal reasons) three unmarried women appointed as trustees; of the original trio, **Jane Martineau** and **Rachel Lydia Notcutt** came from Unitarian families. Jane was the daughter of John Martineau, a cousin of the father of Harriet,[18] and she was Secretary of the college, while Rachel supervised the boarding house. In the twentieth century Unitarian trustees included Rachel Notcutt's niece, the **Revd E. Rosalind Lee**, and **Dorothy Tarrant**.[19] Gradually more women were able to teach to the required standard, and the first woman to become head of a department was **Gertrude Martineau** (daughter of James), who ran the drawing school from 1873 to 1884. The Unitarian **Henrietta Busk** was a student from 1861 to 1864 and became a significant figure in the future of the college, being a member of the council from 1882 almost continuously until her death in 1936. She founded the Old Students' Association, organised the Jubilee celebrations in 1899, and spent much energy in fund raising.[20]

At the time of Elizabeth's death in 1866 the college was still less than secure, but the dedication of her friends and successors ensured that it survived until the present day, having merged with Royal Holloway College in 1985, and provided women with the opportunities for higher education of which she had dreamed.

Endnotes

1   Margaret J. Tuke, *A History of Bedford College for Women 1849–1937* (Oxford, Oxford University Press, 1939), pp.17, 25, 27.

2   Ibid., p.3.

3   Ibid., p.7.

4   Ibid., p.17.

5   Ibid., pp.9–10.

6   Ibid., pp.4–6.

7   Louis Billington and Rosamund Billington, ' "A burning zeal for righteousness": women in the British anti-slavery movement, 1820–1860', in *Equal or Different: Women's Politics 1800–1914*, ed. Jane Rendall (Oxford, Basil Blackwell, 1987), p. 96.

8   'Reid, Elisabeth Jesser', *Oxford Dictionary of National Biography* (ODNB), www.oxforddnb.com, accessed 8 September 2010.

9   L, and R. Billington, op.cit., p.107; Clare Midgley, *Women Against Slavery: The British Campaigns 1780–1870* (London, Routledge, 1992), p.163.

10 Midgley, op.cit., p.164.

11 Tuke, op.cit., pp.28–31.

12 Ibid., pp.33–35.

13 Ibid., pp.62, 281.

14 Dorothy Tarrant, 'Unitarians and Bedford College', *Transactions of the Unitarian Historical Society*, Vol. 9 no. 4 (1950), p.204.

15 Tuke, op.cit., passim.

16 Ibid., p.54.

17 Betsy Rodgers, *Georgian Chronicle: Mrs Barbauld and her Family* (London, Methuen, 1958), pp..9, 188.

18 Tarrant, op. cit., pp.201–6.

19 Ibid., p.205.

20 Ibid., p.206; Tuke, op.cit., p.164.

6 The 'radical unitarians' centred on South Place Chapel, London

Ann Peart

The ministry of William Johnson Fox at Bishopsgate from 1817, and then in the newly built South Place Chapel in London from 1824, attracted a circle of radical thinkers, both women and men. The congregation had Universalist roots and was at first recognised as Unitarian,[1] but Fox's radical views, including advocating easier divorce, coupled with his decision to leave his wife to set up house with his ward, Eliza Flower, led to a distancing between the South Place group (named 'radical unitarians' by Kathryn Gleadle[2]), and the main Unitarian movement. Fox was a powerful speaker and writer, and he edited the Unitarian journal the *Monthly Repository* and other periodicals. He gathered an impressive group of people interested in exploring reform on a variety of issues, notably the social and legal status of women and their rights. He eventually gave up his ministry, presenting his final address at South Place in 1852. Supported from 1847 by a significant lifetime annuity from the Unitarian Samuel Courtauld, Fox was freed to work as a lecturer and writer and was elected as the Member of Parliament for Oldham from 1847 onwards.[3]

William Fox's circle included many recognised Unitarians, such as **Harriet Martineau**, whose early writings he published; the Ashhurst family; William and **Mary Howitt** (who left the Society of Friends and became Unitarian for a time); **Harriet Taylor** (later Mill); and members of the Courtauld family, as well as other social reformers. Between the late 1820s and the 1850s the group based on the South Place Chapel developed the intellectual analysis of issues such as domestic slavery, the relationship between marriage and prostitution, and the legal protection of women which were to undergird feminist activities later in the century. The significance of this initially Unitarian congregation for the changes in women's roles within society is only now being recognised,[4] as illustrated in this chapter by the stories of four Unitarian women: **Margaret Gillies, Harriet Taylor, Eliza Flower**, and **Sarah Flower Adams.**

South Place Chapel, Finsbury
(built 1824, demolished 1927)

Margaret Gillies (1803–1887)

Margaret was one of the most successful portrait painters of her time, a pioneer who paved the way for younger women artists.[5] In common with others in the nineteenth century, in order to gain public approval and support she kept both her Unitarian convictions and her private life secret. Yet it is now recognised that her work is a 'unique example of the Unitarian ethos applied to art'.[6] She and her siblings, though born in London, were raised by family members in Scotland, where she may have met Unitarians, including Thomas Southwood Smith, who served as the minister at the Unitarian Church in Edinburgh from 1812 to 1815 while he studied medicine.[7] When Margaret and her older sister Mary moved back to London in about 1819, Margaret either renewed or began an acquaintance with Southwood Smith, and through him the sisters were introduced to William Fox and his congregation, which they joined. Margaret planned to earn her living as a painter, while Mary pursued writing as a career.[8]

It was difficult for women to find artistic tuition, as there were no art schools open to them, but eventually Margaret found an artist, Frederick Cruikshank, willing to give her lessons. At the same time as studying, she took on commissions for portraits, and she soon began to exhibit her pictures, at first mainly water-colour miniatures on ivory, which were displayed in a variety of galleries in London (including the Royal Academy) and elsewhere. The subjects of her portraits included several Unitarians and members of the South Place circle, including Harriet Martineau. She did not paint solely for money: she claimed a moral and educative motive for her work, writing in a letter to Leigh Hunt in 1837:

> *Artists in general seize every opportunity of painting the nobility of wealth and rank. It would be far more grateful to me to be able to paint what I conceive to be true nobility, that of genius, long, faithfully, earnestly and not without suffering labouring to call out what is most beautiful and refined in our nature and to establish this as the guide and standard of our race.*[9]

For Margaret, 'art was a means of drawing attention to the divine spirit' present in all people.[10]

Meanwhile, her domestic situation had changed. At first she and Mary lived with their father, with Mary taking on the brunt of the domestic responsibilities. Later, as Margaret began to earn more money from her painting commissions, Mary acted as her secretary, and they lived together until Mary's death in 1870. Both sisters were romantically involved with men in the South Place circle. Margaret became the partner of Southwood Smith after he left his second wife in 1824, while Mary became involved with the writer and critic Richard Hengist Horne for a time. The four lived at a variety of addresses in the London area, and often they shared a house together.[11] Early in the 1840s Southwood Smith's young granddaughter, **Gertrude Hill**, came to live with them. Their longest residence was in Highgate, where Margaret, Gertrude, and Southwood Smith lived until 1854, when they moved to Weybridge. (Richard Horne had by this time married another woman.) In order to guard her privacy and maintain her 'respectability', Margaret began working from a separate studio in London, at various addresses in an area just south of Euston Station.[12] (A street north of this area was later named after her.) Her reliance on commissions for much of her income meant that she needed to safeguard her reputation from any suggestion of scandal; for the same reason she also concealed her Unitarianism.

As her standing as a portrait painter grew, Margaret earned enough most of the time to maintain the other members of the household. She enlarged her repertoire to include a wider range of subjects in both watercolours and oils, including biblical themes, literature, and history, usually featuring women. The theme of suffering and its role in developing a moral sense was one of her particular concerns. Her series in the 1830s on the captive Daughter of Zion combined two of her interests: suffering and the status of women.[13] She spent some time in Paris in 1851, studying with Henri and Ari Scheffer, artists whose religious paintings were particularly popular with British Unitarians.[14] In 1852 Margaret was elected to membership of the Old Water Colour Society, which admitted women but gave them no rights or responsibilities. This did, however, enhance her standing and boosted the sale of her pictures, now an economic necessity.[15] Her production of more allegorical depictions of religious themes reflected a development of her religious ideas from the necessarianism of Joseph

Priestley to the more aesthetic and emotional thought of the Martineau wing of the Unitarian movement.[16]

During 1840–42 Southwood Smith served as one of 24 commissioners appointed to an official inquiry into the employment of children in mines. It is probable that Margaret was the anonymous illustrator of many of the pictures and diagrams of what became a very influential report. Women, as well as children, were depicted in the report and in widely circulated summaries of it. These did much to change common perceptions of women workers, and the physical and moral dangers that they faced.[17] Both Gillies sisters were involved in promoting practical reforms. Margaret illustrated a series of educational children's books written by Mary, and both supported the new Whittington Club, opened in 1847 with the aim of promoting the education of both women and men of the lower classes. In the same year the sisters were appointed honorary members of the Co-operative League in Birmingham. Their circle of friends and visitors included Robert Owen, Edwin Chadwick, and others active in improving social conditions for both women and the working classes.[18] Margaret also encouraged younger women artists, including **Barbara Leigh Smith** and **Anna Mary Howitt**, and together with **Eliza Fox** (daughter of William) they signed a petition in 1859, requesting that women be admitted to the Royal Academy Schools.[19]

The death of Southwood Smith in 1861 greatly affected Margaret's life and her art. Together with Mary and Gertrude, she moved to Church Row, Hampstead, the road where **Anna Laetitia Barbauld, Joanna Baillie, and Lucy Aikin** had lived, to a house previously owned by Eliza Meteyard, a writer and historian who had also been associated with the radical unitarians[20] and was an early member of the Whittington Club. For the rest of her life Margaret subscribed annually to the funds of the newly built Rosslyn Hill (Unitarian) Chapel in Hampstead, and she also supported its school. Mary, and later Gertrude, also supported the chapel.[21] Members of the congregation such as **Clementia Taylor** and **Mary Ann Evans** (the novelist George Eliot) became part of the sisters' close network of friends, and when Gertrude married Charles Lewes, son of G.H. Lewes (who was living with Mary Ann Evans), the Leweses became part of the extended family.[22]

Many artists lived in Hampstead, and Margaret now no longer felt the need for a separate studio nearer central London.[23] Her range of subjects included pictures inspired by her travels, often with Mary (until her death in 1870) and then with Gertrude, frequently staying with relatives or friends. The advent of the rail network, and the increasing acceptability of women artists sketching outdoors, resulted in watercolours of local people painted in Wales, Scotland, Italy, and France, frequently shown in exhibitions of the Old Water Colour Society and the Society of Female Artists.[24] Margaret still focused on expressing themes of emotion, intellectual ideas, and character, rather than mere pictures of people in landscapes, and in particular she developed her earlier interest in portraying female suffering in differing contexts. Some of these reflected her loneliness after the deaths of Southwood Smith and her sister Mary, who had been her life-long companion, although Gertrude, with her husband and children, shared a house with her or lived close by for the rest of her life. Margaret continued to travel and led an active social life, including tea parties for her Hampstead friends.[25] She produced a series of paintings on medieval themes, again with an emphasis on women, portraying an altruistic lifestyle with spiritual fulfilment as its goal – a reflection of her own philosophy of life. One particular work, a triptych entitled 'The End of the Pilgrimage', painted in 1873, suggested faith in an ultimate salvation after hard labour. It was exhibited five times in the last years of her life and sold for £105, soon increasing in value to more than double the original price.[26] When Margaret died at Crockham Hill in Kent, she was acknowledged as a leading artist of her day. Her educational and spiritual aims were recognised by many, but the Unitarianism which underpinned her life and work remained known only to a few.[27]

Harriet Taylor (1807–1858)

Harriet (*née* Hardy) was rumoured to have married early (at the age of eighteen) to escape from an unhappy home with a domineering father. Her husband, John Taylor, was a member of the South Place congregation, led by William Fox, and Harriet soon joined it.[28] Fox's views on marriage resonated with her own desire to escape what had become an unhappy marriage to a man eleven years her senior who could not give her the intellectual stimulation that she craved.[29] Within the radical unitarian circle Harriet became known as an advocate of complete equality between women and men. It was through Fox that she met the philosopher and economist John Stuart Mill (at a dinner party given by the Taylors in the late 1830s), who was recovering from a mental breakdown at the time and feeling lonely. Fox's daughter Eliza later remembered Harriet aged 25 as follows:

> Possessed of a beauty and grace quite unique of their kind. Tall and slight, with a slightly drooping figure, the movement of undulating grace. A small head, a swan-like throat, and a complexion like a pearl. Large eyes, not soft or sleepy, but with a look of quiet command in them. A low sweet voice with a very distinctive utterance emphasised the effect of her engrossing personality. Her children adored her.[30]

By this time Harriet had two sons, Herbert (born in 1827) and Algernon (born in 1830), and a daughter, Helen, born in 1831. Harriet and J.S. Mill were immediately attracted to each other and slowly developed a close friendship, sharing their commitment to educational, social, and political reforms, particularly concerning women.[31] In order to maintain an appearance of respectability, John Taylor, Harriet, and Mill agreed that Harriet would remain as Taylor's wife and spend some time in the marital home near Regent's Park, as well as having her own establishment, first in Kent and then at Walton-on-Thames, Surrey. Helen went to live with her mother, while Herbert lived with his father, and Algernon seems to have spent time in both households. Harriet's health began to cause problems, and a lung condition meant that she often spent the winters away, either in Europe, sometimes with Mill, or in the south of England. She returned to John Taylor's home to nurse him through his final illness in 1849, and then, after a suitable interval, married Mill in the spring of 1851. In keeping with their principles, before the marriage Mill formally renounced the legal rights of a husband over his wife and promised a relationship of absolute equality.[32] They set up house together with Helen in Blackheath. But by this time Harriet's lungs were significantly damaged, and she died in Avignon in November 1858.[33]

Harriet had led a quiet life, mixing little with other people after her move away from London, partly because of her wish to avoid scandal, and partly because of her delicate health. She published little in her own name, but was clearly a very significant influence on Mill, who published a great deal, not only on philosophy, but also on social reforms and the position of women. He became an active campaigner for women's rights, including universal suffrage.[34] Authorities agree that Harriet was a more radical thinker than Mill, claiming as she did, from the early 1830s, that women should have complete equality with men. In an essay exchanged privately with Mill at that time she emphasised the degrading effect of women's economic dependence on men and advocated that even married women should be self-supporting. She hoped that such economic equality would make marriage laws unnecessary, and she also advocated that women should take responsibility for their own children. In contrast, Mill's views at this time were much less radical and rather more sentimental.[35]

Harriet's pieces written for the *Monthly Repository* in 1831–2 covered a variety of genres, but most were not directly concerned with reforming the position of women. In 1851 a long essay, *The Enfranchisement of Women*, written by Harriet, appeared under Mill's name in the *Westminster Review*. In it she advocated that women should have 'their admission, in law and in fact, to equality in all rights, political, civil, and social, with the male citizens of the community'.[36] Harriet's influence on Mill's major works is evident, for example in the fact that his 1850s revisions of both *A System of Logic* and *Principles of Political Economy* used inclusive language, for example changing 'a man' to 'a person' , 'men' to 'people', and so on.[37] Together they wrote a series of articles on the subject of male brutality within marriage, published in the *Morning Chronicle* during 1851–2.[38] Even after her death, Harriet's influence was evident in Mill's work for women's suffrage and other rights. Her daughter Helen followed in Harriet's footsteps and did much to advance the status of women. In tribute to Harriet, and at the request of Helen, Mill published his well-known essay, *The Subjection of Women*, as a record of their shared beliefs; this made a significant contribution to the cause of women's rights.[39]

Eliza Flower (1803–1846) and Sarah Flower Adams (1805–1848)

Eliza Flower and Sarah Flower were both at the centre of the South Place congregation and its group of radical unitarians. Eliza was a musician, while Sarah is best known as a poet and hymn writer. They were sisters, the daughters of Benjamin and Eliza Flower. Benjamin was the editor of the radical paper, *The Cambridge Intelligencer,* and had been imprisoned in 1799 for his defence of freedom of expression. Eliza (*née* Gould) had lost her job as a school teacher for refusing to cancel her subscription to the *Intelligencer.* She died in 1810, after giving birth to a son who died prematurely, after which the girls were brought up unconventionally by their father, with lessons from himself and occasionally from village schoolmasters.[40] In 1820 the family moved to Hackney and became neighbours of William Fox, with whom they soon became friends as well as members of his South Place congregation. The sisters remained members of the congregation for the rest of their lives.[41] At this time Fox had suffered a severe mental and physical collapse and was unable to preach for a year.[42] Three years later both families, with Southwood Smith, took a holiday together in Scotland, and, on an outing which included both Eliza and Fox, Sarah broke the record for the fastest ascent of Ben Lomond by a woman (8 September 1823).[43] Back in London, Eliza took a particular interest in the shy Harriet Martineau, who was writing articles for Fox's *Monthly Repository.* Later Harriet would use the Flower sisters as models for the Ibbotson sisters in her novel, *Deerbrook.*[44] Both sisters became friendly with the poet Robert Browning; there was even a suggestion of romance between Robert and Eliza, and to him Sarah confided her doubts about the authority of the Bible (while retaining a belief in an all-wise and omnipotent God).[45] Sarah shared her doubts also with Fox and is sometimes credited with stimulating the development of his thought away from Priestleyan Unitarianism, with its emphasis on materialism and determinism.[46]

Before their father died in 1829, he had arranged for Eliza and Sarah to become wards of Fox, and they went to live with him and his family. Eliza had already been acting as Fox's literary assistant since the Scottish holiday, and the two became increasingly close. This intensified the pre-existing difficulties in Fox's marriage, and in January 1835 he left his wife and set up home with Eliza, first in Bayswater and later in Bloomsbury. Coupled with an article published by Fox advocating divorce on the grounds of incompatibility, this resulted in the resignation of some members of his congregation, and Fox's expulsion from the London group of Unitarian ministers. From this point Harriet Martineau withdrew all contact for a time, but her brother James responded in a rather more kindly manner.[47] Eliza went on to share the hosting of a 'radical salon' which became a centre for discussion of social reforms and feminist ideas. She was described as extremely beautiful and very charismatic, with a spiritual quality which earned her the name Ariel. Literary men such as Robert Browning often sought her advice, and some claimed that she was largely responsible for Fox's success.

In her own right Eliza was a gifted composer and musician. Her first composition, *Fourteen Musical Illustrations of the Waverley Novels,* was published in 1831, and many other pieces followed.[48] In conjunction with the musical director of South Place Chapel, Collet Dobson Collet, she trained choirs, organised lectures, and gave concerts. Her organ recitals were extremely popular, and Sarah contributed to them as a singer. Eliza wrote a great deal of music specially for the chapel, including 63 hymn tunes, and she arranged the work of others for performance at South Place. Words by Harriet Martineau were used for a reform anthem which became popular with many radical groups, and she also composed music for the funeral of Rammohun Roy, the Indian reformer who died while visiting Unitarians in Bristol. At the time of her death she was considered by many to be the greatest British female composer of all time, but her music is rarely heard today.[49]

Eliza and Fox claimed that their relationship was a platonic one, and often it was strained. Surprisingly, Eliza formed a close bond with Fox's wife and daughter, both also called Eliza. For a time Fox and Eliza Flower lived with Sarah and her husband, William Bridges Adams, but London air did not suit Eliza, who suffered from respiratory problems and often needed to rest in the purer air of the countryside. She died from consumption in December 1846.[50] She had used her gifts as a social hostess and above all as a musician in the service of her Unitarian chapel, and she deserves to be remembered for her contributions both to the Unitarian story and to music.

Sarah Flower, known as Sally to her friends, was a gifted poet and author. Eliza Fox (W.J.'s daughter) described her in 1837 as 'tall and singularly beautiful', but in the same year Sarah portrayed herself as 'very thin, very deaf (making me very stupid) and five feet two and a half'. Her adult-onset deafness was inherited from her father, and she shared with her mother and her sister respiratory problems which developed into tuberculosis.[51] While recuperating on the Isle of Wight from a breakdown after her father's death, she composed what may have been her first significant poetry, a long poem called *The Royal Progress* (telling the story of Isabella, the last queen of the Island, who abdicated in favour of her brother, Edward I, in 1293), which was eventually published in 1845.

Sarah met William Bridges Adams, who also belonged to the radical unitarian group, at the home of Harriet Taylor. William, eight years her senior, was a widower who as an engineer had spent some time in Chile and the United States. In 1833 he published in the *Monthly Repository* an article on women which claimed: 'Whatever be the rank of our females, whether high or low, they are, with few exceptions, as much slaves as the inmates of a Turkish Haram [sic]'. He stated moreover that higher-class women were studiously instructed that marriage is not an affair of love, or affection, or judgment, but merely a matter of bargain or sale, and that they were 'trained to undergo... a species of prostitution'; he went on to argue that marriage contracts should be capable of dissolution like any other contract.[52] This much-publicised article outraged many and exacerbated the rift between the South Place group and mainstream Unitarians. It did not alienate Sarah Flower, however, and she married him in 1834.[53]

In the following years Sarah and William both published articles advocating reform on such matters as education and housing, and Sarah also contributed poems and stories.[54] She shared the view of **Harriet Martineau** and **Mary Wollstonecraft** that women had been rendered inferior by their poor education and lack of purpose in society, writing in 1834: 'their energies in being denied full scope, are misdirected. In consequence, they too often become domestic tyrants, or suffer ill health, the consequence of unemployed power.'[55] This was not a problem experienced by Sarah in her marriage, and her husband supported her in her long-held ambition to become an actress. As Fox's daughter Eliza recounted,

After her marriage, with the hearty sympathy and concurrence of her husband, she sought to carry out her youthful ambition of adopting the stage as a profession. She entertained the idea that the life of an actress, a life devoted to the constant expression of the highest poetry, ought to be really – as it was theoretically – a life in unison with the high thoughts to which she had habitually to give utterance. 'The drama', she writes in one of her notebooks, 'is an epitome of the mind and manners of mankind, and wise men of all ages have agreed to make it, what in truth it ought to be, a supplement of the pulpit'.[56]

For Sarah, the stage was another medium for communicating the message of her faith. Since her childhood she had performed songs in costume and acted scenes from Shakespeare at private functions. Her first public performance was as Lady Macbeth at the Little Theatre in Richmond (London) in 1837, followed by appearances in the roles of Portia in *The Merchant of Venice* and Lady Teazle in *The School for Scandal*. These met with enough success for her to be offered roles at Bath, but her health was failing, and she gave up hopes of a theatrical career in order to concentrate on more limited local performances and on writing.[57] Her poems ranged from *Vivia Perpetua,* a five-act drama exploring issues of women's freedom from control by men, to political poetry, such as that for the Anti-Corn Law League, and a verse catechism for factory schools, *The Flock and the Fountain.* She composed thirteen hymns and translated or paraphrased others for a new hymnbook for the South Place Chapel published by Fox.[58] She is best remembered for 'Nearer My God, To Thee', which was used in American Unitarian hymn books from 1844 and is one of two hymns by her still sung by British Unitarians (in *Hymns of Faith and Freedom*). She died in August 1848, less than two years after her sister. An early biographer wrote, 'All who knew Mrs. Adams personally speak of her with enthusiasm; she is described as a woman of singular beauty and attractiveness, delicate and truly feminine, high-minded, and in her days of health playful and high-spirited'.[59] She was a true Unitarian, who wrestled with her doubts, but maintained her theistic faith, and expressed it in words and actions.

Endnotes

1   S.K. Radcliffe, *The Story of South Place* (London, Watts & Co, 1955), pp..2–3.

2   Kathryn Gleadle, *The Early Feminists. Radical Unitarians and the Emergence of the Women's Rights Movement, 1831–51* (London, Palgrave Macmillan, 1995), pp.172–5.

3   R.K. Webb, 'Fox, William Johnson', *Oxford Dictionary of National Biography* (ODNB), www.oxforddnb.com, accessed 1 October 2018.

4   Gleadle, op.cit., pp.172–5.

5   Charlotte Yeldham, *Margaret Gillies RWS, Unitarian Painter of Mind and Emotion 1803–1887*, (Lampeter, Edwin Mellen Press, 1997), p.104.

6   Ibid., p. 105.

7   R.K. Webb, 'Smith (Thomas) Southwood', *Oxford Dictionary of National Biography* (ODNB), www.oxforddnb.com, accessed 4 October 2018.

8   Charlotte Yeldham, 'Gillies, Margaret', *Oxford Dictionary of National Biography* (ODNB), www.oxforddnb.com, accessed 4 October 2018.

9   Yeldham, 1997, op.cit., p.19.

10 Ibid., p.16.

11 Ibid., pp.11–13.

12 Ibid., pp.46, 53, 57, 74.

13 Ibid., pp.28–31.

14 Ibid., pp.68–72.

15 Ibid., p.72.

16 Ibid., p.84.

17 Ibid., pp.47–51.

18 Ibid., pp.56–60

19 Ibid., p.60.

20 Gleadle, op.cit., pp.5-6.

21 Ibid., p.87; Fred Hunter, 'Meteyard, Eliza', *Oxford Dictionary of National Biography* (ODNB), www.oxforddnb.com, accessed 10 October 2018.

22 Yeldham, 1997, op.cit., p. 92.

23 Ibid., p.87.

24 Ibid., pp.88–90.

25 Ibid., pp.92–7.

26 Ibid., pp.98–103.

27 Ibid., pp.104–5.

28 Olive Banks, *The Biographical Dictionary of British Feminists Volume One 1800–1930* (Brighton, Wheatsheaf Books, 1985), p.208; Gleadle, op. cit., p.38.

29 Banks, op.cit., p.208; Janet Murray, *Strong-Minded Women and Other Lost Voices from Nineteenth Century England* (New York, Pantheon, 1982), p.32.

30 F.A. Hayek, ed., *John Stuart Mill and Harriet Taylor: Their Correspondence and Subsequent Marriage* (London, Routledge and Kegan Paul, 1951), p.25, quoted by Ann P. Robson, 'Mill (née Hardy; other married name Taylor), Harriet', *Oxford Dictionary of National Biography* (ODNB), www.oxforddnb.com, accessed 9 August 2018.

31 Ibid.

32 Murray, op.cit., pp.123–4.

33 Robson, op.cit.

34 Banks, op. cit., pp..208–10; Elizabeth Crawford, *The Women's Suffrage Movement: A Reference Guide 1866–1928* (London, Routledge, 2001), pp.408–11.

35 Banks, op. cit., pp..208–9.

36 Robson, op. cit.

37 Ibid.

38 Gleadle, op.cit., pp.126–7.

39 Banks, op.cit., p..210.

40 Virginia Blain, 'Adams, Sarah Flower', *Oxford Dictionary of National Biography* (ODNB), 2004, www.oxforddnb.com, accessed 9 August 2018.

41 Robert Spears, *Memorable Unitarians* (London, British and Foreign Unitarian Association, 1906), p.353.

42 Webb, ODNB, op.cit.

43 Blain, op.cit.; Webb, ODNB, op.cit.

44 R.K. Webb, *Harriet Martineau: A Radical Victorian* (London, Heinemann, 1960), p. 98; Kathryn Gleadle, 'Flower, Eliza', *Oxford Dictionary of National Biography* (ODNB), 2004, www.oxforddnb.com, accessed 8 August 2018.

45 H.W. Stephenson, *Unitarian Hymn-Writers* (London, Lindsey Press, 1931), pp.27–8.

46 Radcliffe, op.cit., pp.21–2.

47 Gleadle, ODNB, op.cit.; Webb, ONDB, op.cit.

48 Gleadle, ODNB, op. cit.

49 Ibid.

50 Ibid.

51 Blain, ODNB, op.cit.

52 Gleadle, 1995, op.cit., pp.34, 116.

53 *Oxford Dictionary of National Biography* (ODNB), 'Adams, William Bridges', accessed 16 October 2018.

54 Blain, ODNB, op.cit.; Gleadle, 1995, op.cit., pp.48–50, 53, 99.

55 Gleadle, 1995, op.cit., p. 95.

56 Alfred H. Miles, 'Critical and Biographical Essay; Sarah Flower Adams (1805–1848)' in *The Sacred Poets of the Nineteenth Century* (1905), https://www.bartleby.com/294/124.html (accessed 15 October 2018).

57 Ibid.

58 Ibid.; Blain, ODNB, op.cit.

59 https://en.wikisource.org/wiki/Adams,_Sarah_Flower_(DNB00), accessed 16 October 2018.

7 Elizabeth Gaskell (1810–1865)

Ann Peart

Elizabeth Gaskell is perhaps the best known of all Unitarian women from the past, with a growing reputation as a significant novelist of the nineteenth century – although in her own life time, and for many years after that, she was remembered mainly for her biography of Charlotte Brontë, as related in her *Manchester Guardian* obituary.[1]

Elizabeth Cleghorn Stevenson, known after her marriage as Lily to her family and close friends,[2] was born on 29 September 1810 in Chelsea, London. Both her parents were from families with a long tradition of dissent. Her father, William, trained as a dissenting minister at Daventry and for a short time served the Unitarian congregation at Failsworth, near Manchester, before trying and failing at farming in Scotland. He eventually settled in London and worked as keeper of records at the Treasury. He was said to be a progressive, radical Unitarian. Her mother, also called Elizabeth, *née* Holland, came from a large family of more traditional, 'respectable', middle-class rational dissenters from Cheshire, linked by marriage to the Wedgwood, Turner, and Darwin families. Elizabeth had one brother, John, twelve years older, but she knew little of him, because after her mother's death in 1811 William sent her to live with her mother's sister, Aunt Hannah Lumb, in Knutsford, Cheshire.

It was there that Elizabeth grew up, attending the Unitarian Brook Street Chapel and receiving her basic education at home.[3] Her father remarried and had two further children; Elizabeth visited them, but never felt happy with her London family. Only John seemed to care for her and visit her in Knutsford, but in 1821 she went to London to see him off as he embarked on his career as a sailor on the India route. After that they met when he was on shore leave, and wrote to each other frequently.[4] That same year Elizabeth went away to a boarding school with an excellent reputation run by the three Misses Bryerley, who had Unitarian connections and were

Elizabeth Gaskell, c.1860, aged 50
(Wikimedia Commons)

related to the Holland family. The curriculum was a broad one; it included outings to nearby places of interest in the Midlands.[5]

Elizabeth spent five happy years at the school and returned to Knutsford as a well-read young woman. But in the next two years she lost both her brother and her father. John apparently disappeared on a voyage to Calcutta in 1828, and no one knew what had happened to him; he was never heard of again. Elizabeth felt both the loss and the uncertainty keenly.[6] William too mourned the loss of his oldest son, and Elizabeth went to stay with him in London for a few months. During this visit he too died, leaving her less money than had been expected. Once again the Holland family looked after her, broadening her education by arranging for her to stay with a variety of friends and relations, including Henry Holland and the Swinton family in London and the Vale of Evesham, with the Revd William Turner and his family in Newcastle upon Tyne, and at various Holland family homes in North Wales, Liverpool, and Birkenhead. Her education was broadened considerably, particularly in Newcastle, where the Literary and Philosophical Society was open to women as well as men.[7]

It was probably on a visit to William Turner's daughter, **Mary Robberds**, who had married the Revd John Gooch Robberds, minister of Cross Street Chapel in Manchester, that Elizabeth met the new co-minister, William Gaskell. Elizabeth was just 21 years old and was considered lively and sometimes 'giddy and thoughtless' according to her Aunt Lumb, while William at 27 was quiet, scholarly, and rather austere. But within six months they were engaged, and married very soon afterwards at the parish church in Knutsford.[8] The Gaskell family also had a long-standing dissenting tradition, with connections to the Cairo Street Chapel in Warrington and the Cross Street Chapel.[9]

William and Elizabeth set up their first home in Manchester, and although they moved twice, they remained in the same small area one mile south of the city centre and Cross Street Chapel. As the minister's wife, Elizabeth met many of the middle-class professional families in the fast-growing city and became involved in their cultural life and their concerns, such as the cholera outbreak of 1832. But the following year they suffered the stillbirth of a daughter, a sorrow which Elizabeth carried with her for the rest of her life. In 1834 she gave birth to a daughter, Marianne, who was followed three years later by another, Margaret Emily, know as Meta. Although her life revolved around her role as a mother, Elizabeth found odd moments in which to write. There were copious letters to her many women friends, although her lively style was inhibited by William's corrections to her grammar. She also composed poems and probably prose pieces, such as descriptions of places she had visited, and perhaps even short stories. She began keeping a diary, chronicling her experiences as a mother and the progress of Marianne.[10]

The first of Elizabeth's pieces to appear in print was *Sketches Among the Poor*, a poem written jointly with William on the experiences and wisdom of an elderly single woman. It was published in *Blackwood's Magazine* in 1837.[11] The birth and death of a second son was followed by the birth of a third daughter, Florence Elizabeth, in 1842. During this time economic problems, coupled with the Corn Laws that controlled the price of bread, led to poverty and unrest among the working-class people in Manchester.

Reports by the Unitarian Domestic Mission gave graphic accounts of extreme suffering; both William and Elizabeth were active in relief work. In the summer of 1840 they escaped for a holiday on the Continent, and in Heidelberg met **Mary Howitt** and one of her daughters, starting a friendship which was to have considerable influence on Elizabeth, introducing her to the world of publishing and the South Place circle of radical unitarians.[12]

Two years later Elizabeth gave birth to a son, William, but in the following year he died from scarlet fever. During her grief over this loss, her husband suggested that she might find distraction in writing something more demanding, and he encouraged her to write a novel. This she did, and in spite of the demands of her domestic life (another daughter, Julia Bradford, was born in 1846) she produced several short stories and a full-length novel, *Mary Barton*. William and Mary Howitt (Quakers associated with the South Place group who became Unitarians) published some of her stories under the pseudonym of Cotton Mather Mills in *Howitt's Journal* in 1847, and helped her find a publisher for *Mary Barton*.[13] This novel, which showed her detailed knowledge of the problems of the poor in Manchester and her sympathy for them, initially appeared anonymously, but was soon attributed to 'Mrs Gaskell'. It created some controversy, because mill-owning Unitarians felt that they were criticised in it. A reviewer in the *Manchester Guardian*, noting that the novel was being widely read, expressed the view that 'its errors have become dangerous' and that ignoring the benevolent acts of the mill owners amounted to a libel. This criticism worried Elizabeth, but it did not stop her writing.[14]

This first novel opened many doors for Elizabeth. She visited London and met many writers and celebrities, including Charles Dickens (who for a time attended the Unitarian Little Portland Street Chapel, where the Revd Edward Tagart was the minister). Dickens was to publish many of her future works, including *Cranford* and *North and South*, mainly in instalments in his periodicals. Her Unitarian friendships increased considerably to include members of W.J. Fox's circle. His daughter, **Eliza Fox**, known as Tottie, became a particularly close friend. Other new friends were the Shaen family, who were to become linked by marriage to the Winkworth sisters whom William tutored. Soon Elizabeth found a group of mainly younger, unmarried Unitarian women actively concerned with women's rights.

Bessie Rayner Parkes, Barbara Leigh Smith, Julia Wedgwood (known as Snow), and the older **Anna Jameson** all stimulated her ideas.[15]

Over the next few years Elizabeth struggled to find time to write in between her domestic and social duties, but she managed to produce a stream of short stories and full-length novels. Her novel *Ruth*, which featured an unmarried mother who had been seduced by an upper-class man and helped by a nonconformist minister, provoked many protests about its alleged impropriety, and was burned by two (male) members of Cross Street Chapel. However, there was also much support for the book, and its publication did a great deal to highlight the plight of the urban poor. In 1850 her domestic responsibilities increased when the family moved to a large house in Plymouth Grove on the outskirts of Manchester, with enough land for a cow, some poultry, and some pigs. Fortunately Ann Hearn, who had become Elizabeth's servant in 1842 and stayed for the rest of Elizabeth's life, took on much responsibility for running the household and looking after the children when their parents were busy or away.[16] Elizabeth's social circle continued to widen; one person who was to become significant for her writing was Charlotte Brontë, whom she met in Manchester and visited at Haworth. After Charlotte's death in 1855, Patrick Brontë asked Elizabeth to write a biography of his daughter. This Elizabeth agreed to do, and she worked hard to strike a balance between discovering the facts and maintaining propriety. However, on its publication Patrick was unhappy about some of the content, and revisions were made.

The strain of Elizabeth's very busy life in Manchester was relieved by frequent spells away, either in Britain, especially North Wales and the Lake District, or increasingly in continental Europe, sometimes with William, always with several of her daughters. In 1854, when she was struggling to finish *North and South*, often considered to be her finest novel so far, Elizabeth went to stay at Lea Hurst, the Derbyshire home of the Nightingale family, who were due to be away. She was in time to meet their daughter Florence and to begin a friendship with her, conducted mainly through correspondence. Early in 1857 a trip to Rome was particularly significant in reviving her spirits, as she met a number of American Unitarians who became life-long friends.[17] The rest of that year was especially busy in Manchester, with a stream of visitors staying with her and William to see the Manchester Art Treasures Exhibition.

Work of a very different kind occupied the whole family during the 'cotton famine' of 1861 onwards, when many Manchester mills were closed due to the British embargo on all goods produced by slaves in the Southern States of America. Elizabeth and her daughters worked long hours, organising fund raising and providing relief and training to out-of-work cotton operatives. It is said that Elizabeth's subsequent ill health, and her death in 1865, stemmed from the strain and over-work of this crisis.[18] However, in the short term she seemed to regain some energy; she enjoyed visits to Italy and France, her usual reward to herself for finishing a novel, in this case *Sylvia's Lovers,* set in a fictional fishing port based on Whitby.[19] She began making plans for William's retirement, away from the unhealthy smogs of Manchester, and with the help of a loan from her publishers she secretly bought a house in Hampshire (The Lawn, in the village of Holybourne near Alton). It was as she was preparing this house for occupation that she suddenly collapsed and died, on 12 November 1865, at the age of 55. She is buried at Brook Street Chapel, Knutsford.

Elizabeth was thoroughly embedded in Unitarianism. She was raised in the Unitarian community, and it remained central to her life as the wife of a prominent minister. Her weekly routine included attending chapel, teaching in Sunday School, and visiting chapel members, as well as hosting fellow Unitarians. The family held prayers on a daily basis; when the children were small, there was one session with the servants, followed by one with the children.[20] Most of her friends seem to have been connected with the movement. Theologically, family friends tended to be from the more conservative wing; this may be a reflection of William's taste rather than Elizabeth's, but it is also evident in their choice of Unitarian-run schools for their teenage daughters, and also in her letters.[21] Elizabeth described herself as a 'sermon hater', and wrote to Charles Norton, one of her American Unitarian friends, 'oh! for some really spiritual devotional preaching instead of controversy about doctrines, – about which I am more and more certain *we can never be certain* in this world'.[22] Although she disliked theological disputes, clearly she was more knowledgeable than she admitted. She described herself as 'more Arian than Humanitarian', meaning that she considered Jesus to be partly divine in nature – though not God – rather than exclusively human.[23] She did not seem to enjoy the company of the Martineau family, finding their conversation too solemn and full of 'sense by the yard'; this may be a reflection on their theology too, but she kept out of denominational controversies.[24]

When away from home, Elizabeth, with her daughters, often attended the local Anglican church (as she had done while at boarding school). On these occasions she wrestled with the competing demands of spiritual satisfaction and reverence for truth, and advised her daughters not to attend the Anglican communion service too frequently, as it would be wrong to deaden one's 'sense of its serious error by hearing it too often'; preferably they should confine their attendance to the evening service, when only the Doxology could offend against 'one's sense of truth'. This emphasis on the importance of truth in the everyday events of daily life as well as in theological questions is an important element of Elizabeth's Unitarianism, and it is reflected in her writing.

Elizabeth's works of fiction do not include any mention of Unitarianism by name, although its values permeate her writing, as well as her life. Her refusal to oversimplify matters sometimes made her appear inconsistent or indecisive, but to overstate this would be to do her an injustice. She considered that she had to study and seek to understand before she could reach an opinion. This went with a typically Unitarian valuing of education and intellectual growth. Her trust in a benevolent God showed itself in many ways; she wrote in a letter of her sense of God 'being above all in His great sense of peace and wisdom, yet loving me with an individual love tenderer than any mother's'.[25] She took care to introduce her children at an early age to this image of a loving God, rather than the typical Victorian parent's insistence on a God who punishes sins. Elizabeth did indeed believe that evil deeds result in consequences, and in this she followed the associationist teaching of Joseph Priestley. She also had a very strong sense of the importance of conscience and duty.[26] In many ways Elizabeth was socially and politically conservative. She thought it wrong to stir up tensions between social classes, and she considered that a woman's primary role was to fulfil her domestic duties, especially when she had children.[27] She was alive to the challenge of trying to fit writing or other creative work around the demands of family, and she discussed this with Tottie Fox on several occasions, writing in 1859:

> *...Women must give up living an artist's life, if home duties are to be*
> *paramount ... I am sure it is healthy for themselves to have the refuge of*
> *the hidden world of Art to shelter themselves in when too much pressed*
> *upon by daily small Lilliputian arrows of peddling cares ... I have felt this*
> *in writing, I see others feel it in music, you in painting, so assuredly a*
> *blending of the two is desirable. (Home duties and the development of the*
> *Individual I mean).*[28]

Tottie was possibly the least conventional of Elizabeth's close friends. She was an artist, and her father had left his wife to live with his ward, **Eliza Flower** (as recounted in Chapter 6). However, as Eliza had died just before Elizabeth met Tottie and her father, this did not seem to impinge on the friendship. Yet Elizabeth was very concerned to learn that **Mary Ann Evans** (George Eliot) was living with George Lewes (of whom she disapproved) without being married to him. The two women never met, but they corresponded, with a mutual respect for their writings. Both believed in working for the gradual improvement of society, rather than in overt political campaigning.[29] This is illustrated by Elizabeth's response to the American anti-slavery campaigner **Maria Chapman**, who visited Manchester in 1856. Elizabeth arranged an impromptu anti-slavery meeting at her home, but wrote to her friend **Mary Green**, wife of the Knutsford Unitarian minister, 'We had a sort of Anti Slavery conference in my drawing room and they sighed over my apathy, but I cannot get up any interest in the *measures* adopted by people so far across the Atlantic.'[30]

Similarly, although at Tottie's request she signed the petition in support of the Married Women's Property Act in 1856, she wrote that she doubted that the law would be effective, as husbands could find ways of getting their own way.[31] Writing to Charles Norton in 1860, she described Barbara Leigh Smith Bodichon as the 'illegitimate cousin of Hilary Carter and F Nightingale' and went on '& has their nature in her (though some of the legitimates don't acknowledge her ... She is, I think in consequence of her birth, a strong fighter against the established opinions of the world, – which always goes against my – what shall I call it? – *taste* – (that is not the word), but I can't help admiring her noble bravery and respecting her – while I don't personally like her.'[32] While Elizabeth respected the pioneering work of many of her more radical London friends, she knew that her place as the wife of a minister and mother of three girls was more circumscribed. Her writing, and her now established place in the literary canon, show how she both used and transcended her situation.

Endnotes

1 *Manchester Guardian*, 14 November 1865, 'Death of Mrs Gaskell'.

2 Alan Shelston, *Brief Lives: Elizabeth Gaskell* (London, Hesperus Press, 2010), p. 8.

3 Ann Peart, 'Elizabeth Gaskell Worship Pack' (London, General Assembly of Unitarian and Free Christian Churches, 2010), p. 11.

4 Jenny Uglow, *Elizabeth Gaskell: A Habit of Stories* (London, Faber and Faber, 1993) p. 21.

5 Shelston, pp.14–15.

6 Ibid., p. 17.

7 Peart, op.cit., p. 11.

8 Shelston, op.cit., pp.20–21.

9 Peart, op.cit., p.11.

10 Ibid., pp.11–12; J. A.V .Chapple and Anita Wilson (eds.) *Private Voices: The Diaries of Elizabeth Gaskell and Sophia Holland* (Keele, Keele University Press, 1996), pp.50–71.

11 Graham Handley, *An Elizabeth Gaskell Chronology* (Basingstoke, Palgrave Macmillan, 2005), p.37.

12 Uglow, op. cit., pp.142–4, 170–1; Shelston, op.cit., pp..35–6.

13 Peart, op. cit., pp.11–12.

14 Ibid., p.12.

15 Shelston, op. cit., pp.40–2.

16 Ibid., p.29.

17 Ibid., pp.62–4, 71–3.

18 Ibid., p.76.

19 Shelston, op.cit., pp.80–3.

20 Uglow, op. cit., p.151.

21 R.K. Webb, 'The Gaskells as Unitarian', in Joanne Shattock (ed.), *Dickens and Other Victorians; Essays in Honour of Philip Collins* (London, Macmillan, 1988), p.154; Peart, op.cit., p.2.

22 J.A.V. Chapple and Arthur Pollard (eds.) *The Letters of Mrs Gaskell* (Manchester, Mandolin, 1997), p.537.

23 Uglow, op.cit., p.51.

24 Chapple and Pollard, op. cit., p.239.

25 Ibid., p.327.

26 Peart, op.cit., p.2.

27 Ibid., p.13; Uglow, op.cit., pp.45–6.

28 Chapple and Pollard, op.cit., p.106.

29 Uglow, op.cit., pp.462–6.

30 Ibid., pp.318–9.

31 Ibid., p.78.

32 Chapple and Pollard, op.cit., pp.606–7.

PART THREE
Disrupting 'Separate Spheres'

Introduction to Part Three

Ann Peart

During the second half of the nineteenth century, radical women were more organised than their predecessors in campaigning for specific rights and on particular issues. Both **Frances Power Cobbe** and **Mary Carpenter** proved extremely effective in gaining publicity for their causes. Although they placed themselves at opposite ends of the widening Unitarian theological spectrum, such differences did not prevent their friendship. After the passing of the 1844 Dissenters' Chapels Act, Unitarian congregations were finally free from legal threats to their property rights, although it took most of the rest of the century to achieve the abolition of all the various restrictions placed on dissenters.[1] At this time the Unitarian movement was described as having two wings, with an increasingly evident split between the scripture-based Priestleyan group and the anti-supernaturalists who followed James Martineau. Apart from Frances Power Cobbe, Unitarian women were not generally prominent in such theological debates; on the whole they tended to devote themselves to practical work, as will be seen in the section about **Lucy Tagart** in Chapter 11.

By the end of the century, the divisions in the movement had deepened still further, due partly to Frances Power Cobbe's promotion of the theism of Theodore Parker, who did not share Martineau's reverence for Christ. They were exacerbated by the existence of two periodicals – *The Inquirer* for the followers of Martineau and *The Christian Life* for the Priestleyans – and two colleges – Manchester New College and the Unitarian Home Missionary Board – with a similar distinction.[2] Paradoxically, as theological diversity increased, attempts to create a practical national identity were more evident, with the British and Foreign Unitarian Association gaining ground, except among the Martineau camp, which refused to accept a doctrinal label. A triennial conference was instituted in the 1880s. Its title embodied the variety of beliefs and nomenclature within the Unitarian movement: 'The National Conference of Unitarian, Liberal Christian, Free Christian, Presbyterian, and other Non-Subscribing or Kindred

Congregations'.[3] The Central Postal Mission, run by Lucy Tagart and **Florence Hill**, and the rise of Sunday School associations and district missionary societies all helped to develop the denomination, which was probably at the peak of its influence and numerical strength from the 1870s to the outbreak of the First World War.

During the nineteenth century the place of women in society, especially women of the growing middle class, was a matter of public and denominational debate. The 'separate spheres' model, whereby men dominated the public realm while women operated in the domestic context, untainted by the outside world, was always problematical and may well have been largely a reactionary protest to the increasing visibility of women in public life. It was always disrupted by congregational activity, as women were expected to have roles outside their own homes, as teachers and visitors caring for the sick and needy.[4]

Unitarians were not always on the progressive side of the debate. In his 1862 essay, *Why Are Women Redundant?*, the Unitarian William Rathbone Greg, assuming that women should be married and restricted to the domestic sphere, categorised unmarried working women as a problem.[5] The national census had revealed larger numbers of women than men, and one solution seemed to be emigration to the colonies in search of paid employment. Frances Power Cobbe, in her essay published later in the same year, *What Shall We Do With Our Old Maids?*, refuted the idea that marriage was possible or even desirable for every woman; instead she promoted the provision of education and professional training for women.[6]

From the middle of the nineteenth century onwards, the cause of women's suffrage attracted a large number of Unitarians, regardless of their theological outlook. A significant proportion of ministers were active in this cause, notably Henry William Crosskey in Birmingham and Samuel Alfred Steinthal in Manchester.[7] Many Unitarian women were members of suffrage organisations. One example is **Agnes Pochin, *née* Heap** (1825–1908), who was a leader in the Manchester suffrage campaign and spoke on the platform at the first public meeting to discuss women's suffrage at the Free Trade Hall in 1868.[8] There is not enough space here to explore such involvement in detail, and much more work needs to be done to bring the fuller story to light.

In this third part of the book, the story of the Langham Place and Kensington groups includes a closer look at the lives of **Barbara Leigh Smith Bodichon, Bessie Rayner Parkes,** and **Clementia Taylor. Mary Carpenter** follows them, and then a chapter on **Frances Power Cobbe,** who had connections with the Kensington Society and also with Mary Carpenter. Finally in this part comes Alan Ruston's account of women in Unitarian administration, to which is added a consideration of the significance of Lucy Tagart.

Endnotes

1 Leonard Smith, *The Unitarians; A Short History* (Arnside, Lensden Publishing, 2006), pp.90–91.

2 Ann Peart, 'Forgotten Prophets: The Lives of Unitarian Women 1760–1904' (unpublished doctoral thesis, University of Newcastle, 2006), pp,153–4. https://theses.ncl. ac.uk/dspace/bitstream/10443/245/1/ peart05.pdf.

3 C.G. Bolam, J. Goring, H.L. Short, and R. Thomas, *The English Presbyterians: From Elizabethan Puritanism to Modern Unitarianism* (London, George Allen & Unwin, 1968), pp. 275–6.

4 Mary Poovey, *Uneven Developments: The Ideological Work of Gender in Mid-Victorian England* (London, Virago, 1989), pp.1–9.

5 Ibid., pp.1–5.

6 Susan Hamilton (ed.), *'Criminals, Idiots, Women and Minors': Victorian Writing by Women on Women* (Peterborough, Canada, Broadview Press, 1995), pp.85–107.

7 Elizabeth Crawford, *The Women's Suffrage Movement: A Reference Guide 1866–1928* (London, Routledge, 2001), pp.153–4, 652–3.

8 Ibid., pp.557–9.

8 The Langham Place Group and the Kensington Society

Ann Peart and Alan Ruston

A network of feminist activists
Ann Peart

Langham Place in central London housed the offices of the *English Woman's Journal* from 1859. It gave its name to a group of women activists who campaigned in a variety of ways for the improvement of the situation of women and went on to form the Kensington Society. Initially the group grew out of the friendship of **Barbara Leigh Smith** and **Bessie Rayner Parkes**, both from progressive Unitarian families (although neither retained her Unitarian identity in later life).[1] Short biographies of Barbara and Bessie, included in this chapter, are followed by Alan Ruston's account of the life of **Clementia Taylor**, the most prominent Unitarian woman associated with the group.

Bessie and Barbara gathered a committee of women to work on the 1856 petition of the Married Women's Property Campaign, and then they founded the *English Woman's Journal* in 1858, financed as a joint stock company mainly by Barbara, but with significant contributions from Samuel Courtauld, Peter Alfred Taylor, and others.[2] The following year Theodosia Monson (Lady Monson) rented accommodation for the group at 19 Langham Place. It included space for a reading room, a coffee shop, and areas for associated groups to meet.[3] They gathered together a group of active and committed women to work on feminist causes. Among the women who worked on the *Journal* were Isa Craig, a Scottish friend of Bessie; Matilda Hays, a writer and companion of the American actress Charlotte Cushman; and Emily Faithfull, who went on to establish the Victoria Press. Finding paid work for middle-class women was a major concern of the group. Barbara Leigh Smith, Jessie Boucherett (a cousin of Florence Nightingale who attended the same Unitarian-run school as Elizabeth Gaskell[4]), and the Catholic poet Adelaide Procter (friend of Bessie and Matilda) were among the founders of the Association (later Society) for Promoting the Employment of Women (SPEW), and were leaders in the establishment of an employment register. Subsequently various members of the group developed training schools to teach skills such as telegraph work and book keeping, and they also provided opportunities for women in the printing trade and as legal copyists.[5] **Clementia (Mentia) Taylor** was on the organising committee of SPEW.[6] Maria Rye was so concerned about jobs for women that she promoted emigration for women to find employment abroad.[7] Some members wanted to concentrate exclusively on the issue of women's suffrage, and this, together with differences in religion and attitudes to divorce, led to the break-up of the group by 1866.[8] While initially many of the women (and the funding for the journal) had come from Unitarian sources, the group became too diverse to remain cohesive.

By this time many of the group had become part of the discussion society that met at the Kensington home of Charlotte Manning (a member of the Unitarian Solly family, and the first Mistress of Girton College). There were more than sixty members, about half of whom had paid employment at some stage. Women living beyond London could become corresponding members. Papers on a variety of women's issues were read, circulated, and debated. Prominent Unitarian members, in addition to Mentia Taylor, included **Frances Power Cobbe, Elizabeth Anne Bostock, Anna Swanwick,** and **Barbara Leigh Smith Bodichon.** Helen Taylor, daughter of **Harriet Taylor Mill,** was an active member, but was no longer part of the Unitarian community. Several members, such as Emily Davies, Frances Buss, and Dorothea Beale, were concerned with women's education, and others campaigned for women to be admitted to medical schools. The society formed a significant network for many of the feminist activists in the later part of the nineteenth century, although it was no longer active after 1868. Its most practical action, in which Mentia Taylor took a leading part, was organising another petition demanding women's suffrage, which was delivered to Parliament in June 1866.[9]

Barbara Leigh Smith Bodichon (1827–1891)
Ann Peart

Barbara was born into a Unitarian family, but she disliked institutional forms of religion and did not become a member of any Unitarian congregation. However, she was brought up as a Unitarian and her life embodied many of the principles of the movement. Her father, Benjamin (known as Ben, son of William Smith, the great Unitarian reforming parliamentarian), never married Anne Longden, the mother of all his five children, giving as his reason that marriage laws were unfair to women. This irregularity caused many mainstream Unitarians, including most of Ben's relatives, who prized respectability, to ignore that branch of the Smith family, which was reason enough for Barbara to distance herself from the movement.[10] Anne died when Barbara, the oldest child, was only seven and the youngest just one year old. Much to his relatives' consternation, Benjamin brought up his children himself, unconventionally, with much freedom and a varied education, including both private tutorials and attendance at Unitarian-run schools.[11] **Julia Smith**, Ben's youngest sister, was a frequent visitor and an important early influence on Barbara, introducing her to Unitarian women activists including **Elizabeth Reid, Anna Jameson**, and **Mary and Anna Mary Howitt**, and taking her on outings to events such as the women's anti-Corn Law bazaar in 1845.[12] **Bessie Rayner Parkes**, whose Unitarian family visited Hastings, where the Smiths lived, became a life-long close friend from childhood.

When Barbara turned twenty-one, her father gave her (as he did all his children) a portfolio of shares which gave her an annual income of between £250 and £300, sufficient to make her financially independent, and also the title deeds to a primary school that he had run on experimental lines.[13] She eventually opened her own school and appointed the young Unitarian **Elizabeth Whitehead (later Malleson)** to be the head; but first she used her independence to obtain more training as an artist at the newly opened (Bedford) Ladies' College, and then went on an unchaperoned trip to Europe with Bessie to study art with Anna Mary Howitt in Germany.[14] In 1850 Barbara had her first pictures accepted by the Royal Academy; this was the start of a career of public exhibitions which was to continue for the rest of her life, with several solo exhibitions at London galleries.[15] She attracted a wide circle of women artists, including **Eliza (Tottie) Fox** and **Margaret Gillies**, and she organised a petition to oblige the Royal Academy to admit women to its schools. Signed by 39 women artists, many of them Unitarians and Barbara's friends, it was initially unsuccessful, but after **Laura Herford** (the Unitarian aunt of **Helen Brooke Herford**) applied for admission using only her initials, and was accepted before her identity was revealed, the Academy capitulated.[16] Together with two other women, in 1857 Barbara founded the Society of Female Artists to help women to get their pictures exhibited and sold, and in 1875 she bought a property in Zennor, Cornwall as a base for herself and other artist friends.[17]

Barbara's personal life benefited from an unusual amount of freedom, derived from her radical upbringing and financial independence. Her father managed to dissuade her from embarking on an affair with the publisher John Chapman, who was already married, and in 1856 Ben took his three daughters on a trip to Algeria. Here they met a French doctor, Eugene Bodichon, 17 years Barbara's senior, and, in spite of her family's concerns, she fell in love and was determined to marry him. Ben insisted that the marriage ceremony should take place in England, and it was held at the Unitarian Chapel in Little Portland Street, London, in July 1857. On the certificate, Barbara gave her occupation as artist. Ben tied up her money in a trust to which her husband had no access.[18] As Eugene hated London, Barbara had a house built on the Sussex estate that her brother Benjamin had inherited when their father died, and she divided her time between London and Algeria until she had her first stroke in 1877, after which ill health prevented her from travelling, and she was confined to England as an invalid.[19]

But Barbara was not only an artist. From her childhood she had been made aware of social problems and campaigns on issues ranging from the relief of famine in Ireland to anti-slavery and women's rights.[20] From 1848, when she wrote articles under a pseudonym for the local newspaper, she became increasingly involved with work on women's rights. Her *Brief Summary of the Most Important Laws Concerning Women*, published in 1854, began a campaign to amend the laws preventing married women from holding property which led to the formation of the Langham Place Group in 1861.[21] For the next five years the activities based on Langham Place occupied Barbara when she was in England; subsequently the debates of the women-only Kensington Society provided a forum for developing both theory and stratagems.[22] Barbara led others in supporting the election to Parliament of John Stuart Mill, who advocated equal rights for women; and in 1866, together with Helen Taylor, she organised the gathering of signatures for another petition calling for votes for women property owners. Her Kensington Society paper, revised and read as *Reasons for the Enfranchisement of Women* at the Social Science Association meeting in Manchester, was a significant factor in the formation of the Manchester Women's Suffrage Committee, the inaugural meeting of which was held at the home of Samuel Steinthal, the Unitarian minister of the Cross Street Chapel, and his wife **Sarah Steinthal**.[23] This committee formed the nucleus of what was to become a national organisation. During the 1860s Barbara began working with Emily Davies and others to establish a college for women at Cambridge, chairing the first building committee and giving the first £1,000 for the construction of a permanent building three miles from the city centre. She remained on the executive committee of Girton College until her stroke in 1877, and later gave several very substantial sums of money and many of her paintings to secure its financial stability.[24] Her infirm old age was brightened by the friendship of a young Jewish girl, Hertha Marks (later Ayrton), a future electrical engineer whom she funded to study at Girton, and who became almost an adopted daughter to her. She also enjoyed the company of the local young men who came to her Sussex home to learn to read and write, taught by her old friend William Ransem, former editor of the local newspaper which had first published Barbara's work. She died in 1891.

Bessie Rayner Parkes (later Belloc) (1829–1925)
Ann Peart

Bessie Rayner Parkes was born into a thoroughly Unitarian family. Her father, a solicitor, was active in government reform and a friend of John Stuart Mill, while her maternal grandfather was Joseph Priestley.[25] She attended a Unitarian school run on liberal lines, but remembered her home life as one characterised by a strict atmosphere, 'chastened by a stern, almost puritanical, sense of duty such as I have seldom elsewhere beheld, infusing a whole establishment'.[26] After the death of her brother Priestley, she was an only child, financially dependent on her father, and expected to lead a conventional middle-class life. Her friendship with Barbara Leigh Smith dated from their holidays at Hastings, and the two young women shared their hopes and frustrations, as well as their pleasure in reading and early writing. Both published articles anonymously in the local Hastings newspaper, and Bessie hoped for a career as a poet. Both women began to reject the theological elements of Unitarianism, although they embraced its values, with Bessie commenting to Barbara that 'my present faith is as yours. In *humanity*.'[27] Bessie's work in founding the *English Woman's Journal* has already been mentioned. She threw herself into the campaigning work of the Langham Place Group of women, finding purpose and friendship in working together with them. When the tensions in the group reached breaking point, she complained to Barbara:

> *I can work with Unitarians, because tho' I am not dogmatically a Unitarian I have been trained in and still retain in great measure their view of life and its duties. And I could work with Catholics because of my intellectual sympathy with their doctrines, and the definiteness of their plans. But I confess that when I get hold of minds which have been trained (or not trained) in the Church of England, I don't know how to deal with them.*[28]

One of the Anglican women with whom she had particular difficulties was Emily Davies, while she developed a very close friendship with the Catholic Adelaide Procter. In 1864 she joined the Catholic Church, and three years later, while on holiday in France with Barbara, she met and married Louis Belloc, a French barrister. After five years of marriage (and two children), Louis died. Bessie resumed her friendship with Barbara, but not her campaigning work. In 1877 she lost money that she had inherited from her uncle, and she retired to a small house in Slindon, Sussex. During her marriage and after it, she continued to publish a variety of literary works.[29]

Clementia Taylor (1810–1908)[30]
Alan Ruston

Clementia Taylor (known to all her friends as Mentia) was born on 17 December 1810 at Brockdish, Norfolk, the daughter of John, a farmer and tanner, and Mary Doughty, and one of twelve children.[31] By the time of her father's death in 1837 this number was down to seven, and then to four by 1842. John and Mary were Unitarian in sympathy and by 1822 were among the chief supporters of the new and short-lived Unitarian cause at Harleston, opened by Revd C.P. Valentine (1794–1861) of Diss.

After Mary's death and her father's re-marriage, it was necessary for Mentia, as a younger daughter, to find a career. The education of the daughters had not been neglected, and the most natural career therefore for Mentia was that of governess. The Unitarian connection was obviously helpful, as she took up a position in the 1830s in the family of Revd J.P. Malleson (1796–1869), the Unitarian minister at Brighton who kept a school at Hove. It seems likely that this position was obtained with the help of the Meadow Taylors of Diss – the main supporters of the Unitarian chapel – who were related to Malleson.

And so it was that Mentia met the latter's cousin, Peter Alfred Taylor (1819–1891). Unitarianism was undoubtedly what brought them together, and they married at Westgate Chapel, Lewes in 1842, with Malleson conducting the ceremony.[32] Peter was the eldest son of the family, his mother Catherine was a Courtauld, and his father, also Peter (1796–1850), was active in the famous textile company of that name. Peter senior had been a member of South Place Chapel, London; his son continued this connection until his own death in 1891. He also entered the family firm and in turn became a director. He was the MP for Leicester (1862–1884). The story of the work done by Peter and Mentia Taylor reflects the social concern of many business grandees of the nineteenth century who combined radical politics with a dissenting religious stance.

The Taylors established themselves in London, where Peter became more and more involved in the family firm. They had no children but shared a passion for political and social reform – in which, with a large income, they were able to engage with zeal and application. Mentia's work

Clementia Taylor
(Public domain, via Project Gutenberg)

spans a period of less than twenty years of her long life: from the late 1850s to 1874, the year in which the couple moved to Brighton to preserve Peter's failing health.

Throughout their marriage the Taylors kept open house for the leading radicals of Britain, as well as Europe and America. Peter was described after his election to Parliament in 1862 as 'anti-everything', and his wife held similar views. They were connected with virtually every English movement for the promotion of freedom in its widest terms. It can be said that their radical 'career' began in 1845, when they moved to Powis Place, Great Ormond Street. Soon afterwards they met Giuseppe Mazzini, the Italian political activist campaigning for democracy and the unification of Italy. This was a friendship which lasted for the rest of Mazzini's life and greatly influenced theirs. The Taylors both became involved in the affairs of Italy, an interest which grew over the years and expanded when they moved into Aubrey House, Notting Hill Gate in 1861.

The move to Aubrey House and Peter's election to Parliament saw an enormous expansion in the Taylors' activities. Mentia wanted to follow her husband into membership of the London Anti-Slavery Society, but she was refused on the grounds that women were not admitted. She immediately formed a Society of Women with the same object, which led the original Society to change its rule. However, Mentia and her group kept the Women's Society going until the abolition of slavery in the USA. During the American Civil War she widened her efforts by organising help for freed slaves, raising large sums of money; her contribution was warmly acknowledged by American abolitionists. She even took into her home escaped slaves who had reached England. One woman developed smallpox while staying at Aubrey House; Mentia attended her because the servants would not – an unusual activity for a rich Victorian lady. It is even said that the Taylors adopted a former slave as their son and had him educated to be a doctor.

She became well known in the 1860s and early 1870s for the many philanthropic movements with which she and her husband were associated. She gathered around her a wide circle of friends and is mentioned in the correspondence of most of the radical women of the period. **George Eliot (Mary Ann Evans)**, for example, wrote to her on 2 August 1880 about their thirty-year friendship:

> *Let me tell you this once what I have said to others – that I value you as one of the purest minded, gentlest-hearted women I have ever known; and where such a feeling exists, friendship can live without much aid from sight.*[33]

Anyone of importance in radical politics attended the Taylors' 'Open Evenings'. Their strong avowal of women's rights, suffrage, and education, and support for almost every radical cause ensured a good attendance. **Louisa M. Alcott**, the American Unitarian novelist, when visiting London in 1871, describes these events (*Shawl Straps*, 1872):

> *Her house is open to all, friend and stranger, black and white, rich and poor. Great men and earnest women meet there: Mazzini and Frances Power Cobbe, John Bright, Rossetti and Elizabeth Garrett. Though wealthy and living in an historic mansion, the host is the most*

> *unassuming man in it and the hostess the simplest dressed lady. Their*
> *money goes in other ways, and the chief ornament of that lovely spot is*
> *a school where poor girls may get an education. Mrs T. gives a piece of*
> *her own garden for it, and teaches there herself, aided by her friends, who*
> *serve the poor girls and lift them from the slough of despond.*[34]

Mentia's twin interests of education and suffrage were not seen as different spheres of involvement but were integral parts of her commitment to improve the lot of women. She was involved in so many women's organisations that she was known by her friends as 'the Mother'.[35] In 1869 an annex, the Aubrey Institute, was built at Aubrey House, complete with classrooms, lecture and reading rooms, and a library.[36] Here were held classes and lectures for boys and girls over 14, and for men and women of all ages. The students chiefly consisted of clerks, dressmakers, and shop assistants who could afford little for their education. This pioneering effort, staffed by friends as well as paid workers, was seen as revolutionary in its time, as teaching men and women together was almost unknown. After the school closed late in 1873, the Taylors wanted to donate the large and excellent library to the neighbouring community. This they did in conjunction with the Unitarian MP James Heywood, who paid for the building and its upkeep to establish the first public library in that part of London.[37]

It is for her role in the early campaign for women's suffrage that Clementia Taylor is chiefly known. Her contribution is acknowledged in some of the key sources on this period, but the most detailed account is in the obituary notice in the feminist periodical *The Englishwoman's Review*, 15 July 1908.

In 1866 John Stuart Mill, the radical MP and early advocate of universal suffrage, undertook to present to Parliament a petition in favour of women's suffrage if one hundred women would endorse it. In little over a fortnight 1,499 signatures were obtained, organised by a small committee which was the first to be formed for this purpose. Clementia was the treasurer and one of the chief driving forces. Encouraged by this move, in 1867 the first societies for women's suffrage were formed in Edinburgh, Manchester, and London. The London National Society for Women's Suffrage Committee met at first at Aubrey House, with Clementia again serving as the first treasurer. She was, in the later evaluation of Millicent Garrett Fawcett (1847–1929), 'its presiding genius, and devoted herself with all the enthusiasm of her gentle and courageous spirit'. The Society held its first public meeting on 17 July 1869 in London; it was reported widely in the national press. Clementia Taylor took the chair, and several sources attest that this 'was probably the first time that a lady has presided over a public meeting of men and women in London'. The closing words of her speech were characteristic, even prophetic:

> *Women are in earnest and will prove before the world that, when in earnest, we are capable of persistent energy which will in the end prove successful.*

An even larger meeting was held on 26 March 1870, which was widely reported by the press, with Clementia again in the chair. Her speech was reported in full.[38]

It was after this that the women's suffrage movement began to split apart over the question of how to deal with the Contagious Diseases Acts (which became a feminist cause because they permitted the police to detain and inspect any women – but not men – suspected of venereal infection). Some believed that the two issues should be dealt with separately, while others saw the two as one. Clementia, possibly for the first time, became a contentious figure and tried to keep a foot in both camps. As might be expected, she was not successful in this, as she regarded women's suffrage as the priority.

In 1874, with increasing age and health problems, Peter and Clementia Taylor gave up most of their interests, sold Aubrey House and retired to Brighton. Peter died in 1891 and Clementia on 11 April 1908. *The Inquirer* remembered her in a long obituary, and particularly her key role in the women's movement of the 1860s. This obituary was reprinted in some non-Unitarian journals.

Endnotes

1 Jane Rendall, 'Langham Place Group', *Oxford Dictionary of National Biography* (ODNB), www.oxforddnb.com/, accessed 9 August 2018.

2 'English Woman's Journal (1858–1864)', *Nineteenth Century Serials Edition* (NCSE), accessed 2 October 2018, www.ncse.ac.uk/headnotes/ewj.html; Rendall, op.cit.

3 Rendall, op.cit.

4 Elizabeth Crawford, *The Women's Suffrage Movement: A Reference Guide 1866–1928* (London, Routledge, 2001), pp.71–2.

5 Candida Ann Lacey (ed.), *Barbara Leigh Smith and the Langham Place Group* (London, Routledge & Kegan Paul, 1987), pp.11–12.

6 Crawford, op.cit., p.674.

7 'Rye, Maria Susan', *Oxford Dictionary of National Biography*, www.oxforddnb.com, accessed 28 October 2018.

8 Rendall, op.cit..

9 'Kensington Society', *Oxford Dictionary of National Biography*, www.oxforddnb.com, accessed 9 August 2018.

10 'Bodichon, Barbara Leigh Smith', *Oxford Dictionary of National Biography*, www.oxforddnb.com, accessed 9 August 2018.

11 Pam Hirsch, *Barbara Leigh Smith Bodichon: Feminist, Artist and Rebel* (London, Chatto & Windus, 1998), pp.8–19.

12 Ibid., pp.21–4, 27–8.

13 Ibid., pp.40, 71.

14 'Bodichon', ODNB; Hirsch, op.cit., pp.43–6.

15 Hirsch, op.cit., p.43, 'Bodichon', ODNB.

16 Hirsch, op.cit., p.165.

17 Ibid., pp.148–9, 284–5.

18 Ibid., pp.106–8, 123, 129–130.

19 Olive Banks, *The Biographical Dictionary of British Feminists Volume One 1800–1930* (Brighton, Wheatsheaf Books, 1985), p. 29.

20 Hirsch, op.cit., pp.25–6, 29–30.

21 Ibid., pp.36, 200, 372.

22 'Kensington Society', ODNB.

23 Crawford, op.cit., p.369; 'Bodichon', ODNB.

24 'Bodichon', ODNB.

25 Banks, op.cit., p.19; Crawford, op.cit., p.527.

26 Jane Rendall, 'Friendship and politics: Barbara Leigh Smith Bodichon (1827–91) and Bessie Rayner Parkes (1829–1925)' in Susan Mendus and Jane Rendall (eds), *Sexuality and Subordination* (London, Routledge, 1989), p.140.

27 Kathryn Gleadle, *The Early Feminists. Radical Unitarians and the Emergence of the Women's Rights Movement, 1831–51* (London, Martin's Press, 1995), p.180.

28 Hirsch, op.cit., p.202.

29 'Parkes [married name Belloc], Elizabeth Rayner [Bessie]', *Oxford Dictionary of National Biography*, www.oxforddnb, accessed 5 November 2018.

30 This section is an abridged version (produced by David Dawson) of 'Clementia Taylor (1810–1908)' by Alan Ruston: an article which first appeared in *Transactions of the Unitarian Historical Society*, Vol. XX, No. 1, April 1991.

31 *Englishwoman's Review*, 15 July 1908, pp.145–58 (obituary by W.T. Malleson); extracts from Brockdish Parish Registers (Norfolk Record Office); Will of John Doughty, proved 5 April 1837, Public Record Office (PROB 11/1876).

32 *Inquirer*, 1 October 1842, p.15.

33 G.S. Haight, *Letters of George Eliot*, Vol. 7, p.309.

34 Quoted in Florence M. Gladstone, *Aubrey House, Kensington 1698–1920* (London, 1922), pp.44–52.

35 *Inquirer*, 18 April 1908, pp.245–6 (obituary).

36 *Englishwoman's Review*, January 1869, pp.148–50; July 1870, pp.226–7.

37 *Inquirer*, 3 October 1874, pp.649–50.

38 *Englishwoman's Review*, April 1870, pp.102–7.

9 Mary Carpenter (1807–1877)

Ann Peart

Unitarianism was the core of Mary Carpenter's life. It gave her the motivation, methods, and support that she needed in her work for disadvantaged children.

She was born in Exeter, where her father Lant was the Unitarian minister and her mother Anna a teacher, and she was raised in a household shared with seven boys who were boarding pupils of her parents.[1] From her early years Mary received a good progressive education, often joining the boys' classes, but also having dolls and dancing lessons. Yet she always seemed to want to be useful rather than merely enjoying herself. Her mother was strict, but privately appreciated the abilities of her oldest child, writing when Mary was eight: 'her little mind is capable of more than most of our lads are capable of'.[2]

When Mary was ten years old the family moved to Bristol, where Lant became minister of the more prestigious Lewins Mead congregation. As they now had a larger house, there was room for more boy boarders, but Lant's ultimate aim was to start a girls' school run by his wife and daughters, and for him to be free to concentrate on ministry, rather than teaching. As the whole family used to read aloud and discuss newspapers, Mary acquired a good grasp of public events and was familiar not only with Waterloo but with Peterloo, and the effects of the Corn Laws, and the campaign for Catholic emancipation.[3] Lant had adopted the associationist theory of education devolved from Joseph Priestley, David Hartley, and Anna Laetitia Barbauld, and he coupled this with the Unitarian belief that all people are capable of both good and evil, depending largely on their own experiences. These core beliefs were to stay with Mary all her life and provide the motivation for her work with deprived children.[4] From childhood, as the oldest in a family of six (three girls and three boys), she was involved in teaching, first in the Sunday school attached to Lewins Mead, and later in her father's schools.[5]

Mary Carpenter
(Photographer: Cyrus Voss Bark; University of Virginia Library)

James Martineau, two years older than Mary, was one of Lant's pupils, and when Lant suffered another of his fairly frequent breakdowns in 1820, Mary, aged fourteen, and James, aged sixteen, deputised for him, apparently successfully. In 1821 Mary herself suffered the first in a succession of illnesses, possibly related to rheumatism but sometimes including difficulties with her eyesight, that were to plague her during much of her life and left her with lasting fatigue and irritability.[6] Once she had recovered from this first attack, her father devolved the running of the school to his wife and daughters, so that he could devote his limited energy to other concerns. When his health broke down completely in 1826, James Martineau, newly qualified as a minister, came to stand in while Lant went on a recuperative sea voyage. Anna, clearly concerned about James's influence over Mary (and possibly Mary's affection for James), sent her to be a governess on the Isle of Wight the following spring. Lant visited her on his way home the following year and arranged for her to return home, but soon Anna sent her off to Hertfordshire to another governess post.[7] By 1828, Lant felt strong enough to resume his ministry, but not his teaching. As James Martineau declined to take this on (instead he went as minister to the Dublin congregation and got married), Lant closed the boys' school and planned for his wife and daughters to run a girls' school instead; Mary and her sister Anna were sent to Paris for some months to improve their French. The school opened to girl boarders in the autumn of 1829, with Mary doing most of the teaching.[8]

In the early 1830s several events occurred which led to Mary recognising her life work. Rioting in favour of the Reform Bill was followed by an outbreak of cholera which was particularly bad in the low-lying areas around the Lewins Mead meeting house, and the Carpenter women were active in trying to relieve some of the suffering with gifts of food, clothing, and fuel. The Carpenter home and school escaped the contagion, partly due to Anna Carpenter's meticulous housekeeping. Then came the visit of the reforming Indian rajah, Rammohun Roy, who had corresponded with Lant. He met the Carpenter family and attended worship at Lewins Mead. When he fell ill and subsequently died, Lant enabled the necessary Hindu rites to be performed at a private burial. A happier visit for Mary was that of an American Unitarian minister, Joseph Tuckerman, who had developed a ministry of visiting the homes of the poorest people in his home town of Boston. He too fell ill, but was nursed devotedly by the Carpenter women and recovered – but not before Mary had accompanied him on his explorations of the poorest parts of Bristol. The story is told that a small ragged boy ran across their path and Tuckerman remarked, 'That child should be followed home and seen after'. Mary remembered this as the great turning point in her life.[9]

Tuckerman's work with deprived and delinquent children was based on the same associationist and Unitarian ideas applied by Lant and Mary. Lant started work on editing a selection of Tuckerman's reports on poverty in Boston for publication in England, and after Tuckerman's second visit the Lewins Mead congregation established a Women's Working and Visiting Society, which engaged in social work in the immediate area, and a needlework group supplying warm clothes to the poor. Mary was the secretary and main organiser of both these groups. Tuckerman's insistence that children should not suffer because of inadequate care became Mary's bible, together with his assertion that 'Human nature is *never* to be given up ... There is no condition so desperate as to forbid recovery, nor does repeated failure justify discouragement.'[10] For the time being she had to work at home, teaching in the family girls' school, which earned enough to put her brothers through college and professional training, not available to Mary and her sisters; but what spare time she had was devoted to poorer children.

In 1839 Lant's health broke down again, with a severe and violent attack of 'melancholia'. His son Russell, having recently completed ministerial training, came to deputise while Lant was sent on another sea voyage, accompanied by a young doctor. The following year Lant disappeared one night during a storm on board a ship in the Mediterranean; he was reported missing, believed dead. Russell insisted that his father must have fallen overboard by accident, and this was the story given to the many who mourned his death. Mary, who had idolised her father and took after him in many ways, was stunned by grief and relapsed into depression.[11] The family's circumstances were changed considerably by Lant's death. He had left all his property to his wife, so in financial terms Mary was totally dependent on her mother. Gradually the siblings left the family home, leaving Mary to run the school (which had moved to new premises) with the help of her sister Anna and her mother. The last sister to marry was Anna in 1848, at which point the school was closed. Anna and her husband took over the main house, while Mary and her mother moved to a side wing.[12]

Up to this point Mary's work with Bristol's poor had been limited to her spare time. Nevertheless it included assisting the man who ran the Domestic Mission set up on Tuckerman's lines. She took on the task of district visiting for the poorest part of the city, between Lewins Mead and the docks, an area where deprivation was increased in the 1840s by the arrival of Irish immigrants escaping the potato famine. Here, in her care for the deprived children, she found an outlet for the love which had never found fulfilment in a romantic attachment, and also for her philanthropic passion.[13] But her outlook was never parochial, and she maintained contact with American Unitarians and reformers, supporting their anti-slavery work, even though the factional divisions troubled her. She paid homage to her two heroes with publications in their honour. Her *Morning and Evening Meditations for Every Day in a Month* was designed to be a non-sectarian tribute to her father. It included contributions from many Unitarians on both sides of the Atlantic, as well as others from different denominations, with much original writing by herself. It was originally published anonymously in 1845, but was so successful that it ran to six editions and was also published in America (1847).[14] This was followed by *A Life of Joseph Tuckerman* in 1848.[15]

The ragged school movement was already underway in England, following the example of John Pounds' school in Portsmouth, and the establishment of a Ragged School Union. Mary was aware of these developments and had already (in 1846) established what she called a 'free school' (rather than a ragged school) for boys, using a room at Lewins Mead, supported by the congregation and John Bishop Estlin, a local Unitarian doctor.[16] Mary insisted that the children should be treated with respect and that there should be no corporal punishment. She provided food and other necessities. The untrained male teacher was ineffectual at first, but order and learning flourished under Mary's guidance. The school soon expanded to new premises and acquired a trained teacher, with girls and boys being taught during the day and also in evening classes, learning a trade as well as school subjects. Once Mary was free of other duties, she herself frequently taught at the school, introducing a wide variety of subjects and activities, always centred on the needs of the children.[17] When the school was officially inspected in 1848 and 1849, the inspector was so impressed that he asked Mary to write more fully about her work; this resulted in a series of anonymous articles in *The Inquirer,* and later a book: *Ragged Schools, by a Worker.*

The school moved again to larger premises, and Mary used her experience of working with the most problematic and criminalised children to publicise both her philosophy and her methods. Her influential book *Reformatory Schools for the Children of the Perishing and Dangerous Classes* (1851) claimed that love and the re-creation of a supportive family environment were more effective than physical punishment.[18] This publication was followed by a conference on juvenile delinquency in Birmingham, where Mary refused to defy convention and speak in public, but she did a lot of preparatory work, especially in conjunction with Matthew Davenport Hill, a lawyer from a Unitarian family. The conference endorsed

Mary's recommendations of three types of school – ragged, industrial, and reformatory – and subsequently many towns tried this scheme. In Bristol she established a reformatory school for both boys and girls at Kingswood, and a girls' school at Red Lodge nearer the centre of Bristol, with much support from Unitarians Russell Scott and her long-term friend and helper **Lady Byron** (the estranged wife of the poet, and the mother of Ada Lovelace, a pioneer of computer science).[19]

From now on Mary divided her time and energy between the practical work of running the schools and caring for individual children and the campaigning work of writing and lobbying for improved understanding and treatment of deprived children. She opened an industrial school in Bristol, and overcame her inhibitions about speaking to mixed audiences, especially at the newly formed National Association for the Promotion of Social Science (NAPSS) from 1857, an organisation with which members of the Langham Place Group were also involved.[20] She became a regular speaker at NAPSS conferences, giving more papers than any other woman in its first twenty years – 32 on her own and two with others – and soon had enough confidence to speak extempore and join in discussions.[21]

Many Unitarians from Bristol and elsewhere supported her work, notably **Frances Power Cobbe**, a lively Irish woman who came to help at Red Lodge in 1858. The two women were both intelligent and strong willed, but otherwise very different: Mary was thin, rather puritanical and austere, with a Priestleyan Unitarian theology inherited from her father, while Frances was from a family of landed gentry, including prominent Church men; large in body and in character, she was a convert to Theodore Parker's brand of theistic Unitarianism, and she was looking for love, warmth, and friendship. After a year it was clear that their contrasting personalities were such that they could not live in the same house, and Frances left, although the two remained friends.

Mary's campaigning work on behalf of disadvantaged children brought her into the public eye, and she overcame her reluctance to step out of the conventional lady's role. In 1860 she gave an address to the statistical section of the British Association for the Advancement of Science, from which, as a woman, she had been barred in 1836. The *Englishwoman's Review* regarded her as a role model for women activists. Ever since the visit of

Rammohun Roy, Mary had been interested in Indian affairs, meeting and hosting a variety of Indian visitors to England, including several from the liberal Brahmo Samaj of Calcutta. She was encouraged to return their visits, and in 1866 she made the first of four trips to various places in India to talk on both girls' education and prison reform, and of course to visit prisons and other institutions.[22] In India she was treated as a celebrity, which was rare for an unmarried woman, and her advice was sought, but her first attempt to start a school was unsuccessful, not surprisingly as it was based on a Western curriculum. However, she did write a memorandum for the Viceroy, asking why the British government was doing more for boys than for girls. On her return to England she continued discussions with India Office officials and wrote an account of her travels which resulted in an audience with Queen Victoria.[23] In order to promote the exchange of knowledge between the two countries she founded the National Indian Association, with branches in various parts of the UK, and edited its journal until her death.[24] On her third visit to India in 1869–70 she established girls' schools in Bombay and Ahmedabad, staffed by English women trained by her to teach in them, but it was in Calcutta that her work survived the longest, supported by members of the Brahmo Samaj.[25]

During Mary's visit to the United States of America in 1873 she saw women active in public offices and in senior roles in hospitals and in education: confirmation of her conviction that, if educated well, women were capable of great things. Earlier that year in England she had refused to chair the executive committee of the International Arbitration Association, because she considered it outside a woman's role, but in the States she began to speak from church pulpits.[26] She had learned to overcome the conventional restrictions on a lady's place in Victorian society, speaking in public to promote the welfare of the children about which she cared so much. Gradually she began to realise that other issues concerning women's rights were relevant in this struggle. At first she rejected the idea of women's suffrage, but, influenced by John Stuart Mill, she changed her mind and in the last year of her life shared a platform with her old friend Frances Power Cobbe at a meeting of the Bristol and West of England Society for Women's Suffrage, when they took turns to propose and second resolutions.[27] Mary had long been concerned about the double standards concerning the treatment and education of girls and boys, women and men, including the condemnation of desperate women guilty of infanticide of illegitimate children whose fathers escaped any censure. This led to her involvement with the National Association against the Contagious Diseases Acts, a mixed group of which she became Vice President. Her struggle to obtain suitable education for women teachers led her to support campaigns for women's higher education, including admission to medical degree courses at the University of London.[28]

At the time of her death in 1877 Mary was considered the 'leading female advocate of deprived and delinquent children' in England; tributes came from both India and America, and a stone memorial in her honour was placed in Bristol Cathedral.[29] Many of the institutions that she founded did not survive into the following century, mainly because of her distrust of state intervention, but her principle of child-centred provision has proved a lasting legacy in both institutions and laws.[30]

Endnotes

1 Ruth Watts, 'Rational religion and feminism: the challenge of Unitarianism in the nineteenth century', in Susan Morgan (ed.), *Women, Religion and Feminism in Britain, 1750–1900* (London. Palgrave Macmillan, 2002), pp.46–7; Jo Manton, *Mary Carpenter and the Children of the Streets*, (London, Heinemann, 1976) p.20.

2 Manton, op.cit., pp.22–3.

3 Ibid., pp. 23-7.

4 Ruth Watts, 'Mary Carpenter: educator of the children of the 'Perishing and Dangerous Classes'", in Mary Hilton and Pam Hirsch (eds), *Practical Visionaries: Women, Education and Social Progress 1790–1930* (Harlow, Pearson Education, 2000), pp.39–40; Manton, op.cit., pp.26–7.

5 Manton, op. cit., pp.54–5.

6 Ibid., p.30.

7 Ibid., pp.29–35.

8 Ibid., pp.36–8.

9 Ibid. pp.43–50.

10 Ibid., pp.50–52; Watts op.cit. (2000), p.42.

11 Manton, op. cit., pp.55–8, 63.

12 Ibid., pp.59–61, 79–80.

13 Ibid., pp.72–5.

14 Mary Carpenter, *Morning and Evening Meditations for Every Day in a Month* (Boston, Wm. Crosby and H. P. Nichols, 1847); J. Estlin Carpenter, *The Life and Work of Mary Carpenter* (London, Macmillan, 1879), pp.65–6.

15 Manton, op. cit., pp.78–9; Frank Prochaska, 'Mary Carpenter', in *Oxford Dictionary of National Biography*, www. oxforddnb.com (2004), accessed 4 November 2018.

16 Prochaska, op.cit., 2004.

17 Manton, op.cit., pp.82–90.

18 Prochaska, op. cit.

19 Ibid.; Manton, op. cit., pp. 112–13; Watts, op.cit. (2000), pp.42–3.

20 Watts, op.cit. (2000), p.48.

21 Watts, op.cit. (2002) p.48.

22 Norman C. Sargant, *Mary Carpenter in India* (Bristol, A.J. Sargant, 1987), passim.

23 Prochaska, op. cit.

24 Sargant, op.cit., pp.102–13.

25 J. Estlin Carpenter, op.cit., p.452; author's personal visit, January 1979.

26 Watts, op.cit. (2000), pp.48–9.

27 Sally Mitchell, *Frances Power Cobbe: Victorian Feminist, Journalist, Reformer* (Charlottesville and London, University of Virginia Press, 2004), p.250; Watts, op.cit. (2000), p.49,

28 Watts, op.cit. (2000), p.49.

29 Prochaska, op. cit.; *Christian Life*, 1877, pp.399–400; *Inquirer*, 1877, p.552; *Christian Life*, 1878, p.128; J Estlin Carpenter, op.cit., p.490.

30 Prochaska, op. cit..

10 Frances Power Cobbe (1822–1904)[1]

Ann Peart

Frances Power Cobbe was not born into a Unitarian family but discovered Unitarianism in early adult life. Her family were Anglican Anglo-Irish landowners with an estate at Newbridge, just to the north of Dublin. Frances was the youngest by five years of five children, and the only girl. Although her parents were well off, her father spent a great deal of time and money overseeing and improving the estate, and her mother became a semi-invalid in the year after Frances was born. Her childhood was rather lonely, as her brothers were away at school most of the time, and she was looked after by a series of nursery maids and then governesses, as was the usual practice in moneyed families; but she was allowed to spend her afternoons reading in the family's extensive library. Although her father was an evangelical Anglican, she was taught to read by the use of Anna Laetitia Barbauld's *Lessons for Children*. In her teens she attended an expensive girls' boarding school at Brighton, intended to 'finish' her as a young lady, but which she hated. The next summer she experienced some sort of conversion to evangelical seriousness and resolved to make religion the focus of her life. During one of the family visits to England in 1842, she apparently encountered Unitarianism for the first time, writing:

> *I can remember Mr Boyd about this period preaching at Cheltenham, and denouncing the Unitarians with such singular vehemence, that it induced me to institute careful enquiries concerning a body of whose tenets at that time I was in total ignorance.*

Frances was taught the management skills needed to run the large household at Newbridge, and she took over the running of the grand house, a task presumably intended as practice for a future role as a married lady. However, she did not enjoy the Dublin balls at which she was supposed

Frances Power Cobbe, 1894
(From *Life of Frances Power Cobbe by Herself*, London, Bentley, 1894)
(Wikimedia Commons)

to meet eligible young men; she preferred to study and do local charity work on the estate. As the potato famine began to be felt, there was much distress to be relieved. She wrote, 'I had the care of our village school ... and the sole supervision of two villages where nobody was ever ill, or dying, or in trouble without being looked after by me'.[2]

Frances continued to take her religion very seriously, but was troubled by doubts about the veracity of the Bible and gave up calling herself a Christian. For a short time she was what would now be called an agnostic, but she began to pray again, and from that time onward never lost her belief in God as the 'Lord of Conscience'. She read widely, including works by Deists and Unitarians such as **Elizabeth Gaskell**, Francis Newman, and James Martineau. But the book that transformed her life was Theodore Parker's *Discourse of Matters Pertaining to Religion*, which she bought as soon as the first British edition was published in 1846. Parker was an

American Unitarian minister who had developed a form of theism which neither depended on biblical authority nor regarded Jesus as other than a great teacher; he was thus on the radical wing of Unitarianism. Parker's position was similar to that being developed by Frances, and she described his book as 'epoch making'. His God was much less distant than the deists', being directly accessible to each person as the revelation of 'God's holiness and love in the depths of the soul'. His belief in the immortality of the soul became especially important to Frances, as her much-loved mother died within the year (1847), and its importance was reinforced in the correspondence that she began with him. Frances's enquiries and her Unitarian reading engaged her curiosity, but her first visit to a Unitarian chapel, in about 1847, was not auspicious. In her autobiography she described it thus:

> *I went to Dublin one 1ˢᵗ January and drove to the chapel of which I had heard in Eustace Street. It was a big, dreary place with scarcely a quarter of the seats occupied, and a middle-class congregation apparently very cool and indifferent. The service was a miserable, hybrid affair, neither Christian as I understood Christianity, nor yet Theistic; but it was a pleasure to me merely to stand and kneel with other people at the hymns and prayers. At last the sermon, for which I might almost say I was hungry, arrived. The old Minister in his black-gown ascended the pulpit, having taken with him – what? – could I believe my eyes? It was an old printed book, bound in the blue and drab old fuzzy paper of the year 1819 or thereabouts, and out of this he proceeded to read an erudite discourse by some father of English Socinianism, on the precise value of the Greek article when used before the word Theos! My disappointment not to say disgust were such that, – as it was easy from my seat to leave the place without disturbing anyone, – I escaped into the street, never (it may be believed) to repeat the experiment.*

After her mother's death, Frances told her father about her rejection of conventional Christianity and adoption of Parker's theism, and as a result she was sent to live with her ailing brother Tom (who taught her Latin and Greek) in the remote Donegal countryside for nearly a year. But her services as an efficient housekeeper were missed, and she returned to Newbridge the following year, with the understanding that religion would not be discussed, and that she need not attend either family prayers or Sunday church services. During this time Frances began to write secretly; while in Donegal she had already written an essay on deism. Back in Newbridge, her wide reading included works by **Harriet Martineau**, **Barbara Leigh Smith (later Bodichon)**, Anna Jameson, and Immanuel Kant. She began writing a work on the latter, eventually published anonymously in 1855 as *An Essay on Intuitive Morals. Part I. Theory of Morals*. In this work she interpreted the philosophy of Kant as providing an ethical system which was intellectually satisfying, yet accessible to thinking people. In the final section she noted some gender differences in 'male and female Codes of Honour', for example that lying is not acceptable for men but counted trivial in women, and that the 'cowardice which would bring ignominy to the Man' is '<u>taught</u> to the woman as the proper ornament of her sex'. Her reading for the second part of this essay, on practical morals, included **Mary Carpenter's** work on reformatory schools, published in 1855. When Part II was published in 1857, it was received favourably by Francis Newman and James Martineau, who both became her friends within a few years. However, later in 1857 her father died – and Frances's world changed completely.

The Newbridge estate was inherited by the oldest son, who then ran it with his wife, and so Frances lost her role in running the household; unless she was prepared to stay on as some sort of redundant dependant, she had lost her home too. Three weeks after her father's death she set out on her travels, moving from a rooted, wealthy way of life to one of comparative poverty and mobility. She had been left an annual allowance of £200, with an additional £100 which she used to travel to the Mediterranean and the Middle East. This journey proved an eye-opener in many ways, taught her different forms of self-reliance, and boosted her confidence in the possibility of living as an independent woman. On her return to England, Unitarians in London provided her with an introduction to **Mary Carpenter**, who was seeking a companion to lodge with her and share in her work with delinquent children. Frances arranged to do this. She found Mary's spartan lifestyle and constant overwork a considerable strain, but she experienced the work, especially visiting poor families and workhouse projects, as fascinating. Frances spent the spring of 1860 in Italy with the women friends she had met during her travels, and visited the elderly scientist Mary Somerville, who became in many ways a mother figure to her. She also spent time with the dying Theodore Parker.

When Frances returned to Bristol later in 1860, she resumed her poorhouse work in conjunction with Margaret Elliot, the daughter of the Dean of Bristol Cathedral, but took lodgings separately from Mary Carpenter. This gave her time to write, and together Frances and Margaret wrote a paper for the 1860 meeting of the National Association for the Promotion of Social Science (NAPSS), one of the few mixed-sex public organisations that allowed women to deliver papers and eat at public dinners. When this paper was published, it appeared with her full name as author, the first of her publications to do so, and she demonstrated her appreciation of the need for publicity to further her cause by organising a further 84 articles and letters in 54 different newspapers, exposing the poor conditions of sick wards in workhouses. The following year, she used her contacts to get an article on workhouses printed in *Macmillan's Magazine*, the first published piece for which she was paid. This set the pattern for Frances's future career as a writer and propagandist on issues of social justice, rather than as a hands-on worker, as she had been when collaborating with Mary Carpenter.

During her next stay in Italy the following winter she reported on the political situation there for *The Daily News* and wrote articles on arts subjects for other publications. She greatly enjoyed the company of the women artists and became particular friends with a Welsh sculptor, **Mary Lloyd**. Although back in Bristol she was still officially doing social work, she concentrated on writing, and gave a paper at the 1862 NAPSS meeting, proposing that women should be admitted to universities: her first public advocacy of women's rights, an issue which consumed increasing amounts of her attention over the years to come. The following year, she began editing the writings of Theodore Parker, producing fourteen volumes with a substantial preface on the religious demands of the age. Published between 1863 and 1871, these remained the only collected works of Parker for fifty years, achieving substantial sales in both Britain and America.

Also in 1863 Frances published her first theological book in her own name: *Broken Lights: An Inquiry Into the Present Condition and Future Prospects of Religious Faith.* In it she surveyed current Christian denominations from the point of view of a theist and found them all, even the Unitarians, to be wanting, as, compared with the theism of Parker, they still placed too much emphasis on the god-like qualities and actions of Jesus. She contrasted the traditional Bible-based Unitarians with the 'New School', noting that Parker worshipped only one God, while many British Unitarians 'have yet persisted in giving to Christ that position which, practically to us as moral beings, is a divine one, namely that of our Moral Lord and Teacher, and future Judge'.

In 1863 the second part of Frances's *Essay on Intuitive Morals*, republished under her own name as *Religious Duty*, attracted considerably more notice. From this time onwards, her writings encompassed social issues, travel, and religion; they are too numerous to consider in detail here, except to note that she developed the practice of writing for a variety of journals and then at intervals collecting articles together to form a book; this maximised both her earnings and her exposure to the book-buying and opinion-forming public. As it was now clear that Frances could earn enough from writing to supplement her allowance from the Cobbe estate, after her next stay in Italy she left Bristol to live in London. There she set up house with Mary Lloyd, and the two spent the rest of their lives together as a devoted couple.

Once resident in London, Frances developed an impressive array of contacts to further both her writing and the causes that she espoused. In addition to her writing and campaigning, she became a very effective public speaker and organiser, and she and Mary enjoyed a lively social life, with frequent dinner and tea parties. Many of the people she worked with had Unitarian connections, including the women associated with the Kensington women's discussion society, such as **Clementia Taylor**, **Barbara Bodichon**, and **Anna Swanwick**; and various members of James Martineau's congregation. Frances was a regular attender at the Little Portland Street Unitarian Chapel when James Martineau was the minister there. In her recollections of James Martineau, she wrote:

> *...when my friend Miss Lloyd and I planned to share a house in London*
> *(about 1864) one of our first and greatest interests was to become regular*
> *attenders at Mr Martineau's services in Little Portland Street Chapel.*
> *It was a long way from our home in South Kensington, and we had no*
> *carriage; yet I do not think we ever missed – rain or shine – a Sunday*
> *morning service when we were in London; nor a week-day evening lecture*
> *(several series of which lectures were delivered in the winter); nor the*
> *Ethical Lectures, to which we were kindly admitted among the students in*
> *Manchester College. We had seats in the gallery of Portland Street Chapel*
> *very nearly opposite the pulpit, and thus had every advantage for hearing*
> *the noble sermons which made up the richest part of our happy lives.*

Manchester New College was based in London during the time that Frances lived there. She petitioned James Martineau to allow women to attend the lectures given to the male theological students. At first he refused, but she persisted, and an undated manuscript list of occasional students in ethics lists seventeen names, fifteen of which are women, including Miss Cobbe, Miss Lloyd, and Miss A. Swanwick. According to one college history, the controversy over the admission of women to the college was settled in London, after a resolute little company headed by Frances Power Cobbe and Anna Swanwick had made their way into Martineau's lecture-room. The debate was prolonged over two years, ending with the vote for admission at an adjourned meeting of the Trustees in February 1876. That was the period in which degrees of London University were opened to women, and for several years, up to the time of his retirement, women, as occasional students, attended Martineau's lectures.

Although after James Martineau retired Cobbe stopped attending the Little Portland Street Chapel on a regular basis and went instead to hear the heretical Anglican Charles Voysey preach, she retained her Unitarian connections, and not only worshipped but also herself began to preach in Unitarian churches and chapels in the London area. Theologically, she described herself as a theist rather than a Unitarian. The principles of her beliefs were 'the absolute goodness of God; the final salvation of every created soul; and the divine authority of conscience', and these, together with her talk of 'the divine spark of divine life within us', became a popular way of expressing Unitarian belief.

Frances's reputation as a journalist and campaigner was considerable. Her campaigns for women's rights included membership of the Married Women's Property Committee and the London National Society for Women's Suffrage. The protection of women from abuse was a major concern, with a popular article on *Wife Torture in England*, and work for various parliamentary bills addressing matrimonial issues.[3] She also wrote two articles on the role of women in the church. The first, 'Women's Work in the Church', was mainly concerned with the Church of England and was published in *The Theological Review* in 1865. In this, Frances dismissed the idea of separate women's organisations and once again attacked institutional religion. The second, 'The Fitness of Women for the Ministry', first published in *The Theological Review* in 1876, promoted the idea that able women could become ministers, and that their ready sympathy and 'special facilities' would give them an advantage in pastoral matters. Women, she thought, were also better at practical acts of religious duty, and at living by their conscience. The last section of the article introduced what would now be called feminist theology, seeing female qualities in both Jesus Christ and God. Frances wrote a variety of works on religion, advocating the use of rational thought and scientific methods, which were taken seriously by the more liberal Christian thinkers, and her regular anonymous leaders in several daily papers influenced a significant proportion of the population. She is reputed to have been the first woman who had a regular staff desk in a national newspaper office. She remained a Conservative in politics.

However, after Frances turned her attention to the treatment of animals and took on the cause of anti-vivisection, her sense of perspective and her always limited ability to make compromises seem to have diminished. She became less convinced that scientific methods and discoveries were leading to a better world. In 1876 she founded and headed the Society for Protection of Animals Liable to Vivisection, commonly known as the Victoria Street Society (from the address of its headquarters), and she spent the next eighteen years working tirelessly on its behalf. She also produced many articles attacking science for undermining spiritual and moral values, and she lost a number of friends over this.

In 1884 Frances and Mary retired to Hengwrt, Mary's large house on the Welsh coast. However, as the house was owned jointly by Mary and two of her sisters and they all needed income from the property, it was often let out, with the couple living in smaller houses nearby. Although Mary and Frances could not be considered to be poor, they always struggled to maintain a middle-class household with servants. They were just about to sign away Hengwrt on a long lease when Frances received a substantial legacy of about £25,000 from **Anna Yates**, a Liverpool Unitarian who had been a pupil at the Carpenters' school in Bristol.

Frances maintained her campaigns against vivisection, but she was involved in increasing tensions with staff members of the Victoria Street Society and resigned in 1898, after losing a vote about whether or not the society should campaign against all vivisection, or only against that which was inflicted with unnecessary cruelty. Although by this time she was in her late seventies, she immediately founded the British Union for the Total Abolition of Vivisection to continue her work. In retirement, she continued to write, and her autobiography, published in 1894, was an immediate success. Two years later, Mary Lloyd died, leaving Frances to live out a rather lonely old age, in spite of frequent visits from friends and relatives, including George Eyre Evans, minister associated with the Unitarian congregation at Aberystwyth, which she had helped to establish and continued to support. At the inauguration of the use of a room in the New Market Hall in Aberystwyth in 1903, Frances invited Unitarian minister **Gertrude von Petzold**, in training for the Unitarian ministry, to preach, and encouraged other women both to preach and to serve as congregational secretaries. Frances died in 1904 and was buried next to Mary in the local parish churchyard, with a service conducted by two Unitarian ministers, George Eyre Evans and Estlin Carpenter (Mary Carpenter's nephew). Harriet Hosmer described her as 'being of proportions ample as her intellect, and possessed of a wit as sunny as her heart'.[4]

Endnotes

1   This chapter is mainly based on
    Ann Peart, 'Forgotten Prophets:
    The Lives of Unitarian Women
    1760–1904' (unpublished doctoral
    thesis, University of Newcastle, 2006),
    pp.182–205, which is fully referenced.
    Additional references are given below.

2   Frances. E. Willard, 'Frances Power
    Cobbe', *Inquirer* 1887, p.634.

3   Sally Mitchell, *Frances Power Cobbe:
    Victorian Feminist, Journalist, Reformer*
    (Charlottesville and London, University
    of Virginia Press, 2004), pp.256–63.

4   Willard, op.cit.

11 Women in Unitarian administration

Alan Ruston and Ann Peart

Chapel governance in the nineteenth century
Alan Ruston

Dissenting chapels and trusts have been dominated by men for centuries. Until the late nineteenth century, women had little formal place in the governance of Unitarian organisations – and even then it was only at the margins; they did not generally sit on main committees until late in the century. The position was little different in other denominations, and it reflected the status of women in wider society. Women may have had considerable influence in certain defined areas, but they had little direct power to mould events in general.

The situation began to change at the margins in the 1840s. Formally elected chapel committees were essentially an early nineteenth-century development; before then, chapel decisions were made by the richer and more dominant men who constituted the governance of the chapel. Open, free elections to the governance of chapel institutions hardly existed, and no examples of the election of women to a governing chapel committee or trust in the first part of the century have been identified.

Women, however, could play a part in governance, in that they were often subscribers to chapel funds, or rented their own pews. Where a chapel depended on income from pew rents rather than relying on a few rich figures or trust funds, then the body of the subscribers often played a key role. Women in the congregation of Birmingham New Meeting appear to have had some influence on its governance from the beginning of the nineteenth century. Several women signed a letter concerning the appointment of a new minister in 1802, and the following year **Sarah Bache** wrote to her sister that she had signed a petition against inviting a new minister. In 1816 the question of appointing a new minister, the Revd James Yates, again caused conflict, and this time the women's vote was decisive. The record of this is as follows:

For the motion	53	Against	62
Ladies present	11	Against	0
	64		62

John Henry Rylands, a prominent member, recalled later that the ladies' vote had been used to ensure the appointment of Yates in the face of considerable opposition.[1]

Another example was the New Gravel Pit Chapel, Hackney. From the 1790s to the 1850s it was among the most influential Unitarian congregations in Britain. Records show that a substantial number of women were subscribers in the late eighteenth century; among the subscribers listed for 1820 there were about 47 women:[2] a sufficient grouping, if taking concerted action, to influence the activities of the chapel, although there is no evidence that they ever did so. An instance where everyone who was a subscriber and a regular attender played a bigger role came in 1846 with the appointment of a minister at the New Gravel Pit, following the death of the long-serving and dominant Robert Aspland in 1845. The consideration of several names had created disputes. In September 1846, the issue came down to a choice between two ministers who had preached acceptably. It was decided that everyone over the age of 18 subscribing one guinea who was a regular attender could vote. In the ballot, 'The chairman requested that those in favour of Mr Harrison to go to the body of the chapel, and for Mr Boucher to go under the gallery'. Mr Boucher received 82 votes and Mr Harrison 79. No further ballot was considered necessary, and Mr Boucher was appointed.'[3] His short ministry was not a success, but the female members played a full part in the vote to appoint him.

The British & Foreign Unitarian Association
Alan Ruston

The British & Foreign Unitarian Association (B&FUA), formed in 1825, was the only national organisation representing congregations that identified themselves as English Presbyterian, General Baptist, and causes created after 1813, when the expression of Unitarian opinions had been legalised. Not all the congregations who identified themselves as being in these categories belonged to the Association. After the 1850s its role was regarded by followers of James Martineau as contentious, and it led to much dispute. Women did not take part in its administration, although they were subscribers to its funds. A change in attitude towards women participating in its governance came late in the century. In the 1880s, among the numerous Vice-Presidents, 96 in all, there were two women: **Lady Deborah Bowring**, *née* Castle (1816–1902), the widow of Sir John Bowring, who had been its President in 1861,[4] and **Miss Anna Swanwick** (1813–1899), the well-known author and translator who came from a long-established Unitarian family and was a leader in the women's movement.[5] The award of a Vice-Presidency was a recognition of the person's importance and Unitarian connection, but there were no women then serving on the much smaller Executive Committee, which actually took the organisation forward.

By 1890, there were six women out of a total of 97 Vice- Presidents; by 1893 there were nine out of a similar number; and in the following year there were 16 out of 154 when all had been re-classified as Members of the Council. In 1894, there were two women on the Executive Committee: **Miss L.M. Aspland** and **Lady Wilson**. The new century saw 19 women members of the Council, and two women on the Executive, one of whom was **Lucy Tagart**, who in 1903 was joined by **Helen Brooke Herford**. These two women played a significant role in the administration of the Association in the early years of the twentieth century. Their stories are told in greater detail elsewhere in this book: Lucy's at the end of this chapter, and Helen's in Chapter 14.

By 1908 Lucy and Helen, both living in Hampstead, had been joined on the Executive Committee by **Miss Annie E. Clephan** (1855–1930) of Leicester. Unlike many women activists, Annie Clephan did not come from the Hampstead/Highgate area or from central London.[6] This group formed a nexus of Unitarian activity in that small area in North London.

Helen Brooke Herford (1854–1935) lived with her two sisters in Hampstead; like Lucy, they were members of Rosslyn Hill Chapel, Hampstead. Significant numbers of active Unitarian women were members at Rosslyn Hill. The only notable exception among these powerful figures was **Mary Edith Martineau**, *née* Nettlefold (1869–1961), the wife of Sydney Martineau: she lived in Ennismore Gardens in South West London and was for decades a member of Essex Church in Kensington. However, they and others involved in the administration of the Unitarian movement would have met regularly and constituted a network, although they would not necessarily have recognised it as such, nor would they have used the term.

The London nexus
Alan Ruston

In 1915, the B&FUA became an incorporated body so that it could hold land and funds on behalf of congregations. The substantial number of council members were replaced with a statutorily regulated body, run by trustees. A register of members was set up which remains open to inspection.[7] Among the first trustees were **Helen Herford, Annie Clephan, Lucy Tagart**, and **Mrs Alice Bartram** (1845–1929, who lived and worshipped in Islington, London), joined by **Edith Martineau** the following year. Those added in the next 25 years constitute a group of women who played a significant role within Unitarian administration. Some also served on the Council of the General Assembly of Unitarian and Free Christian Churches (GA) after its inception in 1928, the successor in certain of its activities to the B&FUA:[8]

- **Rosalind Lee** (whose story is told in Chapter 15).

- **Marian Taylor** (1930), 1872–1947, of Barnet, late of Highgate, and a member of the Rosslyn Hill congregation.

- **Ruth Nettlefold** (1933), 1875–1957, of Birmingham, a member of the GA Council.

- **Gertrude M. Baily** (1937), 1880–1961, always recorded as Mrs Harold Baily. As Miss Slater, she was before her marriage in the 1920s a Fellow and Tutor at Newnham College Cambridge, where she was a research scientist, with the degree of D.Sc. from that University. She was Treasurer of the Women's League from 1927 and a member of the GA Council.[9]

- **Dorothy Tarrant** (1940), whose activity within Unitarianism is separately considered in Chapter 16.

It should be added that Helen Herford was also a member of the GA Council from its inception, as was Edith Martineau. In 1935, of the 34 elected members of the GA Council, 10 were women. In its early years, Rosalind Lee was the representative of the Women's League on the GA Council.

Evaluation
Alan Ruston

Up to 1940, women's role in administration was growing, but was still not extensive. However, five women can be identified as national figures who successfully got things done: Lucy Tagart, Helen B. Herford, Edith Martineau, Rosalind Lee, and Dorothy Tarrant. Each had well-known fathers, and names with historic connections to Unitarian congregations that helped to ease them into influential administrative roles.[10]

The role played by **Edith Martineau** in administration overshadows all the rest. From the 1920s until the 1950s she was involved in each key development which took place, and the extent of her activity requires further study. She was the significant figure in preparing the ground for the creation of the General Assembly in 1928, so much so that she was President in its first full year of operation in 1929, and remains the only person to date to hold the office for two years. Her role is described in an appreciation by an unnamed author, published in *The Inquirer* dated 28 October 1961:

*From 1916 onwards she had been an active member of the Executive
Committee of the B&FUA…Year after year she contributed to the work
of that most important committee and sub-committees, bringing her
gifts of personal enthusiasm and sound judgement. When the First
World War was over she began to focus those gifts upon the question,
vaguely discussed at times and sceptically debated, of the more effective
organisation of our churches. This would obviously involve the
unification of the somewhat overlapping work of the B&FUA and the
National Conference,[11] of whose committee she had been a member from
1915 to 1920. At the triennial meetings of the National Conference in
Sheffield in 1926, she and Lawrence Redfern read papers in a session
which proved to be a turning point in our history. His task was to fire our
enthusiasm, hers to unfold an outline scheme grappling in advance with
practical difficulties and sentimental oppositions and demonstrating that
they could all be successfully overcome if we had the will.*

The result came only a couple of years later, and her contribution was fully
recognised in her appointment as President; no woman was to follow her
in the office until Rosalind Lee in 1940.

The second area in which Edith Martineau played a big part was in the
rebuilding of Essex Hall, the central office of the denomination. Mortimer
Rowe, who had worked with her since the inception of the GA, outlined
her commitment in the address that he gave at her memorial service in
October 1961 (*Inquirer*, 21 October 1961):

*More than thirty years ago she longed to see a new and dignified
headquarters building in place of the old Essex Hall, and even had
plans prepared which proved, alas, impracticable, for its demolition and
rebuilding. Ten years later enemy action accounted for the demolition,
but another dozen were to pass before rebuilding could be entertained.
Then came the ultimate hour of joy and satisfaction, when from all over
the country we crowded into Essex Hall on a sunny June afternoon to
watch her lay the foundation stone of the new Essex Hall, and listen to
the glowing words in which she, now eighty-eight years of age, recalled
the heroic past and proclaimed her confident faith in the future.[12]*

Lucy Tagart (1836–1925)
Ann Peart

Margaret Lucy Tagart was the middle child of three daughters and two sons born to Revd Edward Tagart and his wife Helen, *née* Bourne, the widow of Thomas Martineau (brother of James and Harriet).[13] Edward was the minister of the central London congregation that was established in Duke of York Street in 1824 and moved to Little Portland Street with a new building in the classical style in 1833.[14] The family moved out to a big house on the north side of Hampstead Heath in 1851, the same year that Elizabeth Gaskell discouraged her daughter Marianne from visiting them, as she thought that the family had a 'rude quarrelsome tone'.[15] However, others found the Tagart home warm and welcoming.[16]

Lucy took a keen interest in Unitarianism, and in 1858 she accompanied her father when, as secretary of the British and Foreign Unitarian Association (B&FUA), he toured Transylvanian Unitarian churches (now in north-west Romania, but then part of the Austro-Hungarian empire). She commented on the difficulty of communication with the Hungarian-speaking Unitarians, noting: '...hardly anyone spoke English or German, and the Latin used was so different in pronunciation... that it was impossible to sustain a conversation'.[17] Sadly, on the journey home Edward became ill; he died in Brussels, with Lucy the only member of his family able to be with him. One of her uncles arrived soon afterwards and organised transport back to London.[18] It was left to Lucy, then aged 21, to give a report on the visit. According to her obituary, 'She took up the work in connection with the Transylvanian Unitarians which had been begun by her father ... and she developed it far beyond what could have been foreseen in his time. Her name is well known and honoured in Hungary as it is in this country'.[19]

Lucy visited Transylvania several times and took other British Unitarians, women and men, with her; on her return she wrote reports so that other British Unitarians learned of their Hungarian-speaking co-religionists.[20] In 1901 she led a party of 27 British Unitarians to attend the opening of the new buildings of the Unitarian College in Kolozsvar. In 1910 Lucy was one of the delegates at the fifth congress of what is now the International Association for Religious Freedom, held in Berlin. During these meetings the women formed what is now the International Association for Liberal Religious Women, of which Lucy became an active member.[21] After the Berlin meetings about one hundred people, including Lucy, went on to Kolozsvar to mark the 400th anniversary of the birth of Ferenc Dávid, and she was probably present at the inaugural meetings of the Transylvanian Unitarian Women's League.

In Britain Lucy's major contribution to the Unitarian movement was with the Postal Mission. This was an idea copied from the United States and initiated in 1866 by four women, including Lucy and her friend **Florence Hill**, at a meeting convened by Robert Spears. The aim was to spread Unitarianism using the post for the distribution of tracts and correspondence, and it caught on so quickly that it soon became necessary to co-ordinate activities in various places in the United Kingdom, so becoming the Central Postal Mission and Unitarian Workers' Union. Its headquarters were at Essex Hall in central London, and then at Stepney, and the additional tasks of co-ordination and 'other practical and pioneer Unitarian missionary work' were added.[22] From the outset, Lucy was the President of the Mission, and Florence the Secretary, and although much of the work was done by women, men were also involved, often becoming paid missionaries. It was said that Lucy's chairing of the mission meetings was always 'fair and just', and that she was 'always bright, reasonable and courteous'.[23] Alan Ruston comments that this was the first nationally organised outreach body that put enquirers in touch with Unitarian churches in their locality. The two women continued to run the mission for the rest of their active lives. By 1908 there were thirteen local postal missions, and more than one thousand books were lent each year, in additional to the voluminous correspondence that was conducted with enquirers.[24] Lucy also organised and led summer holidays for Sunday School teachers and members of Unitarian congregations in various places in Britain, as well as continental Europe.[25]

The postal mission's work also included supporting missionaries active in various parts of the country. One such worker was the Revd Alfred Amey, who had himself found Unitarianism through the postal mission. He became the minister at Framlingham, Suffolk, in 1889, and started outreach work in the Bedfield area. Lucy and Florence took a particular

The Committee of the Central Postal Mission.
Lucy Tagart (white hair) is in the centre of the back row, with Florence Hill on her left.
(From the commemorative edition of *The Christian Life*, 1913)

interest in this, and in addition they bought and renovated a number of cottages, one of which they lived in when they stayed in the village, often inviting people from London for a holiday. They built a community centre-cum-chapel, which was opened in 1896. There was a very active Sunday School, and during the week the chapel was used as a reading room and for other community activities.[26]

Lucy's work within the B&FUA has already been described by Alan Ruston above; among all her activities it was 'the widest in its scope, the most varied in the opportunities it gave her', according to her obituary writer,[27] according to whom her 'name has been a household word in our community' – a judgement borne out by the extent of her Unitarian witness: from international work through national activities to support for local congregations in Hampstead, Stepney, and Bedfield.

Endnotes

1 Leonore Davidoff and Catherine Hall, *Family Fortunes. Men and Women of the English Middle Class 1780–1850* (London, Routledge, 1987), p.135; *Oxford Dictionary of National Biography*, 'Yates, James', www.oxforddnb.com, accessed 6 November 2018.

2 London Borough of Hackney Archives Department, New Gravel Pit Chapel D/E/237 GRA Financial Records 1742–1889, Sunday School accounts 1790–1811.

3 Alan Ruston, *Unitarianism and Early Presbyterianism in Hackney*, privately published, 1980, pp.27/28.

4 George Bartle, *An Old Radical and his Brood, Sir John Bowring and his Family* (London, Janus, 1994), pp.113–16; *Inquirer* 1902, p.493.

5 See her entry in the *Oxford Dictionary of National Biography*, and *Inquirer* 1899, pp.728, 734.

6 *Inquirer*, 26 July 1930, p.466.

7 Register of members, from 1915; bound volume maintained by the Secretary of the B&FUA at Essex Hall.

8 The GA Council consisted of representatives of organisations and directly elected members. In 1935/36 there were 11 women out of 63 members and representatives, in 1938/39 14 women out of 60, and similar numbers until the mid-1940s. The women mainly came from the elected group; the Council consisted overwhelmingly of male Unitarian ministers. In 1944, for example, the Council consisted of 17 lay men, 12 women, and 35 male ministers.

9 The role played by key women in administration can be assessed from their obituaries in *The Inquirer*. These can be traced through the Unitarian obituaries index maintained by Harris Manchester College Oxford.

10 Lucy Tagart's father was a leading minister in the mid-nineteenth century. Helen Herford's father, Brooke Herford, was a well-known Unitarian minister in both Britain and the United States whose concluding ministry was at Hampstead; other Herfords were also ministers. Edith Martineau was born a Nettlefold; her father had been President of both the B&FUA and the National Conference. And she married into the Martineau family. Rosalind Lee was the daughter of Grosvenor Lee, a Unitarian manufacturer in Birmingham who left her with ample funds to allow her freedom of action. Dorothy Tarrant's father, Revd W.G. Tarrant, was twice editor of *The Inquirer* and was the most admired hymn writer of his day among British Unitarians.

11 The National Conference of Unitarian, Liberal Christian, Free Christian, Presbyterian, and other Non-Subscribing or Kindred Congregations had been set up in 1882 by the B&FUA on an American model, to provide a focus different from its own. Meeting triennially until 1926, it was dissolved on the creation of the GA. It maintained advisory committees on ministry and a Ministerial Settlements Board.

12 For a full account of the opening, see Mortimer Rowe, *The Story of Essex Hall* (London, Lindsey Press, 1959), concluding chapter and epilogue.

13 Ann Peart, 'Forgotten Prophets: The Lives of Unitarian Women 1760–1904' (unpublished doctoral thesis, University of Newcastle, 2006), pp.153–4. <https://theses.ncl.ac.uk/dspace/bitstream/10443/245/1/peart05.pdf >.

14 Judy and Graham Hague, *The Unitarian Heritage: An Architectural Survey of Chapels and Churches in the Unitarian Tradition in the British Isles* (Sheffield, privately published, 1986), p.67.

15 J.A.V. Chapple and Arthur Pollard (eds), *The Letters of Mrs Gaskell* (Manchester, Mandolin, 1997), p.145; John Chapple and Alan Shelston (eds), *Further Letters of Mrs Gaskell* (Manchester, Manchester University Press, 2000), p.60.

16 Revd Dr Bellows, *Inquirer*, 1871, p.193.

17 M. Lucy Tagart, *The Hungarian and Transylvanian Unitarians* (London, Unitarian Christian Publishing House, 1903), p.3.

18 *Inquirer*, 1858, p.684.

19 *Inquirer*, 1925, p.359.

20 Tagart, op.cit., passim.

21 Ann Peart, 'Links Through Time and Space: Connections between British and Transylvanian Women of the Past Hundred Years', unpublished presentation at the centenary meeting of the Transylvanian Unitarian Women's League, Kolozsvar, October 2010.

22 *Christian Life*, June 6, 1908, p.299; *Christian Life*, May 10, 1913, p.233.

23 Cliff Reed, 'The Continuing Mission: The Story of Bedfield Unitarian Chapel, Suffolk; Addresses given at the Centenary Service, 17 November 1996', unpublished, p. 2.

24 *Christian Life*, 1908, op.cit.

25 *Christian Life*, 1913, op.cit.

26 Reed, op.cit., pp.1–3.

27 *Inquirer*, 1925, p.359.

PART FOUR
Suffrage and
Public Service

Introduction to Part Four

Ann Peart

During the twentieth century (up to about 1970, when we reach the limit of the scope of this book), Unitarianism suffered a gradual decline, both numerically and in terms of its wider influence. The First World War and its aftermath dealt a blow to the optimistic belief in the progress of humanity which had characterised Unitarian attitudes during the previous century. Church attendance in general declined rapidly after the Second World War, and the Unitarian movement suffered from this, in common with most other denominations. The influence of American Unitarianism, with its inclusion of humanist stances within the movement, was one aspect of the broadening of the spectrum of beliefs (or lack of them) within British Unitarianism. Increasing knowledge of, and respect for, other religions led to the growth of Universalism, in its new sense of seeing value in all religions. Women played an increasingly important role in the administration of the movement, and were significant right from the start of the formation of the General Assembly of Unitarian and Free Christian Churches in 1928. This body brought together the British and Foreign Unitarian Association (which continued as a trustee body) and the National Conference.[1]

During the twentieth century it was probably in the area of social service, including its ecumenical developments, that women were most prominent. But women's suffrage was still a major concern before the First World War. The activism that began in the nineteenth century continued, with most women, such as **Margaret Ashton**, favouring law-abiding campaigning, but some, including **Margaret Brackenbury Crook** and **Helen Watts**, joining the more radical Women's Social and Political Union (WSPU). Helen was imprisoned several times for her suffragist activities and was visited by the Revd Fred Hankinson, who made a point of visiting suffragette prisoners of all denominations.[2] Essex Hall, the central London organisational headquarters of British Unitarianism, regularly hosted large suffragist meetings.[3]

Alongside the campaigning for national suffrage, Unitarian women were active in local government. Some, like **Helen Herford**, and **Mary Ethel Leach** of Yarmouth, were elected as Poor Law guardians; some (including Ethel Leach) served on Education Boards. **Annie Leigh Browne** spearheaded the campaign to enable women to be elected as local councillors, in her role of Secretary of what became the Women's Local Government Society, from 1888 to 1921. Unitarians were among the first women to be elected to town and city councils, and some (including Ethel Leach) became mayors.[4]

This fourth part of the book first considers the achievements of the suffragist, politician, and peace campaigner Margaret Ashton, and then, in a chapter by Alan Ruston, the artist **Helen Allingham**. The chapter on the Unitarian Women's League includes stories of three prominent League presidents, Helen Herford, **Rose Allen** (told by Alan Ruston), and **Annie Beard Woodhouse**. Then comes a chapter on women ministers, with **Gertrude von Petzold**, **Rosalind Lee**, and **Margaret Barr** given prominence. Alan Ruston has the last word with an account of the life of the distinguished classicist **Dorothy Tarrant**.

Endnotes

1   Alan Ruston, 'British Unitarianism in the 20th century: a survey', *Transactions of the Unitarian Historical Society*, Vol 25, no 2, 2012, pp.77–83.

2   Elizabeth Crawford, *The Women's Suffrage Movement. A Reference Guide 1866–1928* (London, Routledge, 2001), pp.72, 267–9.

3   Crawford (2001), op.cit., p. 68.

4   Elizabeth Crawford, *The Women's Suffrage Movement in Britain and Ireland: A Regional Survey* (Abingdon, Routledge, 2006) p.93; Crawford (2001) op.cit., pp. 85–6; Jaime Reynolds, 'Madame Mayor: the first wave of Liberal women in local government leadership 1918–1939', *Journal of Liberal History* 89, Winter 2015–16, pp. 6-19.

12 Margaret Ashton (1856–1937)
Ann Peart

Described in her obituary as 'one of the most notable women in the North of England', Margaret Ashton was a suffragist, philanthropist, politician, and peace campaigner.[1] She was a life-long Unitarian: a member and regular worshipper at Hyde Chapel, in what is now Greater Manchester. Her long life of service demonstrates how she put her faith and ideals into practice, even when it meant sacrificing much for which she had worked.

The Ashton family were prominent mill owners in Hyde (seven miles to the east of Manchester city centre), and active in many philanthropic and educational schemes. Margaret was one of nine children, the third of six daughters, and was the only daughter not to marry. The boys of course went to school and college, but the girls were mainly educated at home, with a governess, although it is possible that Margaret attended a school for a short period. As the only adult child remaining in the parental home, she was particularly influenced by her father; she often helped him with his public work and accompanied him on engagements.

When she was two the family moved from what was then Cheshire into the southern suburbs of Manchester, firstly to Rusholme, and then to a rather grand house (now demolished) in Didsbury. Here the Ashtons entertained the great and the good, including in 1889 William Gladstone.[2] Their social circle encompassed a wide variety of intelligent and prosperous middle-class Mancunians, including members of the university, artists and musicians (notably Charles Halle), and Unitarian families such as the Scotts, Gaskells, and Philips. (C.P. Scott was the owner and editor of the *Manchester Guardian*, his wife, Rachel, had been one of the first Girton students at Cambridge; William Gaskell was minister of Cross Street Chapel, and his wife Elizabeth a noted author). Thus Margaret grew up with knowledge of local service and politics, a commitment to liberalism, and a sense of responsibility towards humanity.

It was made clear that the family businesses, with cotton mills in Hyde and a trading firm in Manchester, would be run by her brothers, even

Margaret Ashton, photographed in 1914
(Handbook of the Grand Suffrage Market, ref. M50/1/12/6, held by Manchester Archives)

though Margaret asked to join the family firm, arguing that her brain was as good as her brothers'.[3] Her second choice of occupation was nursing, but this also was rejected, because her health was considered too delicate. However, she did take an interest in the Hyde 'Sick Kitchen' established by her father, and for many years maintained a nursing institution 'for the benefit of all classes in the town'.[4] She spent much of her time as her father's companion in his public work. This gave her considerable insight into such service, as he was the first mayor of Hyde, High Sheriff of Lancashire, a member of the Manchester branch of the National Education League, a prominent member of the Liberal Party, active in the formation of Manchester University, and instrumental in the founding of Manchester High School for Girls.[5] Margaret began to follow in his footsteps in 1875 by taking over the management of Flowery Field School, which catered for the children of the mill workers. She took a keen interest in the living conditions of the families, and when new houses were built nine years later she supervised their construction. When she discovered that they were too small, with too few bedrooms, according to an eye witness she 'marched down to the site, raised Hell, and made the builder pull down what had been done and rebuild them to her own design'. She had studied sanitation and building design – evidently to good effect, as the houses are still standing. Then for six months with a companion she toured the west coast of America, and Canada, hosted by many local contacts. She gained a reputation for being forthright and asking questions about society which were considered rather unladylike.[6]

On her return she plunged back into her busy social life and local philanthropy. She joined the newly formed local branch of the Women's Liberal Association, which involved canvassing for the male candidates and organising social and fundraising events such as 'at homes', bazaars, and tea dances.[7] At this stage Margaret was clearly active only as a supporter of others, for she remarked that she had never made a public speech and 'at my age I am not going to begin'. She was 38 at the time.[8] However, she became increasingly involved in regional activities, and then with other organisations concerned with improving the lot of poorer families and women in particular. In 1884, with Olga Hertz, she helped to found the Women's Guardian Association, aiming to get more women elected as Poor Law Guardians, a post for which they had been eligible since 1875. Then in 1895, along with others, including Unitarians C.P. Scott and his wife **Rachel Scott**, and **Julia Gaskell**, she initiated the Women's Trade Union League, with the aim of improving wages and conditions for women workers.[9] Although the Manchester Women's Suffrage Society had been formed in 1867, Margaret did not join it until 1894, probably prompted by a local MP's refusal to help on a matter concerning women because, he said, he was too busy – and 'any how you have no vote'.[10]

A turning point came with her father's death in 1898, when Margaret was 42. Her mother decided to sell the family home and move to London to live with one of her sons, Thomas Gair Ashton, the Member of Parliament for South Bedfordshire, and Margaret was invited to go too. This would have meant giving up her local activism, and although she had hobbies such as fine needlework which would have helped her to fill in her time, she decided that she wanted to do more with her life. She had absorbed her father's expression of their Unitarian faith, with its love of freedom and hatred of injustice, a concern for education and civic affairs, and above all, a 'tiresome conscience'.[11] She wrote: 'born and brought up on the city's atmosphere of public service, who could escape the inspiration of, and joy of, work for the prosperity and progress of the people?'.[12] All her sisters had married men who were active in public affairs, and through her two Lupton brothers-in-law she met Anne Clough, the founder of Newnham College, Cambridge. Her uncles in the Greg and Rathbone families also provided examples of Unitarian activism. But for a single woman to throw herself into public campaigns, especially for the unpopular cause of women's suffrage, was a dramatic change which created some tensions in her relations with her much-loved family. One brother-in-law, James Bryce, was a noted anti-suffragist.[13] Her obituary observed, 'It is difficult to realise now what it meant for the daughter of a freeman of Manchester in those days to speak from lorries, give out handbills in the street, or chalk on pavements'.[14]

Margaret moved to a substantial semi-detached house (which her mother described as 'a hovel') in Withington, mainly in order to have more money to contribute to the suffrage cause, and also to stand for election to the Withington Urban District Council in 1900. (Women ratepayers had been able to stand as candidates for local district councils since 1894.[15]) She was successful and joined its education committee, for which she was eminently suited, with her experience of managing the primary school in Hyde.[16] One of her significant achievements was persuading the committee of the need for more school places, and organising the building and opening of a large new primary school in West Didsbury.[17] From 1904 onwards she was co-opted to serve on the Manchester city education committee.

The local branch of the Women's Liberal Association had joined the Lancashire and Cheshire Union of Women's Liberal Associations ('the Union'), which was affiliated to the national body and so had a voice at the national annual meetings, a status of which Margaret made use in 1905 when she was President of the Union. As a general election seemed likely, she organised many meetings to promote Liberal policies. At one such meeting, in October 1905 at the Free Trade Hall in Manchester, Christabel Pankhurst and Annie Kenney of the Women's Social and Political Union disrupted the meeting by asking if the Liberal government would give votes to women. The two were ejected for unfurling a banner and were later convicted of obstruction. This was the first time women had used such attention-seeking tactics in the suffrage campaign, and it led to a split in the movement.[18] The International Labour Party supported the action of Christabel and Annie, with Philip Snowden writing, 'their action on this occasion has done more for the women's cause than all the continued work of such as Mrs Mills and Miss Ashton'.[19] Margaret felt very strongly that it was important to campaign by persuasion and legal means only, and she was particularly angry at this criticism. She wrote to the *Manchester Guardian* defending the Liberals, and then to Millicent Fawcett, maintaining that if the latter knew the facts she 'would have been compelled to condemn the actions of these few violent women who have so much injured the reputation of women politicians in Lancashire... It ... has made it more difficult to approach the Government with dignity.... we Women of Lancashire have suffered much from these disturbers who have spent their time shouting while we have been at work.'[20]

After the Liberals won the election, Margaret was part of an unsuccessful deputation to Campbell-Bannerman, the new Prime Minister, asking for the parliamentary franchise to be extended to women. For the next two years she worked within the Liberal Party and its women's associations for a policy that included women's suffrage, but they failed to achieve this, and she left both the Union and the party as a result.[21] In 1906 she became chairperson of the North of England Women's Suffrage Society and campaigned tirelessly, speaking at both indoor and outdoor meetings in all parts of the country, and assiduously attending executive meetings of the National Union of Women's Suffrage Societies (NUWSS) in London. The Manchester demonstrations that she organised were particularly well attended, involving thousands of women. So a typical middle-class lady who had refrained from speaking in public learned to address crowds of thousands in open-air demonstrations. No wonder some of her family found this difficult to appreciate.

Meanwhile, in 1907, Parliament passed a bill allowing single-women ratepayers to stand for election to borough and county councils.[22] There was little time to organise a sustained campaign, but Margaret stood as a Liberal in a Conservative-held Hulme ward, emphasising her long record in public service, with special interests in education, housing, and sanitation; however, she was defeated. The following year she stood successfully as an independent in her home ward of Withington, taking the seat from a Conservative, and subsequently served on the education and sanitary committees. She also served as the city council representative on the governing body of Manchester High School for Girls (MHSG) and remained as a governor for 25 years with only one short break.[23] Across the city she worked to ensure that good education was provided for girls as well as boys, and that the teachers were properly trained and appropriately paid. She also protested against a new rule banning the employment of married women teachers; she argued that their experience made them particularly valuable, and that they would lose their right to a pension and thus face a more precarious future. Her work on the sanitary committee included supporting the work of lady inspectors and exposing cases of sweated labour. She was particularly involved with housing – getting slums demolished and building new council homes, with three bedrooms instead of two, and with bathrooms.

One area which had previously been ignored was the provision of housing in central Manchester for working women in need of safe and clean accommodation. She organised the building of a hostel providing beds for 220 women, each with her own cubicle in a self-contained dormitory, with water closets on all floors. On the ground floor were a large dining room, a recreation hall, a shop selling basic necessities, and the superintendent's home; in the basement were laundry facilities, baths, a locker room, and boot-cleaning room.[24] She insisted that women were accepted as lodgers 'without any inquiries being made into (their) character, where they slept the night or what they had been doing with themselves'.[25] This was the first such municipal provision in the country, and it was named Ashton House in her honour.

The other area in which Margaret was particularly active was women's and children's health. With the Medical Officer of Health, and women doctors such as Catherine Chisholm, she established clinics for new babies, with education and other support for mothers. In 1914 she funded from her own resources a babies' hospital which developed into a larger children's hospital known for its pioneering work on childhood illnesses.[26]

During these years Margaret's friendship with Annot Robinson, a younger working-class activist, informed and influenced her work, and brought her into contact with Independent Labour Party members as well as many working-class women. This may well have started with their work on the Election Fighting Fund campaigns of 1912, and was deepened in the years of shared campaigning during the First World War and after.[27]

With the outbreak of the war, Margaret's 'tiresome conscience' created difficulties. She campaigned tirelessly for peace; the day before war was declared the *Manchester Guardian* published her letter calling for men to 'preserve peace and prevent the destruction of countless homes both in our own and other countries'.[28] Her pacifism caused her (and others) to resign from the NUWSS in 1915 when it failed to pass a resolution promoting work for international law and understanding; she resigned also from the Manchester Women's Suffrage Society. She was elected as a delegate to the women's international peace congress in Amsterdam, but the closure of the English Channel to shipping prevented British women from travelling. They responded by forming the Women's International League, loosely based on the branch network of the NUWSS, committed to civil liberties, a just peace, and votes for all. Margaret was a leading figure and became President of the Manchester Branch in 1922. This became a life-long concern, as it developed into the Women's International League for Peace and Freedom (WILPF).[29] However, such a commitment to peace was not respected during 1914–18, and Margaret was vilified as a traitor to her country, and worse. She responded with these words: 'If we go into public life we must take what the public gives us, plenty of knocks and little praise .... work on, our Peace message will be needed later'.[30] She was not an absolute pacifist, as she worked for better conditions for the women munitions workers, but she argued for a negotiated peace. She was active in organising and speaking at large anti-militarist demonstrations of the Women's Peace Crusade in 1917–18. Manchester city councillors were hostile to the peace message, and they removed her from a sub-committee in 1916, and then from the education committee the following year, as a person unfit to be responsible for children.[31]

In 1921, aged 65, Margaret retired from the City Council on medical advice and went to live briefly with one of her brothers in Gloucestershire.

But she found bed rest tiresome and felt cut off from her friends, so she returned to Didsbury and resumed work for the WILPF, the babies' hospital, and MHSG, although hampered by increasing heart trouble and eyesight problems.[32] She became a member of the court of governors of Manchester University, and was awarded an honorary MA degree for her services to the city.[33]

To mark her seventieth birthday C.P. Scott commissioned a portrait of Margaret and presented it to the City Council, which, together with the City Art Gallery, refused to accept it. This is what she wrote to her friend Annot Robinson about the occasion:

> *I wish you could have been at the party given to me with the portrait. It was such a happy occasion, and everyone (even myself) enjoyed it. Mr C.P. Scott made the presentation and lightened his remarks with a few sound digs at my unyielding and obstinate character which delighted us all. ... The Town Council had to go in for a great deal of manoeuvring and finally to pass a new bye-law before they could decline the portrait.*

The portrait was given to the Women's Union of the University and placed in their debating hall.[34]

Margaret died aged 81 in 1937. By then much of the hostility to her peace work had died down, and she was honoured as 'Manchester's greatest woman citizen' with a memorial service held in the cathedral, as well as a Unitarian funeral. Throughout her life she was a practising Unitarian. She was a generous benefactor to her congregation, and the bicentenary celebrations of Hyde Chapel in 1908 record her as being a speaker at the afternoon social event, and a committee member as well as a seat holder.[35] It is clear from other records that Margaret was on the chapel committee for a good number of years.[36] Her obituary in the *Manchester Guardian* ended: 'Her religion was a broad and simple spiritual aspiration, finding its fullest satisfaction in personal beneficence and common worship',[37] but this hardly does credit to her courage in defying convention and her dedication in her commitment to work for the causes in which she believed, guided always by her 'tiresome conscience'.

Endnotes

1   *Inquirer,* 23 October 1937, p.521.

2   Jane Bedford, 'Margaret Ashton: Manchester's "First Lady"', *Manchester Regional History Review,* Vol. 12 no. 4 (1998), p. 4.

3   Lady Simon of Wythenshawe, *Margaret Ashton and Her Times,* The Margaret Ashton Memorial Lecture for 1948 (Manchester, Manchester University Press, 1949), p.15.

4   Thomas Middleton, *The History of Hyde and Its Neighbourhood* (Hyde, Higham Press, 1932), p.54.

5   Bedford, op.cit., p.3.

6   Ibid., p.4.

7   Ibid., p.5.

8   Simon, op.cit., p.10.

9   Ibid., pp.10–11.

10 Ibid., p.10.

11 Ibid., pp.14–15.

12 Bedford, op.cit., p.5.

13 Simon, op.cit., p.14.

14 *Manchester Guardian,* 16 October 1937.

15 Kathryn Gleadle, *British Women in the Nineteenth Century* (Basingstoke, Palgrave, 2001), p.157.

16 Simon, op.cit., p.15; Bedford, op.cit., p.9.

17 R. D. and T. Boyle, *A Century Scored: Cavendish School, A History of the Early Years 1902–1945,* (privately printed, 2001).

18 Ray Strachey, *The Cause: A Short History of the Women's Movement in Great Britain* (London, Virago, 1978 (1928)), pp.293–5.

19 Bedford, op. cit., p.5.

20 Ibid., p.5.

21 Ibid., pp.6–7.

22 Ibid., p.10.

23 Ibid., pp.11–12; Simon, op.cit., p.8.

24 Bedford, op.cit., pp.12–13.

25 Alison Ronan, *'A Small Vital Flame'. Anti-War Women in NW England 1914– 1918* (Saarbrucken, Scholar's Press, 2014), pp.106–7.

26 Bedford, op.cit., p.14.

27 Ronan, op.cit., 2014, pp.104–10.

28 Alison Ronan, *Unpopular Resistance; The Rebel Networks of Men and Women in Opposition to the First World War in Manchester and Salford 1914–1918* (Manchester, North West Labour History Society, 2015), p.8.

29 Ronan, op.cit., 2015, p.11, Bedford, op.cit., p.9.

30 Bedford, op.cit., p.9.

31 Alison Ronan, 'Hanging the Pacifist' (leaflet, n.d.), p.3.

32 Bedford, op.cit., p.14.

33 Simon, op.cit., p.8.

34 Ronan (n.d), pp.3–4; Bedford, op.cit., pp.14–15.

35 Thomas Middleton, *A History of Hyde Chapel* (Manchester, Cartwright and Rattray, 1908), pp.46, 153; Anon, *Souvenir of Bi-Centenary Hyde Chapel* (Hyde, Cartwright and Rattray, 1908), pp.12, 19.

36 Presentation Album to Rev Enfield Dowson, 1905, Hyde Chapel archives.

37 *Manchester Guardian,* 16 October 1937.

13 Helen Allingham (1848–1926)

Alan Ruston

At the turn of the nineteenth century Helen Allingham was the most well-known British woman painting in watercolours. She specialised in rural scenes, and her works enjoyed considerable popularity. Her idealised view of the countryside went out of vogue in the forty years after her death, but in recent decades her work has regained its popularity; her paintings now reach high prices at auction and are much in demand for use on greeting cards. However, her rural scenes were only part of her prodigious output. She also painted domestic scenes, children (particularly her own three children, Gerald, Eva, and Henry), seaside holiday scenes, and famous literary people.[1] She was also a book illustrator.

Helen Mary Elizabeth Paterson was born in Swadlincote, Derbyshire, the eldest of seven children. Both sides of the family were Unitarians. Her father, Alexander Henry Paterson (1825–1862), a medical doctor, was the son of a Unitarian minister who had a thirty-year ministry at Stourbridge. Her mother was **Helen Chance Paterson**, *née* **Herford** (1824–1894), with connections to the Unitarian Herfords of Lancashire, Cheshire, and the Midlands. Her mother painted landscapes and portraits in oils, as did her aunt, **Laura Herford** (1831–1870), who was the first woman to attend the Royal Academy Schools in 1860,[2] became a professional painter and was Helen's role model. Helen followed her into the Schools in 1868. As her biographer Ina Taylor notes:

> *Helen was surrounded by her Herford Unitarian relations whose family connections included Mrs Gaskell, the descendants of Joseph Priestley and prominent contemporary figures like the Rylands and the Martineau family... She was educated at the Unitarian boarding school in Altrincham that her mother had attended and which had originally been set up by Helen's grandmother, Sarah Smith Herford (also an artist).*

Helen moved to London in 1866 to attend the Royal Female School of Art, staying with other women artists in Bloomsbury. By the early 1870s she was working as a freelance illustrator of children's magazines, as well as holding a permanent post on *The Graphic* from 1870.[3] It was at *The Graphic* that she met the Irish writer and poet William Allingham (1824–1889), and they married at Little Portland Street Unitarian Chapel in London in 1874. From then onwards she concentrated on her painting. She moved in William's artistic and literary circles, which included Edward Burne-Jones, William Morris, Thomas Carlyle, Alfred Lord Tennyson, and John Ruskin.[4] They lived in Chelsea near Thomas Carlyle, who finally yielded to her persistent persuasion and agreed to sit for her. Her portraits of Carlyle, Tennyson, and Ruskin are in public art galleries; her portrait of her husband is in the National Portrait Gallery.

The Allingham family (they had three children) moved to Sandhills in Surrey in 1881, which gave Helen an opportunity to paint different countryside scenes; it was a turning point in her art. She became widely recognised as a fine painter and was the first woman to be made a full member of the Royal Society of Painters in Water Colours, in 1890. She exhibited annually at the society's shows from 1875 to 1925. At Sandhills she became a friend of Gertrude Jekyll, the artist and garden designer; this contact encouraged more garden scenes in her pictures, and she then painted flowers in greater detail. Tennyson, who lived not far away, became another friend with whom she went on long walks.[5]

In Surrey she depicted the cottages around her new home with great attention to detail: her figures became smaller, while the cottages assumed greater significance. She could create a romantic view with a precision that captured the public imagination of rural life. Her work was so popular that in 1886 the Fine Art Society held a one-woman exhibition of 66 of her pictures of Surrey cottages, with a second one six months later. She exhibited twice a year at the Fine Art Society until 1913, as well as elsewhere.

It can be said that from her marriage until 1888 for the first time in her life Helen was not under the direct Unitarian influence of the Herfords and the Patersons; before that it had been strong. She still had Unitarian friends, even though she was not a regular member of a congregation in London. This changed in 1888 because a decline in her husband's health necessitated a return to London. They made their new home in Eldon House, Eldon Road, Hampstead, where many of their friends and many Unitarians resided. In 1889, not long after moving to London, William died. Helen needed emotional support, and found it in the close-knit Unitarian networks in Hampstead. Kate Taylor, writing about Helen Allingham, describes some of those connections:

> *For Unitarians the Herford, Paterson and Allingham family connections with Rosslyn Hill Chapel Hampstead are significant. Laura Herford, her aunt, who lodged at the home of the then minister Rev Thomas Sadler, seems to have been the first of the family to attend Rosslyn Hill, but in the 1880s her widowed sister, Helen's mother Mary Paterson, moved to Hampstead. In 1892 Helen's uncle, Rev Brooke Herford, the brother of Mary and Laura, became the minister at Rosslyn Hill until he resigned in 1901. Helen's brother, novelist Arthur Paterson (1862–1928), was the treasurer of the chapel between 1909 and 1915.[6]*

And there were even more Unitarians in the immediate locality. According to Helen's biographer Ina Turner:

> *The Allinghams took a large house on the corner of Eldon Road, opposite their friends the Martineau family. Basil Martineau, son of the great Unitarian preacher and writer Dr James Martineau, was William's solicitor, and his wife Clara and sisters Edith and Gertrude Martineau were all artist friends of Helen and lived in the same road. Nearby was Carlyle's niece Mary, by then married with a young family...and Kate Greenaway. Not only was Helen surrounded by friends but most of her family lived in Hampstead as well, with her uncle minister of the Unitarian Chapel. The presence of so many friends and relatives were to be reassuring to Helen.[7]*

Undoubtedly the Unitarian networks, both in her early life and after 1889, helped to sustain her. Female Unitarian friends were there to encourage her. Throughout the 1890s Helen worked at a remarkable pace, painting and exhibiting several hundred pictures; as she needed to earn her living, she continued to produce images of cottages. She was still very active when she died suddenly on 28 September 1926, while staying with friends at Haslemere, where she had gone to paint.[8]

A memorial to Helen Allingham, erected in Rosslyn Hill Chapel, includes part of a poem by Robert Browning:

> *For, don't you mark, we're made so that we love*
> *First when we see them painted, things we have passed*
> *Perhaps a hundred times nor care to see,*
> *And so they are better, painted – better to us,*
> *Which is the same thing. Art was given for that –*
> *God uses us to help each other so,*
> *Lending our minds out.*

Endnotes

1 Ina Taylor, *Helen Allingham's England* (Caxton Editions, 2000, first published 1990). An excellent biography with a large number of her paintings reproduced in colour.

2 'Helen Allingham', Kate Taylor, *National Unitarian Fellowship Newsletter* No 286, January/February 1993, pp.8–9.

3 *Oxford Dictionary of National Biography* (www.oxforddnb.com), articles on Helen and William Allingham.

4 'Watercolour pioneer, Helen Allingham', *Camden New Journal*, 16 June 2016, profiling an exhibition of Helen's paintings at Burgh House, Hampstead, most of which were donated by her grandson Patrick in 1989.

5 Anthony Begley, 'Helen Allingham, the artist, and her Ballyshannon connections', *Annual Journal of the County Donegal Historical Society*, No 58, 2006, pp.112–25.

6 Herford family trees and related material, in the Herford MSS, Harris Manchester College Oxford.

7 Ruth Rowntree, *'Religious Devills' of Hampstead. Individually Respected, Collectively Reviled* (Oxford, Harris Manchester College, 2004). Of greatest significance for this study are the family trees showing the connections between members of Rosslyn Hill Chapel.

8 Obituary, *The Times*, 30 September 1926; *The Inquirer*, 2 October 1926, p.619.

14 The Unitarian Women's League

Ann Peart and Alan Ruston

The founding of a national organisation
Ann Peart

One of the most significant events for Unitarian women was the founding in 1908 of what is now called The British League of Unitarian and Other Liberal Christian Women (WL). There had been women's groups in congregations before that, but they had concentrated on social events, sewing, fund raising, or social work of various kinds. One example was the Ladies' Auxiliary Society, formed at the Stockport Unitarian Church in 1883, with the object of 'the financial advantage of the congregation especially with a view to the improvement of the musical services'. The ladies took it in turns to prepare tea at 5 pm for a mixed-sex gathering once a month, at which a collection was taken, and they also organised other fund-raising activities.[1] In the Hampstead (London) congregation, **Hannah Herford**, wife of the minister, Brooke Herford, established the Women's Union in the winter of 1894–5, with the object of bringing together both older and younger women of the congregation to share experiences of active work; activities included talks by speakers from a variety of professions, and voluntary projects.[2]

In contrast to local groups, the WL was envisaged as a national body right from the start. The initiative came from **Helen Brooke Herford**, daughter of **Hannah**, both of whom had experience of the American **Alliance of Unitarian Women**, which had been active since 1890.[3] Helen, together with the Revd Copeland Bowie (Secretary of the British and Foreign Unitarian Association (B&FUA)), had attended the meetings of the International Council of Unitarians and Other Liberal Christians in Boston, USA in 1907, and in the autumn of that year they proposed the idea of a national Unitarian women's organisation to the B&FUA meetings in Liverpool. The proposal was agreed, and in June the following year the first public meeting was held at Essex Hall in London. Helen was appointed Secretary to the first committee; other committee members included many prominent Unitarian women, such as **Lucy Tagart**, but also younger women such as **Rosalind Lee**, who was eventually to succeed Helen as Secretary in 1929.[4]

The League's aims were to 'quicken the life of the churches' and to bring Unitarian women into closer co-operation and fellowship. It was to form branches in congregations and districts, and promote Unitarianism.[5] During the first year 26 branches had been formed and the League grew rapidly, in both numbers (78 branches in 1912) and activities, with appeals, hospitality, publications, fellowship, and international sub-committees.[6] One very important aspect of the League was to train women in organising meetings, including the skills of secretary and treasurer. These skills were then available to the congregations, and they became particularly needed during the First World War and after, when men were not available to fill the roles that they had traditionally undertaken. The full story of the WL has been told elsewhere,[7] and will not be repeated here. Instead, this chapter will focus on three individual League presidents, to illustrate its importance to the Unitarian movement and the wider world.

Helen Brooke Herford (1854–1935)
Ann Peart

Helen, the second child and oldest daughter of the Revd Brooke Herford and his wife Hannah, *née* Hankinson, was born in Todmorden but moved to Sheffield and Manchester as her father changed ministries. She was educated at schools in Knutsford and Manchester, and spent a year in Germany learning the language. As the oldest girl in a large family, she was much in demand to help with the younger children. In 1876 the family moved to a ministry in Chicago and then to Boston in Massachusetts. Helen moved with them, but visited England frequently, until 1892, when they moved back to England, where Brooke took the ministry at Hampstead.[8] Helen played an active part in the Women's Union established by her mother, and took on other roles within the congregation, including running a boys' club at her parents' house, and teaching a Sunday School class at the nearby Rhyl Street mission. Her work within the administration of the national Unitarian movement has already been noted by Alan Ruston in Chapter 11. She also began to take on voluntary roles in the Hampstead community, starting with responsibilities as a Poor Law Guardian, a position that she held until 1930, when the post was abolished. It entailed both committee work and visiting poor families and also sick people in the workhouse. In 1895 she founded a branch of the Brabazon Society, helping to find activities for those workhouse inmates deemed to be unemployable. After the 1930 reorganisation she played an important part in establishing a radio service for patients in the local hospital. She volunteered at the Hampstead subscription library, and was also very active in the Liberal Party, being for some time assistant secretary in the town ward. After the death of their mother in 1901, Helen and her two sisters kept house for their father until his death two years later, after which the sisters lived together in Hampstead for the rest of their lives.[9]

Helen described herself as a 'dyed in the wool' Unitarian, and her greatest work was for the Women's League. In its early years she travelled extensively, encouraging groups of women to form branches, starting a newsletter, and ensuring that the organisation ran smoothly. She said of the early days, 'It was very very hard at first to find women able and willing to overcome their shyness and their Unitarian reserve and stand up and take their part'; this included learning to conduct meetings, take minutes, and write reports.[10] International work was also important to Helen; during the First World War she was one of the few individuals allowed to correspond with people in Germany, and she was also able to get news through a Dutch contact in the International Union of Unitarian and Other Liberal Christian Women (IU). She even managed to visit the Netherlands in 1915 and was able to see her sister Laura, who had married a German. After the war Helen was instrumental in helping Hungarian and German Unitarian women by selling their needlework to raise funds, and also by raising money for children in Budapest. Her international work with the IU resulted in much travel, including a visit to the USA in 1923 for the centenary of the American Unitarian Association, and visits to Prague, Amsterdam, Geneva (to see the General Assembly of the League of Nations at work), and other European destinations. She only relinquished the secretaryship in 1934, when she was becoming too frail to travel abroad, and handed the task to Rosalind Lee.[11] Rosalind had already succeeded Helen as Secretary of the WL in 1929, but not before Helen had visited both Wales and Ireland to foster new branches. By this time there were 171 branches, eleven District leagues, and two Neighbourhood leagues.[12] Helen became national President of the League for 1930–2, so was able to open the League hostel for women visitors near Essex Hall. She was still active in other good causes, such as organising a meeting of all the Hampstead churches in favour of disarmament, serving on the Women's Advisory Council, and on the Hampstead hospital committee. She died in 1935. At her funeral Copeland Bowie praised her 'breezy vitality' and her selfless service in bringing joy to others.[13]

Rose Allen (1870–1946)[14]
Alan Ruston

Rose Allen showed imagination, determination, and considerable organising ability in her work to support those affected by the First World War. Born in Portsmouth in 1870 into a middle-class family, Rose Eliza Cooke married Bernard Meredith Allen (1864–1951) in 1895 at Edmonton, London. The couple began their married life in Hampstead, joining Rosslyn Hill Chapel in the early years of the twentieth century; after trying several mainly Anglican churches in the area, 'we came definitely to the conclusion that the only place of worship where we could find intellectual freedom was the Unitarian Chapel in Rosslyn Hill'.[15] There was an active Unitarian group centred in the Hampstead area, with the particularly strong support of leading women who lived in neighbouring roads. The Allens' home from 1904 was 14 Gainsborough Gardens; this address would be the centre of activity from 1915 to 1919 for the war-relief work that Rose was to organise.

Britain had gone to war in August 1914 because of the threat to Belgian neutrality, and that country was quickly over-run. Many Britons felt strongly about the parlous condition of the Belgians, resulting from the impact of the German onslaught. Bernard Allen takes up the story:

Naturally, like most of our friends, we took into our home a Belgian refugee... But we wanted to play a more active part and before long the opportunity presented itself... During the first Christmas holiday of the war my wife and her younger sister managed to get permission to cross over to the North of France to visit the hospitals in that region. My wife was most anxious on her return to launch an appeal for helping the Belgian wounded, who, after being driven into France before the German advance, had had to take refuge in any building that could be used as a hospital. It was our connection with the Unitarian congregation at Hampstead that gave her the opportunity she was seeking. The editor of The Inquirer, Rev W.H. Drummond, a friend of ours, also attended Rosslyn Hill Chapel, and lived within a few doors of us. My wife approached him and asked if he would insert a letter she had written about the plight of the suffering of Belgians in France. He read it, and said her appeal was just what he had been looking for, as he wanted the Inquirer to take on a piece of war work of its own. So, on 9th January 1915, my wife's letter appeared in full.[16]

Rose Allen reported a shortage of bedding and clothing, and appealed to readers of *The Inquirer* and to working parties connected with the Women's League for donations of warm underclothing or gifts of money to buy absolute necessities. The response was prompt, and clothes and money poured into 14 Gainsborough Gardens:

From the first we determined that our house should be the centre for carrying on the work, none of the money contributed should be spent on offices or clerical assistance, no charge should be made on the fund for travelling, and that we ourselves would meet the cost of all printing, stationery and postage. As the work grew, the help of additional workers became necessary, but these were all found among our personal friends who came to our house to unpack, sort and despatch to hospitals. My wife always wrote personal letters for gifts and there was no typewriter.[17]

W.H. Drummond kept his promise to give the Belgian Relief Fund as much prominence as possible. While he was the editor there was a weekly progress note, which turned into a longer monthly note, written by Rose Allen, with a list of the donors of money and parcels. The last Fund Report, after the end of the war, appeared in *The Inquirer* at Christmas 1918. The extensive, mainly weekly reports, written over three and a half years, are key sources which provide the story of the war-relief effort made by Unitarians, mainly women.

The Belgian Relief Fund was almost entirely supported by members of the Women's League throughout the country. Well-known Unitarian men did give to the Fund, but it was a female cause and run entirely, it appears, by women. By February 1915 donations for the appeal had reached £1,003. The report published on 15 May 1915 included a reference to £100 sent from 'a reader in thankfulness of a deliverance of a relative on the Lusitania'; whatever was given was acknowledged. By 25 December 1915 the cash raised totalled £9,664. The Fund's objects in 1915 and for much of 1916 are set out in *The Inquirer*, 22 July 1916:

> *The Belgian Relief Fund is recognised by the Local Government Board*
> *to appeal for funds to provide the Belgian Military Hospitals in France*
> *with surgical instruments, medical and nursing requisites, bed-linen, and*
> *clothes for the patients, and for aiding the Convalescent Depots for Belgian*
> *soldiers, and maintaining a Hospice for civilian refugees in Calais.*

The following extracts from weekly reports in *The Inquirer* for 1915, 1916, and 1917 give a flavour of the scope and detail of Rose Allen's work in this period. From the issue dated 13 November 1915:

> *On our visit to Brittany in August, we found that the convalescent depots*
> *were in need of considerable help to make them really comfortable and we*
> *heard that there were ten more of these in Normandy... the most urgent*
> *needs there were for lamps and blankets. There was no means of lighting*
> *the bedrooms after dark, about 4pm in winter, and only very poor light in*
> *the refectory. We are sending here a number of small safety lamps and a*
> *few large ones as they had no means of obtaining any, and the prospect of*
> *long winter evenings in total darkness seemed insupportable.*

From the issue dated 22 July 1916:

In response to my appeal for games we have received several parcels and a large case. These have all been despatched to three institutions – one to a hospital for tuberculous soldiers at Montpellier (200 beds and not one game or book), one to a convalescent depot at Honfleur, and to a depot des invalides at Le Havre. A large bale came ... from the Essex Church Working Parties containing 50 shirts and 30 children's nightgowns among other items; the High Pavement Nottingham War Relief Committee 59 articles, and Mill Hill Leeds Sewing League, 84 articles, both very large. All the contents have been sent off this week.

From the issue dated 14 April 1917:

Our Maternity home here in Calais is about to open. The doors will be opened when the last of the equipment arrives...It is already looking very nice, with its wards of three or four beds each with its pretty coverlet... The Belgian doctors say that it will always be full, and already there are applications for beds. There are ten little cradles. It is proposed to have consultations on one or two afternoons a week, when mothers can bring their babies to be weighed and for advice.

A report, rather than a monthly note, in the issue dated 2 November 1918 provides a survey of what had been achieved since the inception of the Fund in January 1915:

While other funds set up at the start of the war to aid Belgians have languished and ceased, we are proud to say ours has been maintained and extended. The money contributed to date is over £21,400, and the value of gifts in kind is estimated as fully equal to that sum. Thus, we may say that the readers of THE INQUIRER have devoted to this purpose considerably over £40,000.

There follows an account of what was done with the donations:

> *Here are some but by no means all of the items: Surgical instruments,*
> *beds, furniture, drugs, clothing, and comforts have been given, regularly*
> *or at intervals, to 137 Military Hospitals and Convalescent Depots. Over*
> *500 doctors at the front have been aided with surgical outfits or refits. The*
> *Hospice Belge, which afterwards became the Maternité Belge at Calais,*
> *has been and is wholly maintained by the Fund. In addition, a Hospice at*
> *Waton was maintained for six months in 1915. Aid has been given to more*
> *than 30 Colonies Scolaires, for orphans, and complete equipment for a*
> *children's hospital. Many canteens have been supplied with books and games;*
> *20,000 francs was expended on the Hut at Calais, and 8,000 on tents for the*
> *front. At Chambery, an excellent water supply has been provided at the cost*
> *of 20,000 francs, and a steam laundry furnished another hospital, costing*
> *10,000 francs. In addition, seven motor-cars and ambulances have been sent*
> *out in connection with these and other works of aid.*

With the war over, Rose Allen described in *The Inquirer*, 7 December 1918, what was to happen now that hostilities had ceased:

> *The hut at Calais is to go on, as long as the Belgian base is there, and*
> *even beyond, as soldiers will be passing to and fro for some time. It*
> *is further proposed to keep it open to feed the returning refugees from*
> *France, as the refugee trains generally stop some hours at Calais and*
> *our hut is only about five minutes' walk from the station ... We have*
> *already sent out a store of clothing to Calais for parcels to be made up for*
> *each soldier passing through the hut and going to his home in Belgium,*
> *according to the number and ages of his family. The maternity home will*
> *continue as it's very busy now ... The hospitals will continue for a while*
> *and I will keep in contact with them until they disappear or are made*
> *permanent ... I hope to be able to do something for them, and especially*
> *for the tuberculous and the paralysed, as I have all along been keenly*
> *interested in them ... I have arranged with the Director of the Service de*
> *Sainté to go over to Belgium when things are a little more settled.*

The Inquirer records the names of those who donated items or money to the Fund, but it fails to make any mention of the volunteers, that large group of

Hampstead helpers who must have gathered at 14 Gainsborough Gardens regularly to sort the items and then despatch them, plus much else. One of Rose Allen's helpers would undoubtedly have been **Helen Brooke Herford** (1854–1935), who lived nearby, one of the active female Unitarians living in Hampstead who were in constant contact with each other. Correspondence was initiated with relatives and friends of interned prisoners in Austria, Germany, and Hungary which 'called forth the gratitude of a large number of people in the countries concerned'. Such activity brought her and others, as well as Essex Hall, to the attention of the Home Office; it was suspected that privileged information was being passed to the enemy. However, the government was reassured, no doubt with the help of H.G. Chancellor, MP for Haggerston, who was a leading figure on the B&FUA Executive.[18]

Rose Allen was awarded the Croix de Chevalier de l'Ordre de Léopold by the King of the Belgians for her work on behalf of the Belgian people. The Queen of the Belgians had already conferred a decoration on her. A double decoration is a remarkable testimony to her work, while the award of the Croix de Chevalier to a woman is probably unprecedented. In 1922 she sent a comprehensive report on the work of the fund to the Imperial War Museum in London, now available in their archive at EN1/3MED/002/43. Their response shows a high regard for the work and achievement of Rose Allen:

> *I am enormously impressed by the amount of money you were able to raise, and the apparent ease with which you overcame all difficulties with the Belgian authorities ... I know of no other fund which seems to me so self-effacing. You never seem to have thought of doing things for yourself, but only to help others to do this more efficiently.*[19]

Bernard and Rose Allen moved away from Hampstead in 1925 and relocated to a flat in central London. This was not the end of Rose Allen's activity on behalf of the Women's League to aid the welfare of others. In 1924 **Frieda Tayler** had drawn the attention of the Women's League to the need for suitable lodgings for women in London. Lawrence House had been set up in 1917 at 1 Essex Street for soldiers and young men connected with Unitarian churches.[20] It was clear that something similar was needed for women. The initiative to create such a hostel began in 1926, and

Rose Allen, Rosalind Lee, and Helen Brooke Herford worked out a plan to provide accommodation for Unitarian women from the provinces when they came to London. Rose, as treasurer of the organising group, sent out a special appeal to the hundreds of friends who had given her support in the First World War, asking for their help in this new venture. The effort was successful, and a house in Devereux Court near Essex Hall was obtained and furnished. A later source states that 'largely by her efforts the hostel was established on a sound financial basis. She played an active part in all the arduous labour of furnishing and planning the hostel and helped to give it its unique character.'[21]

After the Second World War broke out, the Allens moved to Torquay. Here Rose saw another opportunity to help, organising a Red Cross working party to support evacuated schoolchildren from London. She died on 1 July 1946. Her obituary in *The Inquirer* concluded:

> *She was something more than an efficient organiser and raiser of money.*
> *Her courtesy and graciousness won the hearts not only of those she helped,*
> *but also of her supporters, to whom she was generous in her gratitude.*[22]

Annie Beard Woodhouse (1869–1939)[23]
Ann Peart

Many Unitarians may know of Annie Beard Woodhouse as the woman who gave the Barn at Flagg, Derbyshire, to the Foy Society (formerly the Fellowship of Youth), but there is more to tell.

Annie Beard was born on 27 December 1869 to James Rait Beard (a prominent Manchester businessman, founder and partner in the textile firm of Beard Agate and Co) and his wife Mary (*née* Wilkinson, from Northumberland). She was the oldest of three children, two girls and a boy. [24] A year after her birth the family moved within what is now Greater Manchester, from Cheetham Hill to Bredbury, and then to nearby Godley in 1874. She was a pupil at Manchester High School for Girls from 1879 to 1882,[25] and then attended a school in Germany in that year. Little is known of her early adulthood.

Annie Beard Woodhouse (artist: BNS; no date)
(Courtesy of The Flagg Trust)

In September 1909 (aged 39) she married Samuel Thompson Woodhouse, then aged 67, who was apparently her landlord at the time. She changed her name by deed poll to include her maiden name of Beard, to emphasise her family of origin. Samuel died in 1912, aged 70, leaving Annie comfortably off. It is probable that she was in Germany in the summer of 1914 and was urged to cut short her stay in order to get home before the outbreak of war. That year she was living in Knutsford, where she was a member of the Unitarian Brook Street Chapel, and also of Knutsford's Women's Suffrage Society. In that capacity Annie, along with approximately one hundred other women, signed an open letter of Christmas goodwill to the Women of Austria and Germany in December of that year. [26] In her last home, in Old Broadway, Manchester, which she bought in 1926, she was celebrated for her hospitality to overseas and other visitors. [27]

Annie took a keen interest in the Unitarian work done by her father and grandfather (the Revd John Relly Beard, the founder, with William

Gaskell, of the Unitarian Home Missionary Board), and she collected their personal papers. Her own collection of letters from interesting people is preserved in the Unitarian College Collection in John Rylands Library. One particular lifelong concern of Annie's was the Collyhurst Guild of Social Service, continuing her father's work with young people in a very deprived area of Manchester.

Annie's Unitarian activities included membership of several congregations: Gorton, Longsight, and Platt in the Manchester district, Knutsford in Cheshire, and Torquay, where her family often spent summer holidays. [28] The village chapel at Flagg in Derbyshire was especially close to her heart. It had been founded as part of the village missionary movement in which her grandfather had been prominent, and her father preached there on several occasions. Annie recalled visiting it in 1890–1 with her father, who was then President of the British and Foreign Unitarian Association. 'We decided then that although we had only returned that week from Switzerland, we had found nowhere in that country such invigorating air as we had that day enjoyed. The smallholding at The Green presented possibilities.' They subsequently rented The Green as a weekend retreat. By 1929, the then disused chapel was in a sorry state, and there was a possibility that it might be sold. At Whitsuntide Annie invited members of the newly formed Fellowship of Youth, then camping at Whaley Bridge, to visit Flagg with the idea of her buying The Green to provide a campsite for the young people who would support the chapel and bring it back into use. The location had another attraction for Annie in that it was not far from Buxton, where treatment for her neuritis and heart trouble was available. She hoped that The Green would become a Unitarian centre.

Within the Manchester area Annie worked actively for Unitarian causes and served on a variety of committees, being the first woman to become President of the Manchester District Association of Unitarian and Free Christian Churches in 1929–31. She was also President of the Manchester District League of Unitarian and other Liberal Christian Women, and then President of the National Women's League in 1926. Her support of the Unitarian College was both practical and financial, and she became a vice-president. Nationally she supported the Central Postal Mission and other philanthropic societies. In the 1920s she was one of only two women members of the joint committee which promoted the union of the two national Unitarian bodies, the British and Foreign Unitarian Association and the National Conference.

Annie travelled widely, and one particularly fruitful journey was to the Unitarians in the Khasi Hills in north-east India in October 1928. This must have been an extremely arduous expedition for a woman of 58 in not particularly good health. Of the small group of British Unitarians, the main speakers were Annie herself, and Dr Drummond. Annie's booklet describing their visit and the Khasi Unitarian community did much to persuade the British Unitarians to provide support. She wrote:

> *We are a small community; we can't do much (but the disciples of Jesus numbered twelve). Here is a still smaller community, without any learning or wealth or any natural advantages except the goodness and kindness of their hearts, who are begging and praying us to come to their aid, and have been doing so for years. They feel themselves to be ignorant and inefficient, and the help and comfort which a spiritually minded and sympathetic minister or teacher could give them is incalculable. Must we refuse them? I will not believe it.* [29]

She remarked that Unitarian vision was limited to its own institutions, and she wrote: 'Give us something bigger and wider to think about, and our own church activities will be strengthened and enlarged'. [30] The General Assembly responded by sending out the Revd Magnus Ratter to explore the possibility of sponsoring a project. The principle was accepted, but the relevant committee refused to accept the offer of the **Revd Margaret Barr**, as although it agreed that she was eminently qualified, it considered that 'no committee would take the responsibility of sending a woman alone to such a lonely post'. The fact that eventually Margaret Barr became a community worker in the Khasi Hills is due in no small measure to the activities of Annie, who rallied support and finance, with the help of the Women's League.

Clearly Annie had great influence, although she was not necessarily easy to work with, described as 'a woman with a will and a mind of her own, whilst ever ready to appreciate the good works of colleagues, she was never a mere detached observer of others' efforts'. At her funeral at the Manchester Crematorium in 1939, the Revd Dr Herbert McLachlan described the Unitarian tradition of service, both social and religious, as 'her life's work'. [31]

Endnotes

1   *Unitarian Church, Stockport. Minutes of the Ladies' Auxiliary Society (1883–1892)*, Unitarian College Collection, John Rylands Library, Manchester.

2   Ruth Rowntree, *'Religious Devills' of Hampstead. Individually Respected and Collectively Reviled* (Oxford, Harris Manchester College, 2014), pp.187–8.

3   Unitarian Universalist Women's Federation, https://www.uuwf.org/who-we-are, accessed 27 November 2018.

4   Marjory G. Mitchell, *History of the British League of Unitarian and Other Christian Women* (London, British League of Unitarian and Other Christian Women, 1958), pp.2–3, 22; Judy Hague (ed.), *A Century of the Unitarian Women's League 1908–2008* (Sheffield, British League of Unitarian and Free Christian Women, 2014), pp.2–3.

5   Hague, op.cit., pp.3–4.

6   Mitchell, op.cit., pp.4–7; Mrs Bernard Allen, *Helen Brooke Herford and the Women's League*, (London, British League of Unitarian and Other Christian Women, n.d. c. 1936?), p.19.

7   Mitchell, op.cit.; Hague, op.cit.

8   Allen, op.cit., pp.1–6; Rowntree, op.cit., pp.185–6.

9   Allen, op.cit., pp.6–11.

10 Ibid., p.16; *Inquirer*, 1935, p.274.

11 Allen, op.cit., pp..21–27, 29.

12 Ibid., p.28.

13 Ibid., pp.25, 29, 30–1.

14 This section is an abridged version (produced by David Dawson) of 'Supporting Belgium: Unitarian heroine of the First World War' by Alan Ruston: an article first published in *Transactions of the Unitarian Historical Society*, Vol. 26, No. 4, April 2018.

15 Bernard Allen, *Down the Stream of Life* (London: Lindsey Press, 1948), p.99.

16 Ibid., pp.110–11; *Inquirer*, 9 January 1915, pp.17 and 20.

17 Bernard Allen, op cit., pp.112–13.

18 Mrs Bernard Allen, op.cit., pp.22–23.

19 Bernard Allen, op cit., p.117.

20 *Inquirer*, 9 June 1917, pp.272–3.

21 *Inquirer*, 3 August 1946, p.222.

22 Ibid.

23 An earlier version of this piece appeared in *Foy News* Spring 2012.

24 Much of the information for this section comes from manuscripts and typescripts lent to me in 2010 by Joy Winder, Annie's great-niece. These have now been deposited in the Unitarian College Collection of the John Rylands Library (University of Manchester).

25 Manchester High School for Girls, record for Annie Beard, 1879–1886, archives of Manchester High School for Girls.

26 www.wilpf.org.uk/wp-content/ uploads/2015/03/Hobhouse-Xmas-letter.pdf, accessed 26 November 2018.

27 H McLachlan, 'Annie Beard Woodhouse', *Inquirer*, 1939, p.554.

28 Ibid.

29 Annie B. Woodhouse, *A Visit to the Unitarians of the Khasi Hills, Assam, India* (General Assembly of Unitarian & Free Christian Churches, 1930) pp.12–13.

30 Ibid., p. 13.

31 McLachlan, op.cit.

15 Unitarian women ministers[1]

Ann Peart

Although in the second half of the nineteenth century women began to speak from Unitarian pulpits, they encountered much resistance; in the words of Ruth Watts, 'because of their anxious quest for "respectability" in a world which anathematized their religious beliefs, they [Unitarians] tended to mind the proprieties which restricted the lives of middle-class women'.[2]

Public speaking by women was associated with lower social classes, Quakers, and dangerously 'enthusiastic' sects. Nevertheless, some women did speak out and were accepted in some sense as ministers. People heard Lucretia Mott, the American Quaker anti-slavery campaigner, speak from Unitarian pulpits in 1840,[3] and they learned of women ministers in America from 1853 onwards.[4] By the 1870s women such as **Frances Power Cobbe** were invited to preach to middle-class Unitarian congregations, while the more working-class Methodist Unitarians had fewer inhibitions about women speaking; George Fox, minister of the congregation in Mossley, north-east of Manchester from 1857 to 1865, commented, 'From their connection with Methodism, quite a number of people, both men and women, could pray and speak at meetings'.[5] In south Wales **Mrs R. J. Jones**, still spoken of with respect in Aberdare, was active in educational, philanthropic, and political spheres and also, according to her 1899 obituary, 'When her husband was prevented from preaching, she often occupied the pulpit for him'.[6]

But speaking at meetings, or even preaching, is of course by no means the same as being recognised as a minister. Unitarians had prided themselves on having a learned ministry, and for this a formal higher education was seen to be required. For a considerable time it was not easy for male nonconformists, let alone women, to achieve this, excluded as they were from the traditional universities on account of their unwillingness to subscribe to the Thirty-Nine Articles of the Church of England. And even when women did gain access to higher education in the second half of the nineteenth century, it was not generally to faculties of theology.

The opening of Manchester New College to female occasional students in 1876 has already been noted in Chapter 10. In 1892, the college formally accepted two American women ministers for a year's study and was even prepared to grant them a certificate. The college records list them as occasional students, and the annual report for 1893 states 'The **Rev Marion Murdoch** and the **Rev Florence Buck** of USA have been admitted free to such lectures and classes as, under the direction of the Principal, they may desire to attend'.[7] It is most likely that this was one of the factors that encouraged **Gertrude von Petzold** to attempt to become a minister, and her story is told later in this chapter.

The second woman to appear on the Unitarian General Assembly (GA) roll of ministers, in 1907, was **Mrs T. B. Broadrick** (1850–1925), who was the widow of the minister at Bridgewater, Somerset. She took over his ministry for the year after his death. In 1905–7 she was minister in charge of Lewins Mead Domestic Mission in Bristol, and after that served as a supply preacher in the Western Union. There seems to be no record of her having undergone formal ministry training, or even a record of her own first names. In the *Christian Life* of June 6 1908, she signed an article headed 'Message from Mrs Broadrick' in support of the Unitarian Van Mission with the initials A.A.B. Her 1925 obituary describes her as Mrs rather than Revd, but perhaps as the first British married woman minister there was no understanding of which title should have preference.[8]

After Mrs Broadrick there was a gap of ten years before **Helen Phillips** was recognised on the ministry roll in 1917. Her story is told briefly in Chapter 17. Then the next year came **Margaret Brackenbury Crook** (1886–1972), who did the full training at Manchester College Oxford (MCO), with a break during the First World War, when she spent time in France doing welfare work with the Friends War Relief Committee. Margaret ministered successfully at Norwich for two years, but moved with her widowed mother and brothers to America, where at that time the Unitarians did not accept women ministers. She became an academic in the field of religious studies and produced one of the earliest books of feminist theology in 1964.[9] **Rosalind Lee**, whose story is told later in this chapter, was the fifth woman to enter the roll. By the end of 1927 eight women had trained for the ministry at MCO, but then the college decided that it was too difficult to accommodate women, and it accepted no more until 1936; between then and 1959, only three women were trained there. **Lillian Preston** was the first woman to train at Unitarian College, Manchester (UCM) in 1929, and she was followed by four more, after which there was a gap from the 1930s to the 1960s. The number of women actively ministering slowly rose from three in 1920 to fifteen in World War Two, and then declined to five in 1960, not reaching double figures again until 1981, so the proportion of women was not high enough to have a very significant effect on the character of British Unitarian ministry during the time span covered by this book.[10] Short accounts of three of the most significant early women ministers, **Gertrude von Petzold**, **Rosalind Lee**, and **Margaret Barr**, follow.

Gertrude von Petzold (1876–1952)

Gertrude von Petzold is celebrated as the first woman to be accepted for official training and recognition as a Unitarian minister in Britain (or indeed as a minister in any denomination). She was born (as Gertrud – she added the 'e' during her time in England) in what was then Thorn in East Prussia (now known as Torun in Poland) in 1876. Her father was in the army, and she had a conventional Lutheran upbringing, and was rather a pious girl with a great respect for and knowledge of the Bible.[11] By the time she was eighteen, Gertrude had passed the exams which qualified her to teach, but, feeling that she was not sufficiently well prepared, she aspired to a higher education. So she decided to come to Britain, which she said 'had long recommended itself to me as a land of freedom'.[12] She spent two years learning English and teaching part-time as a governess,[13] and then began to read for a degree at the University of St Andrews in Scotland. She began to study medicine, but theological questions seemed more important, and she switched to studying theology. It was then that she developed a calling to enter the ministry, of which she wrote:

At the same time the determination had arisen within me to dedicate myself, if it were possible, to the practical work of the ministry. It must naturally be a free church; for in the first place only such a church would

Revd Gertrude von Petzold
(Unitarian Historical Society)

appoint a woman to its ministry, and, secondly, my theological studies had convinced me of the untenableness of the dogmatic faith of my school-days. Having myself struggled up to perfect freedom in religious matters, I felt that only in such a free atmosphere could I pursue my chosen vocation.[14]

So Gertrude applied for entry as a ministry student to Manchester College, by then based in Oxford. Portraits show her to be a beautiful young woman; she was described as having a 'pale, spiritual, classically-featured face, whose pallor was emphasised by the dark mass of black hair resting above the wide, white brow, a graceful, gracious presence, full of dignity and charm'.[15] As a student she is described in a university reference as a perfect lady, by birth and by feeling, character, and behaviour at all times. Her St Andrews reference also describes her as having a keen clear intelligence, as a fearless thinker, desiring nothing but the truth, Morally, she was high-minded and straightforward, and 'No folly or silliness of any kind have ever appeared in her'. The only criticism made is that she was not always conciliatory enough, or considerate of others.[16] Her letter of application, in early September 1897, sent from a Southampton address, shows that she was not unduly subservient or modest in her attitude: she explained that she did not know any Unitarian ministers who would give her a reference, and wanted to continue her course at St Andrews with funding from Manchester College. Gertrude got her bursary and went on to read moral philosophy at St Andrews and an MA arts course in classical languages at Edinburgh University, all the while receiving grants from Manchester College, and also from the Hibbert Trust to enable her to study for two terms in Germany.

It was the autumn of 1901 before Gertrude finally took her place in Oxford as a regular student for the ministry. She was the only such student who was not in residence in college; there was, however, another woman, Harriet Johnson, who was admitted to classes, but not apparently for ministerial training. The college appeared to be gracious in its welcome.[17] However, all did not go as smoothly as this might suggest. Gertrude had a mixed reception. Fred Hankinson, a fellow student, wrote:

> *I was a student at MCO at the same time as Gertrude von Petzold when the other male students refused to have her sitting at the refectory table with them, so I championed her, and talked them round so that she was able to eat with the rest of them. I supported the suffragettes as she did.*[18]

The only report of her college career in the college archives is submitted by the elocution and voice-production tutor, who criticised her German accent.[19] Gertrude clearly worked on this, as it was said of her in her first ministry that she had a rich, clear voice, with excellent elocution.[20] Indeed, R.J. Campbell in 1911 described her as 'one of the most brilliant women speakers of the day, a scholar of repute, and I think, the only ordained minister of her sex in the country'.[21]

Fears that no congregation would appoint a woman minister proved groundless, and in 1904 Gertrude was chosen unanimously out of nine candidates at the Narborough Road Church in Leicester.[22] During the four years of her Leicester ministry the congregation flourished, with huge attendances at services, Sunday School, the Women's Friendly Society, and the Men's Meeting (which she initiated). This in spite of her absences in Berlin, where she was the first woman ever to conduct a service, and Boston, USA, where she gave several addresses, including one to the women's work section of the Fourth International Congress of Religious Liberals in 1907.[23] Gertrude evidently liked America, which had many women ministers by this time, and the following year she left England to undertake various short-term ministries in the USA, some with the group of women ministers in Iowa. She returned to Britain in 1910 and accepted a ministry at the Waverley Road Church in Birmingham, where the pattern was repeated, with a huge increase in numbers, and Gertrude taking time away to preach and speak in Germany, Switzerland, and various places in Britain.

However, this foreign travel was to present a problem when Gertrude, and her friend and helper Rosa Widman (a German woman who had been in Britain for 24 years) applied for naturalisation in 1915 during World War One (Gertrude having failed to complete her 1908 application). Their application was unsuccessful, and both had to leave for Germany by 31 July (rather than the United States, which they would have preferred). In Germany, after a temporary ministry at the American Church in Berlin, Gertrude went to Tubingen and studied for a PhD with a dissertation, 'Images of the Saviour in the German Novel of the Present Time', dedicated to Rosa. In 1918 Gertrude accepted a ministry with the Protestant Free Churches in Konigsberg and Tilsit, and served as a socialist town councillor until 1923. After that she found work mainly as an academic, as Free Church communities were banned after 1934. Her frequent visits to Britain during the 1920s and 1930s caused her to fall under suspicion, and she was investigated by the Gestapo. However, she was regarded as a 'harmless...eccentric spinster' and survived.[24] Since the first decade of the century Gertrude had had contacts with the Quakers, and in Germany she was a formal member of that denomination for a time, After the war she worked to help refugees from Prussia and East Germany, and continued to write; one article on Harriet Martineau was published in 1941, and she contributed an article entitled 'English refugees in Germany' to *The Inquirer* in 1947.[25] She died in 1952.

It may be that Gertrude's primary loyalty was to religious liberty rather than the British Unitarian denomination, and her vocation was to ministry rather than specifically Unitarian ministry. However, she was an extremely effective Unitarian minister for the time that she was in post, and her pioneering determination changed British Unitarianism for good.

Rosalind Lee (1884–1959)

Emma Rosalind Lee was one of the most prominent women in the Unitarian movement in the first half of the twentieth century. Her parents, Thomas Grosvenor and Winifred Hannah (*née* Notcutt), belonged to a well-known and respected Unitarian family in Birmingham, where her father was a solicitor.[26] After graduating from Cambridge (Newnham College) in 1906, she wanted to enter the ministry, but her father persuaded her to wait ten years and gain more experience before committing herself. So she spent some time doing social work in Birmingham and widened her Unitarian experience by becoming involved in the formation of the British League of Unitarian Women, serving on its first committee from 1908. The following year she became a Reid Trustee of Bedford College, continuing until at least the 1940s.[27]

During the First World War she worked in the Voluntary Aid Detachment (VAD).[28] The war resulted in a shortage of male preachers, and as part of her ministerial training she served, first as lay charge, then as minister of the Glanrhondda Unitarian Chapel in Pentre, near Treorchy in south Wales. As her war work prevented her from going to either Manchester or Oxford for ministry training, she studied at home, passing all the examinations with such high marks that she was awarded a Hibbert Scholarship in 1920.[29] This enabled her to travel to the United States and study for a year at Radcliffe College, Cambridge (Massachusetts). She then toured Canada, Australia, and New Zealand, visiting every Unitarian congregation in those countries, and spending six months as co-minister of the Melbourne congregation.[30]

On her return to England she was appointed to serve the Narborough Road Church in Leicester (where Gertrude von Petzold had ministered

Revd Rosalind Lee
(Stourbridge Unitarian Chapel)

twenty years earlier).[31] This congregation had fallen on hard times, but Rosalind was able to restore it to a healthy state, with much hard work. While she was in Leicester (1923–9), she served as a co-opted member of the City of Leicester Education Committee. After five and a half years she left Leicester to become the Honorary Secretary of the Unitarian Women's League, based at Essex Hall in London.[32] For two years she combined this with ministry in the service of the Hackney congregation, but then moved to Wales to become District Minister of the South East Wales District (1932–46), while continuing her work with the Women's League.[33] She had maintained her interest in the Welsh communities and, as National Secretary, had organised relief parcels to be sent to Rhondda Valley congregations suffering unemployment in the depression of the late 1920s; she continued to support those most in need during her district ministry.[34] For a number of years she combined her work in Wales with her Women's League activities, and in 1931 her generosity enabled a house near Essex Hall to be bought and staffed as a hostel, known as League House, to accommodate members and foreign visitors.[35]

Rosalind maintained her interest in international affairs, becoming Secretary of the International Union of Liberal Religious Women in 1934, but her plans for its expansion were prevented by the Second World War, and it was not until 1947 that she achieved its reorganisation.[36] In 1938 British Unitarians, concerned about the plight of Sudetenland refugees in Czechoslovakia, raised funds to support them, with Rosalind appointed by the Women's League to go and investigate how the money could be best used. She flew to Prague (where there was a Unitarian congregation) in October 1938 and together with John McLachlan, another British Unitarian minister, set up and ran for several months a relief centre with the Quakers, working with Nicholas Winton to co-ordinate transport for refugees trying to leave the country. Many children managed to reach England and were looked after by guarantors in all parts of the British Isles.[37] Rosalind herself fostered two or three Austrian refugee children and brought them to live on the Gower coast, eventually supporting them through university.[38] Her reports of the Czech situation and the plight of the refugees did much to rally British Unitarian support for the work.[39] In order to concentrate on it, Rosalind had relinquished much of her work as Secretary of the Women's League, and was about to be nominated as its President when she was elected President of the British Unitarian General Assembly (1940), the second woman (and first woman minister) to hold this post.[40] Throughout this time Rosalind had maintained her Welsh district ministry and is remembered fondly in these words, recorded in 2004: 'a truly generous and gracious lady, usually dressed in black and with a deep carrying voice' ... 'a strikingly masculine-looking person in a plain tweed suit, shirt and tie, stiff brimmed hat and no-nonsense presence' ...'she always wore black, with big boots; she thought nothing of walking over 10 miles over the mountains to take a service'.[41]

In 1946 Rosalind left Wales for her final ministry in Stourbridge. This was near the land, Kinver Edge, that she and her siblings had donated to the National Trust in 1917 in memory of their parents, and she enjoyed hosting Unitarian gatherings there on the campsite that she set up. Suffering from severe arthritis in her hands, she retired in 1953 and two years later moved back to the Gower, where she died in 1959. She bequeathed more land on the Gower peninsula and at Kinver to the National Trust, and left her house at Penmaen to the congregation of Swansea Unitarian Church.[42] Her most important legacy is probably in the lives of the children whom she rescued from Czechoslovakia, and in the transforming power of her ministries in England and Wales, where her words and deeds were remembered for many years.[43]

Margaret Barr (1899–1973)

Annie Margaret Barr became a legend in her own life time, and her work among the Khasi Unitarians of north-east India brought about a close connection between the Khasis and British Unitarians. She was born in Yorkshire into a Methodist family and joined the Unitarian church while at Girton College, Cambridge (where she read English and Moral Sciences, and was President of the Cricket Club), inspired by the minister, Cyril Flower, and his respect for other religions.[44] She contemplated a career in caring for people with learning difficulties, but eventually trained as a teacher and taught for a year.

Margaret had a special concern for disadvantaged people, and also for religion as a way of faithful living. This led her to train for the ministry at Manchester College Oxford (MCO), with a posting to Rotherham for a year as lay pastor and then ministry there from 1928 to 1933. At the 1931 meeting of the Old Students' Association of MCO in 1931, under the overall theme of *Sex Problems of Today*, Margaret gave a paper entitled 'The Social Consequences of the Feminist Movement', in which she concluded that there was no question of 'seeking to oust men or asking for a "spurious 'equality'"', ending with these words:

> *The thing which the Feminist Movement is giving them is the thing which is calculated to have the most wide-spread and beneficial social consequences – freedom to develop fully, physically, mentally, and spiritually, thus enabling them to bring their own unique contribution to the development of the race, not as women merely, but as citizens and human beings.*[45]

Revd Margaret Barr at the Taj Mahal in 1968
(Courtesy of John Hewerdine)

A plea from **Annie Beard Woodhouse** for aid to the Khasi Unitarians, and Magnus Ratter's subsequent visit to their community, fired Margaret's enthusiasm, but the Unitarian General Assembly (GA) council vetoed her offer to minister there, saying that it was too lonely and isolated a post for a woman. As Margaret said of herself after an earlier conflict over membership of ministers' fraternals in Rotherham, 'I always enjoyed giving battle, or watching others do it for me. And there's a sorry confession for a pacifist to make.'[46] On this occasion Margaret took matters into her own hands, resigned her Rotherham ministry, and took up a teaching post in Calcutta, from where she could reach the Khasi Hills (by train and road) and tour the village churches (on foot), while Annie and the Women's League battled for her in England. The GA gave in, and Margaret took up her work in 1936, spending the next 37 years as Unitarian worker with the Khasis. She insisted that she was not a missionary, but an educator and worker along the lines of Gandhi (whom she had met) and Rabindranath

Tagore. She set up schools in the town of Shillong and developed a rural centre with both educational and medical facilities near the village of Kharang, where she lived in very basic conditions, sharing the life of the local people. She described this vividly in *A Dream Come True: The Story of Kharang*.[47] A good number of British (and American) Unitarians have spent time working with the Khasi Unitarians, both with Margaret and after her death. She kept up a steady stream of reports which were published in *The Unitarian,* in addition to individual correspondence, and she was supported by fund raising, especially by the Women's League. She visited Britain from time to time, notably in 1951 and in 1963, when she preached the sermon at the GA annual meetings, and then in 1971, when she was made an Honorary Member of the GA and Honorary Fellow of Manchester College Oxford.

Margaret was a true pioneer. She devoted her life to the Khasi people, living out her faith of service to those most in need. She firmly believed that there is good in all people and in all religions, and that children should be taught to know and respect other faiths. Her advocacy of teaching such universalism can be found in her 1937 book, *The Great Unity*.[48] Her commitment to village work and the simple life was learned from Gandhi.[49] Margaret summed up what religion meant to her in the following words:

> *To be sure of the voice that guides me and the experiences in my daily life that 'Sense of Joy in God' which can weather all storms, make the heaviest burden seem light and be the kindly light that brightens even the darkest and loneliest path, that is what religion means to me.*[50]

Her Unitarianism also meant service in the tradition of **Mary Carpenter** to the most deprived and needy of her fellow humans.[51]

Endnotes

1 Much of this section is taken from Ann Peart, 'Forgotten Prophets: The Lives of Unitarian Women 1760–1904' (unpublished doctoral thesis, University of Newcastle, 2006), <https://theses.ncl.ac.uk/dspace/bitstream/10443/245/1/peart05.pdf>, and Ann Peart, '"Deconsidered by men": women and the British Unitarian movement before 1904', *Transactions of the Unitarian Historical Society*, Vol 24 no 2, 2008, pp.61–80.

2 Ruth Watts, 'Rational religion and feminism: the challenge of Unitarianism in the nineteenth century', in Susan Morgan (ed.), *Women, Religion and Feminism in Britain, 1750–1900* (London, Palgrave Macmillan, 2002), p. 41.

3 E.B. Tolles (ed.), *Slavery and the 'Woman Question'. Lucretia Mott's Diary of her Visit to Great Britain to Attend the World's Anti-Slavery Convention of 1840* (London: Friends' Historical Society, 1952).

4 *TUHS*, 1997, p.7.

5 George Fox, 'Sketch of my Ministry at Mossley from March 8th 1857 till December 7th 1865 (1910)', in the Unitarian College Collection (unlisted), John Rylands University Library, Deansgate, Manchester.

6 *Inquirer*, 1899, p.167.

7 MCO Annual Report for 1892–3.

8 Keith Gilley, 'Women and the Unitarian ministry', Arthur Long, 'Unitarian women ministers', both in *Growing Together: The Report of the Unitarian Working Party on Feminist Theology* (London, GA of U&FCC, 1984), sections 4.4, 4.3; 'Obituary, Mrs T.B. Broadrick', *Christian Life*, 1925, p.245; A.A. Broadrick,, 'Message from Mrs Broadrick', *Christian Life*, 1908, p. 293.

9 Ann Peart, 'Forgotten prophets: Unitarian women and religion', in George Chryssides (ed.) *Unitarian Perspectives on Contemporary Religious Thought* (London, Lindsey Press, 1999), pp.61–4; Claudia Elferdink, 'Margaret Brackenbury Crook', *Dictionary of Unitarian and Universalist Biography*, http://uudb.org/, 2014, accessed 1 December 2018.

10 Gilley, op. cit., 1984; GA Directory, 1971–2.

11 Keith Gilley, 'Gertrude von Petzold – the pioneer woman minister', *Transactions of the Unitarian Historical Society*, Vol. 21, no.3, 1997, p.157.

12 Ibid., p.158.

13 Claus Bernet, 'Gertrude von Petzold (1876–1952): Quaker and first woman minister', *Quaker Studies*, 12.1 (2007), pp.129–33.

14 Gilley, op.cit. 1997, p.158.

15 'British Unitarian women ministers' in Keith Gilley, 'Worship Material To Mark The Centenary Of The Induction Of Gertrude Von Petzold As England's First Woman Minister' (Worship Panel of the General Assembly of Unitarian & Free Christian Churches, 2004), p.4.

16 HMCO MS MNC. MISC. 12/iii p. 22, reference from St Andrews University, illegible signature, 26 September 1897.

17 HMCO 1902 Annual Report.

18 Gilley, op.cit., 2004, p.4.

19 HMCO MS MNC MISC. 85, appendix 3, p. 290.

20 Gilley, op.cit., 2004, p.4.

21 Cited in Gilley, op.cit., 2004, p.4.

22 Gilley, op.cit., 1997, p.160.

23 Ibid., pp.159–61.

24 Bernet, op.cit., p.131.

25 Bernet, op.cit., pp. 131–2, Gilley, op.cit., 1997, pp.166–9.

26 Peter Hodges (ed.), *Kinver Edge and the Rock Houses: Centenary Guide 2017* (National Trust, 2017), p.7.

27 Margaret Stevenson, 'Rosalind Lee', *Inquirer*, 1959, p.346; Margaret J. Tuke, *A History of Bedford College for Women 1849–1937* (Oxford, Oxford University Press, 1939), p.330.

28 Stevenson, op.cit., p.346.

29 D.M. Northcroft, *Women Free Church Ministers* (London, Edgar G. Dunstan & Co, 1929), p.15.

30 Ibid.

31 John Kielty (ed.), *Year Book of the General Assembly* (London, Unitarian and Free Christian Churches, 1954), p.82.

32 Northcroft, op.cit.

33 Kielty, op. cit.; Stevenson, op. cit.

34 'The distress among the miners in the Rhondda Valley' (February 1928) in Judy Hague (ed.), *A Century of the Unitarian Women's League 1908–2008: The British League of Unitarian and other Liberal Christian Women* (Sheffield: British League of Unitarian and Free Christian Women, 2008), p.137. My thanks are due to Rory Castle Jones for citations from the work of Judy Hague and John McLachlan.

35 Marjory G. Mitchell, *History of the British League of Unitarian and Other Christian Women* (London, British League of Unitarian and Other Christian Women. 1958) pp.24–5.

36 Stevenson, op.cit.

37 Stevenson, op.cit.; Hague, op.cit., pp.12–13; John McLachlan, *The Wine of Life: A Testament of Vital Encounter* (Sheffield, John McLachlan, 1991), pp.71–3.

38 Mollie Jones, Mary Burns, and Jack Thomas, 'Rosalind Lee' (September/October 2004) in Hague, op.cit., p.51.

39 Rosalind Lee, 'Refugees in Central Europe' (March 1939) in Hague, op.cit., pp.101–2.

40 Stevenson, op.cit.

41 Jones, Burns, and Thomas, 'Rosalind Lee', op.cit., p.51.

42 Stevenson, op.cit.; Hodges, op.cit., p. 9; Jones, Burns, and Thomas, op.cit., p.51.

43 Jones, Burns, and Thomas, op.cit.

44 H. John McLachlan, 'Margaret Barr – a vision and a hope', *Inquirer*, 1 September 1973, pp.1–3; Winifred Laurie and Margaret Barr, in Y. Surrendra Paul (ed.), *Margaret Barr: A Universal Soul* (Udaipur, India, Unitarian Inter-faith Fellowship of India, 1975), pp.5–7, 15–17.

45 Margaret Barr, typescript notes, 'The Social Consequences of the Feminist Movement', Harris Manchester College, MS MOSA 1.

46 McLachlan, op.cit., 1973.

47 Margaret Barr (ed. Roy Smith), *A Dream Come True: The Story of Kharang* (London, Lindsey Press, 1974).

48 Margaret Barr, *The Great Unity* (London, Lindsey Press, 1937).

49 Barr, op.cit., 1974, p.4.

50 Gwyneth Thomas in Paul, op.cit., p.14.

51 McLachlan, op.cit., 1973.

16 Dorothy Tarrant (1885–1973)

Alan Ruston

Dorothy Tarrant was among the most academically brilliant Unitarians of the twentieth century. She was a pioneer in classical studies, a field which at the time was almost wholly dominated by men. She was the first woman to be appointed a professor of Greek in Britain (in 1936 at the University of London). Since the First World War Dorothy had been an internationally recognised authority on the works of Plato. When she was made a Fellow of Bedford College in the University of London in 1969, the citation stated, 'To paraphrase outrageously an unknown third century Greek, writing on a very different character, "Had it, fifty years ago, been rather more of a woman's world, we might have been putting up bronze statues to her honour in the market place".'[1]

Dorothy was born into London Unitarianism, the only daughter of Revd William G. Tarrant (1853–1928) and his wife Alice, *née* Stanley (1863–1936). He was the minister of the newly founded Wandsworth Unitarian Christian Church in London, and Dorothy was the first child to be baptised there.[2] William became a well-known figure within Unitarianism, twice the editor of its weekly newspaper *The Inquirer*, and a recognised and published hymnwriter, not only within the Unitarian movement but also in other denominations. She followed on from her father in most of his chief interests, becoming not only a director of *The Inquirer* board but also an expert on hymnology and devotional life.

> *Educated first at home, and then for a time at Clapham High School, she took first-class honours degrees in Classics at the universities of London (Bedford College) and Cambridge (Girton College). She had to wait until 1927 for the award of the Cambridge degree, as women before then could take the examination but did not receive the actual award. She received an MA from the University of London in 1909, the same year in which she joined the staff at Bedford College; her doctorate was awarded in 1930, and on becoming Professor in 1936 she became head of the department of Greek.*[3]

Before her retirement in 1950 she wrote numerous articles and reviews, mostly on ancient Greek thought, and was recognised as one of the finest teachers of classics in the country. She had a clear style in teaching, as in everything, and took a personal interest in the progress of her students. Dorothy was notable as one of the first women to develop a full academic career. In the 1950s she received the accolade of being made President of both the Hellenic Society and the Classical Association, as well as becoming an Honorary Fellow of both Girton College and Manchester College Oxford.[4]

Throughout her life Dorothy Tarrant was devoted to the Unitarian movement in Britain and served it in a remarkable number of capacities. As her obituary in *The Inquirer* states, 'she never slackened in her devotion to the church at Wandsworth, which moved to Putney in 1968, of which she had been a life-long member. She was secretary from 1950 until her death. In addition, she was secretary of the trustees, deputy organist, treasurer's assistant and chief tea maker. She was virtually unfailing in her attendance at worship. The church was hers in a very real sense – and she belonged to the church and its members.'[5]

She was a pioneer of Sunday School activity, producing material of various kinds for children, and was always willing to play the piano whenever asked to do so. She was remembered as being full of fun in her early years, and she could tell stories to children superbly well. The temperance movement was another enthusiasm of hers, and she travelled widely to speak in its support. Lorna Hardwick, in the appreciation of Dorothy that she contributed to the *Oxford Dictionary of National Biography,* states that 'her interest in the relationship between ancient and modern thought infused her lectures and publications on Unitarian topics. She explored Plato's contribution to free religious thought, while her writings on temperance examined biblical and classical sources for evidence of social attitudes to alcohol and to the practical and ethical shortcomings of policies of moderate drinking.'[6] Nevertheless, the tide of later times flowed against her position of total abstinence.

Dorothy held many offices within Unitarianism, but the one that probably meant most to her was the presidency of the General Assembly of Unitarian and Free Christian Churches during 1952–1953. She held signal positions in both the two main colleges for the training of Unitarian ministers, and was the first woman to be appointed a trustee of Dr Williams's Library and Trust. She was never National President of the Unitarian Women's League, despite many invitations to accept the role. She said that her work precluded it, and after she retired she claimed that she was too old. This however did not deter her from serving on its governing committee for many years. In addition, she provided the prayers and readings in the devotional section of its Newsletter for a remarkable 47 years.[7]

With Revd Mortimer Rowe, Secretary of the General Assembly, Dorothy helped to create the *Golden Treasury of the Bible,* which was first published in 1934. The collection, extracted from the Revised Version, was to be found in most Unitarian pulpits for decades, and was not displaced until the 1980s. Her obituary records, 'She was deeply involved in the production of hymnbooks, for the young as well as adults, particularly *Hymns of Worship Revised* (1962); she had strong likes and dislikes in both hymns and tunes.' Dorothy perhaps did not deal with criticisms of the book with her usual aplomb; its content exemplified her vision of Unitarian Christianity.

Her prestige, learning, and knowledge of the Unitarian movement could be intimidating, and many meeting her for the first time were apprehensive. But further contact revealed an honest, down-to-earth person who could be humorous but insisted that things should be done correctly and in a proper order. She would undertake any task, even if merely addressing envelopes for the common Unitarian good as she saw it. A superb proof reader, she corrected every Lindsey Press book for decades. At times, particularly in the 1950s, she appeared ubiquitous within Unitarianism: wherever you turned she was there in one way or another, and her command of seemingly everything could appear daunting.

Some ministry students at the Unitarian College Manchester were grateful for her instruction, as the University of Manchester required them to reach a certain level of classical Greek, which they found very difficult. She stepped in to coach them. Her tuition invariably got them through the examination; the process of getting there may not always have been easy with such a task master, but her kindly persistence produced the necessary result. As the late Revd Peter Short put it, 'Greater than my perpetual admiration for her complete command of the subject and her

joy in it, was my respect for her unbending discipline which found in me
an ability for application which hitherto I knew not.'

Both Revd Peter Hewis and I recall her in the 1960s within the London
District and South Eastern Unitarian Assembly. Several people reported to
us that she thought we were 'such nice young men'. I recall conducting
worship in a service at Wandsworth Church (all efficiently managed, for
she was well known as consistently replying to correspondence by return
of post), and I was invited to wear the preaching gown kept in the vestry.
It supposedly had some connection with her father. I did so, but, when
leaving the pulpit at the conclusion of the service, I caught it on part of the
pulpit, and there was a loud ripping sound; it never could have been the
same again. She responded in a kindly, understanding way and assured me
it was not my fault. Her memory into her eighties was superb: on another
occasion I was travelling back with her by train from a national Unitarian
occasion in the north and asked if there was a way of obtaining a copy of
a Unitarian Year Book for around 1916. When I came to take the service
at Wandsworth some months later, there was a copy from her collection
waiting for me in the vestry, and I have it to this day.

One of her less appreciated characteristics was to express occasional
disapproval with utterances of 'tch, tch'. Sydney Knight in her obituary says
'it was heard quietly whenever a proposal came up for discussion of which
she disapproved. You knew when she thought a speaker was going on for
too long. She snorted at travesties of language, Greek or English.' By the
1960s the 'tch, tch' had grown louder, as she had become rather deaf. Now
it was heard whenever someone got up to speak with whom she habitually
disagreed, or who spoke too quickly. She disliked ostentation of any kind;
she was a Puritan in the best sense of the word.[8]

In 1967 Dorothy gave her recollections of Unitarians in the past in an
address to the London Unitarian Club, which met at Essex Hall. The text
was published as a four-page leaflet, and its tone and style reflect the person
she was. A couple of her early memories of the 1890s are of interest:

*At the time of the Boer War, I recall that at school I had some early
training in the heretical attitude. I followed my father in disapproving
of this War and I told my school friends that I didn't approve it. I was*

called a pro-Boer and a Little Englander. I shared this unpopularity
with two of Mr Lloyd George's daughters who were at the same school. ...
My little brother Stanley [she had an elder brother, Arthur George, who
was an active Unitarian lay preacher in the 1950s and 1960s], when he
was about six, encountered with my father on the steps of the old Essex
Hall the venerable Dr Martineau, who was one of father's teachers. My
brother had a pat on the head and a blessing from the grand old man.
I've always envied him that.[9]

Dorothy was very much a Unitarian Christian, as is exemplified in her short pamphlet *What Unitarians Believe*. First written for young people in 1926, it was expanded and issued as a booklet for adult use (eighth impression 1963).[10] It remains worth reading, for it sets out her religious position with her usual clarity of thought and expression. She saw things in Biblical terms; she wrote to me in 1968, after having been asked to look over some modern attempts at hymn writing, 'I'm glad they do all lean to the theistic side – I've never expected Humanists (pure) to be lyrical!'

While at Cambridge she encountered the Unitarian group, which had started to meet only the year before. She recalled, 'I shall always be thankful that I found the group led by Mr Stratton (later Professor), Miss Slater (later Mrs Harold Bailey) and Miss Rosalind Lee. I found there a Unitarian "home" to follow on the tradition of the home I had left behind me. I shall always be thankful that the habit of Unitarian worship was made possible for me in that way.'[11] Sunday was the day of rest, and Peter Hewis recalls her telling him that she never studied or did anything like work on the Sabbath, a practice that she had followed since her Cambridge days.

These recollections are concluded with a paragraph that is in many ways a summary of how Dorothy Tarrant saw the Unitarianism of her day:

Reminiscences crowd in, and it has been very pleasant to share some of
these memories with you. It is as a family of friends that we do try to
function in our work, and the more we know about each other and joke
about each other, the better for the spirit of all we do.[12]

Endnotes

1 Obituary, *Inquirer*, 29 September 1973, by SHK (Revd Sydney Knight): the longest single obituary to appear in *The Inquirer* in the second half of the twentieth century.

2 Ibid.

3 Lorna Hardwick, *Oxford Dictionary of National Biography*. This long and excellent profile has been amended in the on-line version (www.oxforddnb.com), which correctly records her presidency of the Unitarian temperance association, which is wrongly stated in the printed version.

4 *Who Was Who, 1971–1980* (Bloomsbury Yearbooks, 1990).

5 Obituary, *Inquirer* (see note 1).

6 Hardwick, op.cit.

7 Obituary, *Inquirer* (note 1).

8 Personal recollections and letters.

9 Dr Dorothy Tarrant, *Recollections*, given to the London Unitarian Club, 1967 (copy in Ruston MS at Dr Williams's Library).

10 Dorothy Tarrant, *What Unitarians Believe*, 1963 impression (on line at unitarian.org.uk/documents).

11 Tarrant, op.cit., 1967.

12 Ibid.

PART FIVE
Untold Stories from Scotland, Wales, and Ireland

Introduction to Part Five

Ann Peart

All the women featured so far in this book practised their Unitarianism mainly in England. **Helen Herford**, who in her promotion of the Women's League toured all parts of Britain and Ireland, and **Rosalind Lee**, with her ministries in Wales, are the exceptions to this. This final part introduces women who were active in Scotland, Wales, and Ireland. While each of these countries had very close links to the English Unitarian movement, sharing ministers, literature, and often institutions such as the British and Foreign Unitarian Association, they also had their own distinctive history and culture. In Scotland most of the smaller congregations have died out, leaving only four extant Unitarian congregations. The Universalist causes promoted by **Caroline Soule** were short lived, but they were part of the Universalist tradition that has been documented for England, Scotland, and Wales by Andrew Hill.[1]

Rory Castle Jones has discovered some of the women whose stories have been missed in most accounts of Welsh Unitarianism. Most of the women whom he portrays were English speaking, but some took part in the struggle for the recognition of the Welsh language, a dimension unique to this part of the British Isles. Derek McAuley reveals some almost-forgotten women from Irish Unitarian history, with a brief introduction to the complexities of religious groupings and nationalist tensions which make Irish religious history so distinctive.

Endnote

1   Andrew Hill, 'The obscure mosaic of
    British Universalism: an outline and a
    bibliographical guide', *Transactions of
    the Unitarian Historical Society*, 23 part
    II (2003), pp.421–44.

17 Unitarian women in Scotland
Ann Peart

Very little is known about Unitarian women in Scotland before the late twentieth century. L. Baker Short's *Pioneers of Scottish Unitarianism* refers only to men, except for one mention of Henry Williamson helping and supporting 'Mrs Soule, the American Universalist woman preacher, when she came on various missionary tours to Scotland', and commenting that she conducted the funeral of Williamson's wife.[1] **Caroline Augusta White Soule** (1824–1903) was indeed an American Universalist missionary, but she also ministered to Scottish Unitarians, and was the first woman to be formally ordained in the UK, in March 1880.

She came from New York State, where her family made a considerable financial sacrifice to send her to school and then to the Universalist Albany Female Academy, from which she graduated with a gold medal for a theological essay at the age of seventeen. Her minister described her as 'so small, slender, timid and shrinking that she looked even younger'.[2] She took an unpaid post as head of the girls' section in a Universalist secondary school, where she met the Revd Henry Soule. Her teaching was cut short by illness after seven months, but the following year she married Henry, and spent the next nine years as a minister's wife and mother to five children in various part of New England. Henry died suddenly from smallpox in 1852 and Caroline turned to teaching for a time, and then to writing, as a means of earning a living. She had already published some stories before her marriage, and had helped her husband with editing work. She moved to a log cabin in Iowa in order to live more cheaply and concentrate on writing; her output ranged from novels and short stories to journal articles and editing a children's magazine.[3] Ten years later, when her children reached adulthood, she returned to New York, partly in order to get treatment for failing eyesight, and then did mainly editorial work for the next four years.

In 1869, at the Universalist General Convention, she helped to organise a women's group formed to raise money for denominational projects, including funding women's ministerial education. This became known as the Women's Centenary Association (WCA), the first national women's organisation in the United States. From the outset, Caroline, as its President, toured the United States, speaking at fundraising meetings. This was a huge success, with the Universalist General Convention women's group reaching a membership of 13,000 and raising $36,000 by 1870.[4] Public speaking was not easy for the shy Caroline; she wrote to a friend, 'I was necessarily obliged to speak to our women; but my sufferings were intense always, and only my love for our cause carried me through'.[5] Nevertheless, she continued to speak, and gave her first sermon in January 1874 at the age of 49.[6]

Caroline's delicate health suffered from all this work, and she took time off to visit England and Scotland in the summer of 1875 to recuperate. During this visit she continued her presidential work, as the WCA was then responsible for raising money for missionary outreach in Scotland. She preached several times, helped to organise the Scottish Universalist Convention, and participated in the dedication of a Universalist Church building in Larbert, near Falkirk, the first in Scotland.[7] On her return to America, she became minister of a congregation in Elizabeth, New Jersey.

The WCA sent Caroline back to Scotland as their missionary in 1878. In the first year she preached in Dunfermline, Larbert, Braidwood (near Carluke), Lochee (Dundee), and Glasgow, as well as England and Northern Ireland. And then in her second year she settled in Glasgow, helping to found St Paul's Universalist Church. The Scottish Universalist Convention formally ordained her in 1880, and made her its secretary for 1881–2. She returned to the States for four years from 1882 to 1886, preaching in New Jersey and throughout New England and the West, while her friend **Marion Crosley**, a minister from New York, took her place in Glasgow. On her return she served until her retirement in 1892 as the minister of the Glasgow St Paul's Church, with additional responsibility for the Unitarian church in Dundee for 1886–7 while its minister, Henry Williamson, visited America. Williamson said of her, 'she was most devoted to making the common people share her great hope and faith'.[8] Caroline was made honorary president of the Scottish Universalist Convention in 1888. She stayed in Glasgow after her retirement, a well-known and respected figure, continuing to preach where needed and to help with the Larbert congregation. She wrote in the *Universalist* of 1894, 'I was always tired, for there was never a chance to rest...but fatigue in the cause of Universalism is infinitely better than inaction, apathy, indolence'.[9] She died in December 1903.

Caroline was not the only woman to preach in Scottish Unitarian churches in the nineteenth century. In 1883 **Martha Turner,** the minister of the Melbourne Unitarian Church in Australia, came to Britain and preached in many English and Scottish congregations, including Glasgow, Dundee, Edinburgh, and Aberdeen.[10]

An American Unitarian woman who paid just one visit to Scotland but had a lasting impact was **Dorothea Lynde Dix** (1802–1887). She is known for her work in improving conditions for the mentally ill, and when she visited Edinburgh on a recuperative holiday she investigated the provisions for the insane and found them to be wanting. Discovering that the real power to change things was with the government in London, she immediately hastened there and lobbied the Home Secretary and other influential people, with the result that a royal inquiry was instituted that year, and the Scottish lunacy laws were reformed in 1857. No wonder she was described as a tornado.[11]

In the twentieth century the **Revd Helen Phillips** went to Dundee at the request of the British and Foreign Unitarian Association as assistant minister to the Revd Henry Williamson, who died shortly afterwards in 1925. She remained there for about a year, and became much liked and well respected. She and many of the congregation hoped that she could remain there as minister, but the B&FUA considered that the position was not suitable for a woman minister; they put forward their own candidate, who was duly elected, but not without division and some bad feeling, as it was considered that Helen had given 'splendid service' to the church.[12] She had trained for the ministry at Manchester College Oxford. She had ministries in Nottingham, Carlisle, Newbury, Moseley (Birmingham), and Tamworth before her short ministry in Dundee. After it she served in Poole (1931–44) and then became Secretary of the Central Postal Mission until her retirement in 1952. She died in 1961, having been an active member of the Maidstone church during her last years.[13]

Grace Mewhort (1884–1974) was born and brought up in Edinburgh, in a Baptist family. She felt drawn to overseas missionary work from an early age, but as a worker in the interdenominational Edinburgh Free Breakfast Mission she got to know the appalling conditions in Edinburgh's slums and decided to stay in Britain to try to improve conditions of the poor locally. She campaigned for women's suffrage and was particularly active in the Trade Union and Labour movements, becoming the representative of the National Union of Clerks on the Trades Council. She went on to represent the Council on numerous other bodies, such as Juvenile After Care, and War Pensions, becoming the first woman Vice President. She also served on the Parliamentary Committee of the Scottish Trades Council.

Grace's reaction to the First World War was to link social reform with the need for a religious base, and in 1917 she joined St Mark's Unitarian Church in Edinburgh, influenced by its minister, Raymond Holt. She continued her work in trade unionism and politics for a while, standing for election as a city councillor in 1919, and was also very active in the Women's International League for Peace and Freedom. When the government set up the Scottish Committee on Women's Employment in 1920, she served as one of its members. Grace decided to train for the Unitarian ministry and began her studies at Manchester College, Oxford, in 1922. Her subsequent ministries were all in England, at Banbury, Boston, Carlisle, Nantwich, and Crewe. She retained her passions for education and social welfare. One of her enthusiasms was for Esperanto, as a possible common language to enable people from different parts of the world to understand one another better. She became a vegetarian and worked for the welfare of animals, campaigning against blood sports and vivisection. Her last home was in Boston, Lincolnshire, where she died in 1974.[14]

Endnotes

1 L. Baker Short, *Pioneers of Scottish Unitarianism* (privately printed, 1963), p.132.

2 Alan Seaburg, 'Caroline Soule' in *Dictionary of Unitarian & Universalist Biography* (2002), http://uudb.org/, accessed 24 November 2018.

3 Seaburg, op.cit.; Caroline F. Hitchings, *Universalist and Unitarian Women Ministers* (Boston, USA, Unitarian Universalist Historical Society, 1985), p.134.

4 Seaburg, op.cit.

5 Hitchings, op.cit., p.135.

6 Seaburg, op.cit.

7 Ibid.

8 Ibid.

9 Hitchings, op.cit., p.136.

10 Dorothy Scott, *The Halfway House to Infidelity: A History of the Melbourne Unitarian Church 1853–1973* (Unitarian Fellowship of Australia and Melbourne, Unitarian Peace Memorial Church, 1980), pp.57, 144,

11 Andrew Hill, 'The American Invader or what Dorothea Lynde Dix did for Scotland', sermon preached at St Mark's Church, Edinburgh, on 31 July 2005.

12 Colin H. Wicker, 'Unitarians in Dundee: Williamson Memorial Unitarian Christian Church' (stencils from typescript, 1983), pp.59–60.

13 *Inquirer,* 1961, p.192.

14 D.M. Northcroft, *Women Free Church Ministers* (London, Edgar G. Dunstan & Co, 1929), p.18; *Inquirer,* 1975, January 18, p.4; Alan Ruston, *Obituaries of Unitarian Ministers 1900–204 Index and Synopsis,* Unitarian Historical Society website, www.unitarianhistory. org.uk, accessed 24 November 2018.

18 Unitarian women in Wales

Rory Castle Jones

Of the 98 Welsh Unitarian 'giants of the faith' who appear in the wonderful book *Cewri'r Ffydd* by the late Revd Dr D. Elwyn Davies, only two are women.[1] Similarly, of the 80 or so individuals associated with Unitarianism who have entries in *The Dictionary of Welsh Biography*, just one is a woman.[2] In the histories of our denomination and of individual Unitarian congregations in Wales, as on the memorial plaques honouring ministers in our chapels, women rarely appear.[3]

Can it be that the great Welsh Unitarian movement has been led, organised, and supported only by men over the past two hundred years or so? When we look at our 21 congregations across Wales today, do we see all-male chapels with services led only by men? No, of course not. It is perhaps sufficient to say that historians of Welsh Unitarianism have not been immune to the unconscious biases of their times. Almost all Welsh Unitarian ministers have been men, and congregational and community leaders too were almost exclusively male until recent times. Where women appear in our denominational history, they are usually only marginal, supporting characters. Now we must delve back into our history to discover, or rediscover, the stories of the Welsh Unitarian women who have contributed so much to our denomination and to our country's history.

Unitarianism in Wales is a denomination with deep historical roots and great impact, despite its small numbers. Today, there are 13 congregations in rural Ceredigion – the famous 'Smotyn Du', or Black Spot, making up the South Wales District – and all of them are Welsh-speaking. In South East Wales there are seven congregations, mostly English-speaking and including the major cities of Cardiff and Swansea. In the north, there is one (relatively new) congregation near Bangor.

The stories of a handful of women of importance to the history of Unitarianism in Wales survive. Here an attempt is made to sketch the lives of some of these women, from the earliest days up to the close of the twentieth century. Doubtless, the lives of many others have been lost to us for ever.

The eighteenth century

Mary Rees Bevan (*née* Howell) was born in 1718 near Swansea into a family of non-conformists well known for their support of Cromwell and parliament during the Civil War. Mary inherited from her ancestors 'a spirit of independence, and a love of freedom, especially in respect to religious matters'.[4] She married Revd Owen Rees, a Protestant preacher, and moved first to Llandovery, Carmarthenshire, and then to Trecynon, near Aberdare, where Owen was minister at Hen Dŷ Cwrdd ('The Old Meeting House') and where the two of them became Arminians.

Widowed in her fifties, Mary re-married; her second husband was the respected Aberdare surgeon Rees Bevan. From then on, she was known as Mary Rees Bevan. Widowed for a second time at the age of 80, she moved to Pontardawe in the Swansea Valley to live with her only child, Revd Josiah Rees, minister of Gellionnen Chapel. There, liberated from

Mary Rees Bevan (miniature, painted early 19th century)
(© Dick Robinson, used with permission)

housework and wifely duties, and with all her needs provided by her children and grandchildren, Mary engaged in serious study of the Bible and the latest theological books. Plunging into the religious controversy of the day – Unitarianism – Mary became a Unitarian, perhaps the first at Gellionnen Chapel to do so. Her son Josiah followed her example and with him, eventually, the entire congregation (albeit only after debate, splits, and even physical fighting in the churchyard).

Mary believed that God embodied 'in himself everything that is perfect and amiable and engaging', that people were accountable for their actions, and that a more equal world was possible 'wherein men shall receive according to their works'.[5] She lived to the age of 100, outliving two husbands and her son, and she astounded all with her powerful faith, her intellect, knowledge of the Bible, and composition of Welsh verse. She selected the verse for her funeral herself: 'With long life will I satisfy him, and show him my salvation' (Psalm 91:16).[6]

Mary's daughter-in-law, Josiah's wife, was also called Mary. This **Mary Rees** (*née* Jones) (1747–1829) was well respected and a prominent independent woman in her community after her husband's death in 1804. The daughter of Thomas Jones of Pen-y-Glog, Carmarthenshire, she was Josiah's second wife and the mother of ten children.[7] She was known for her understanding, cheerfulness, kindness, and extensive charity work among the local poor.[8]

Catherine Rees (1760–1841) was a member of the congregation at Hen Dŷ Cwrdd in Cefn Coed y Cymmer, near Merthyr Tydfil. Born in Cefn Coed, Catherine was the daughter of John William Thomas, a long-standing member of the Hen Dŷ Cwrdd chapel, which was first built in 1747.[9] According to an 1841 article in *Seren Gomer,* Catherine was 'brought up among wicked and blasphemous people ... who reviled the Christian Religion and persecuted its adherents'. We might assume that this refers not to her own family, but to her neighbours and the community in Cefn Coed at that time.[10] At the age of fifteen, she attended the chapel's renowned Sunday School and learned to read the Bible in her mother tongue with other girls. Aged 24, she married Edward Rees, a stone mason and member of the congregation.

Catherine became a leading figure in Hen Dŷ Cwrdd and the community. Her one passion was to 'save souls', and she spent much of her time accosting drunken neighbours and appealing to them to find religion. The historian of Hen Dŷ Cwrdd, Tom Lewis, records that 'armed only with the courage of her convictions, nothing deterred her from carrying the "message" to the roughest of her neighbours'. Catherine 'attacked the "wicked and the lost" relentlessly, and beseeched them to abandon their unsober and sordid way of living'. Evidently, she was a fearless woman, accosting drunken mobs 'without a tremor', with a flow of biblical verses, scoldings, and encouragements to change their ways.[11] Interestingly, she earned the respect of other Christian denominations (as evidenced by her obituary printed in the *Seren Gomer,* a publication strongly associated with the Baptists), and Lewis writes that 'denominational barriers were broken down' by her work.[12]

Catherine was the village midwife and nurse, delivering more than 1,000 babies and spending endless nights comforting the sick and the dying, earning the love and respect of her neighbours and community. In fact, she was more than a midwife, having studied 'medical subjects' more broadly.[13] She had no children of her own, but following the deaths of her sister and brother-in-law she adopted their four orphaned children without hesitation.

What else do we know about this unusual woman? She had a beautiful singing voice and led her congregation in song during services, dedicating her musical gifts to 'the glory of God'.[14] Catherine died in 1841 and on the day of her funeral 'there was not a dry eye in the village'.[15] Her favourite biblical verse was 'Come unto me all ye who are weary and heavy laden and I will give you rest'.[16] The historian of her chapel concluded that Catherine was 'a personality of exceptional virtue', a woman of 'inherent saintliness' characterised by 'love of her fellows'.[17]

Women play an important part in the story of a Welsh Unitarian hero, Tomos Glyn Cothi (1764–1833), who was imprisoned for two years in 1797 for singing a song *On Liberty.* As well as imprisonment, he was condemned to stand in the pillory and face humiliation and abuse from the public. His daughters walked many miles from their home to Carmarthen, where they stood beside their father in the pillory in order to protect him. So impressed were the mob by his daughters' loyalty and courage that Tomos Glyn Cothi was left unharmed.

The nineteenth century

Lucy Thomas (1781–1847) was a colliery owner, businesswoman, and member of the Hen Dŷ Cwrdd congregation in Cefn Coed y Cymmer. Known as 'the mother of the Welsh steam coal trade', she took over her late husband's business in 1833 and was extremely successful, despite being illiterate.

Originally from Llansamlet, near Swansea, Lucy was the daughter of Job and Ann Williams.[18] In 1802, she married Robert Thomas and moved to Merthyr Tydfil, where he supplied coal to the ironworks, and they had eight children. When he died in 1833, she took over his thriving business. One story goes that when Lucy went to the famous Coal Exchange in Cardiff she was refused entry because she was a woman. She sent in one of her male employees with the message: 'My coal is equal to any man's; failure to grant entry will lead to my business lining another's pockets'.

Lucy fell ill with typhoid and died in 1847. She was buried at Hen Dŷ Cwrdd, and a beautiful fountain commemorating her and her family still stands on the High Street of Merthyr Tydfil today.[19]

Caroline Elizabeth Williams (1823–1908) was a member of an important family of industrialists, scientists, and politicians and was a descendant of Dr Richard Price, the famous philosopher and Unitarian minister. She was born in Bridgend and educated at the Bristol boarding school run by the mother of the Unitarian social reformer Mary Carpenter. Following the early death of her parents, Caroline was taken in by her wealthy uncle Walter Coffin, of Llandaff Court, and after his death she inherited both his estate and his colliery at Dinas in the Rhondda Valley. Considered a 'radical', Caroline devoted her energy to the struggle for women's rights and education. In 1892 she commissioned and paid for the building of a Workmen's Institute and reading rooms for both men and women. Caroline also gave large donations to fund scholarships for women to study at the University College of South Wales. She never married, and in her will she left her money to the University, to her five servants, and £100 to the cause of women's suffrage. Her ashes were interred in the Unitarian chapel in Bridgend.[20]

Emily Higginson (*née* Thomas) (1826–1895) was born in Carmarthen, the daughter of George Thomas, a solicitor and town clerk. When her father died, Emily's mother moved with her eleven children to Ferryside, a fishing village on the coast eight miles away. Emily was educated at home and then worked as a governess for a number of prominent Unitarian families, before taking a teaching post at a school in Wakefield, Yorkshire. There in 1857 she married Revd Edward Higginson, a Unitarian minister. The two moved to Swansea when Edward became minister of Swansea Unitarian Church the following year. Emily played an active role in supporting her husband's ministry work, and together the couple translated from French and published *The Fine Arts in Italy* (1859) by Althanase Josué Coquerel.[21]

Emily was a teacher and a member of the Swansea School Board (1879–1882) when only a handful of women in Wales held such positions, and she helped to introduce modern kindergarten methods of teaching young children.[22] She placed strong emphasis on the education of her own children and took responsibility for educating many others in her home. After her husband's death in 1880, she took on an increasingly public role in advocating women's education.[23]

Her obituary records that besides her support for women's education 'her interest extended further to the whole range of women's questions, as to occupations, public work, and political rights'. She actively supported younger women in their struggles, and 'her friendship was given with special readiness to such young women as were endeavouring to make careers of their own'.[24] She has been described as Swansea's 'leading feminist' in her day.[25] In 1890, Emily left Wales to live with her son in Manchester, where two years later she was struck down by a 'terrible illness' which she suffered with 'great courage and calmness', and during which she continued her work. She died in 1895, aged 69.[26]

Anne Adaliza Puddicombe (1836–1908) is better known under her male pseudonym 'Allen Raine'.[27] She was born and raised in Newcastle Emlyn, Carmarthenshire. Her father, Benjamin Evans, was the grandson of the famous Unitarian minister and educator Dafydd Dafis Castellhywel. Anne spent some years studying with the family of her father's cousin, Revd David Davis, a Unitarian minister in Cheltenham. She married Beynon Puddicombe, a London bank clerk, but for ten years suffered from ill health. When eventually her health was restored, her husband experienced a mental breakdown, from which he never recovered, and they returned to Wales.

Anne turned to writing, both to find a source of income and, it seems, as a source of escape and solace. In 1894, one of her stories won a prize at the National Eisteddfod. In 1896, after repeated rejections by publishers of her first novel, she submitted it under a male pseudonym and it was published in the following year. *A Welsh Singer*, which sold more than one million copies, was followed by many successful novels, including *Torn Sails*, *A Welsh Witch*, and *Queen of the Rushes*, set during the religious revival of 1904–05. Her novel *All In A Month* was based on her experiences of her husband's mental illness, and *Under The Thatch* drew on her experiences of suffering from cancer, from which she died in 1908, aged just 58.[28] *The Inquirer* reported that she 'would be sincerely mourned throughout Wales, of which she has become the most popular novelist'. 'She loved her native country and its people', her obituary records, 'and was familiar with its traditions, legends, and folklore. Her stories are wholesome and genuinely human throughout.'[29]

The twentieth century

Sarah Helen Davies (1905–1972), better known as Sali Davies, was the deputy headmistress and teacher of Welsh at Lampeter Grammar School. When she retired in the 1960s, she returned the pension forms that had been sent to her in English and requested them in Welsh. When this was refused, she declared that she would live without her pension until Welsh-language forms were made available. The case became symbolic of the struggle for Welsh-language rights, and eventually Sali won her battle in 1966.

Beyond the classroom, she was a very active member of Caeronnen Unitarian Chapel in Cellan, near Lampeter, and in her South Wales district. Some locally called her 'Sali Sosin' – or Sali the Socinian, which Unitarians in Y Smotyn Du were still called even then by their opponents. For her companions, she was the 'conscience of Unitarianism' and remembered as such long after her death. As well as her work in education and religion, Sali

Davies was active with the Urdd (the Welsh youth movement), Cymdeithas yr Iaith (the Welsh-language society), and Plaid Cymru (the Welsh nationalist party). Sali Davies died in 1972 and was buried at Caeronnen Chapel.[30]

Dorothy Lloyd (1905?–1995), from a family who had been Unitarians for more than two centuries, came to Wales from Birmingham to work as a teacher during the Second World War. Her close family were killed during a bombing raid on Birmingham in 1940. She settled in south Wales and was active in the Unitarian movement, serving as National President of the Women's League and attending the Peace Conference of the International Women's Year in East Berlin in 1975. Her call for 'more toleration, freedom and understanding between world faiths' was reported in the East German press. She was a supporter of the Guide Movement, the United Nations, and Save The Children, as well as the India Fund, which supported Margaret Barr's work in the Khasi Hills of India (described in Chapter 15 of this book).[31]

Women in leadership roles

To date, only two women have served as Unitarian ministers in Wales: Revd Constance Harris and Revd Rosalind Lee, neither of whom was born in Wales.

Revd Constance Harris was the first female Unitarian minister in Wales, taking up her post in 1927, 23 years after the Unitarian Revd Gertrude von Petzold became the first woman minister in England.[32] Raised and educated in Leicester, Harris was trained for the ministry at Manchester College, Oxford (1922–25) and was the eighth woman to be trained for the Unitarian ministry in Britain.[33]

Her first ministerial positions were in London and Birmingham, and she undertook and published research into social conditions in Bethnal Green, east London, one of the poorest districts in Britain.[34] In 1927 she went to Highland Place Unitarian Church in Aberdare as a 'supply' for twelve months, impressing the congregation sufficiently to be offered a permanent position in February 1928. Her ministry at Aberdare was 'very active and fruitful', and Harris was 'well-known for her effort to alleviate the sufferings of those impoverished by the depression'.[35] She opened a food bank and clothing-distribution centre in the chapel for the unemployed and their families. Constance Harris left Aberdare in 1931 and served in Sidmouth and Derby before retiring to Leicester in 1952.[36]

The story of **Revd Rosalind Lee** has been told in Chapter 15. Her time in lay charge at Glanrhondda Unitarian Chapel in Pentre, near Treorchy in the Rhondda Valley (1917–20), and later as district minister for South East Wales (1932–46), is significant for Welsh Unitarians.

Welsh women may not have had ministerial status so far, but they have played a significant role in lay leadership positions, which became much more accessible in the twentieth century. The first woman elected President of the South East Wales Unitarian Society was **Mrs Reid**, of Swansea Unitarian Church, in 1910–12. She was followed over the years by many women presidents. In the interwar period were **Mrs Lewis** (Pontypridd), **Sophia George** (Aberdare), and **H.E. Hargrove** (Swansea). In the 1950s and 1960s came **Revd Rosalind Lee**, **E.A. James** (Trecynon), **Edna Dando** (Swansea), and **Alice Howells** (Trecynon). Then in the 1970s and 1980s followed **Gwyneth Thomas** (Pontypridd), **Dorothy Lloyd** (Cardiff), **Julianne Symons** (Swansea), and **Margaret Evans** (Cardiff). Since then, a further six women have served as District President. In the South Wales district numerous women have served in leadership roles. Gwyneth Thomas from the Pontypridd congregation was the first Welsh woman to serve as President of the British General Assembly, in 1974–75.

Conclusion

In this short chapter I have attempted to provide a glimpse into the stories of some important Welsh Unitarian women. It is incomplete, selective, and focused much more on my own South East Wales district than on the larger South Wales district. Despite these failings, it is hoped that it can contribute towards a better understanding of women's role in the Unitarian movement in Wales, and perhaps encourage other professional and amateur researchers to discover more. The future is bright for women in the Welsh Unitarian movement, and all Unitarians can find strength, hope, and inspiration in the stories of our female forebears.

Endnotes

1   D. Elwyn Davies, *Cewri'r Ffydd: Bywgraffiadur y Mudiad Undodaidd yng Nghymru* (Giants of the Faith: A Biography of the Unitarian Movement in Wales) (Llandysul: Gwasg Gomer, 1999).

2   *The Dictionary of Welsh Biography* (Aberystwyth: The National Library of Wales, 2007) at http://yba.llgc.org.uk/en/index.html [accessed 24.September 2018].

3   The outstanding history of Welsh Unitarianism is D. Elwyn Davies, *Y Smotiau Duon: Braslun o Hanes y Traddodiad Rhyddfrydol ac Undodiaeth* (Llandysul: Gwasg Gomer, 1980); published in English as D. Elwyn Davies, *'They Thought For Themselves': A Brief Look at the History of Unitarianism in Wales and the Tradition of Liberal Religion* (Llandysul: Gwasg Gomer, 1982). Most individual congregations also have their own published histories.

4   Thomas Rees, Obituary of Mary Rees Bevan (11 February 1818) in *The Monthly Repository of Theology and General Literature*, Vol. 13, January to December 1818 (Hackney: Sherwood, Neely and Jones, 1818), pp.143–4.

5   Ibid.

6   Ibid.

7   Geraint H. Jenkins, Ffion Mair Jones, and David Ceri Jones (eds.), *The Correspondence of Iolo Morganwg*, Vol. 3, 1810–1826 (Cardiff: University of Wales Press, 2007), p.146.

8   Obituary of Mary Rees in *The Cambrian*, 21 November 1829, p.3; Obituary of Mrs.Mary Rees in *The*

Christian Reformer, or, New Evangelical Miscellany, Vol. 15, January to December 1829 (Hackney: Sherwood, Gilbert and Piper, 1829), pp.528–9.

9   Tom Lewis, *The History of the Hen Dŷ Cwrdd, Cefn Coed y Cymmer* (Llandysul: J. D. Lewis & Sons, Gomerian Press, 1947), p.136.

10 Quoted in Lewis, *The History of the Hen Dŷ Cwrdd*, p.136.

11 Ibid., p.136.

12 Ibid., p.137.

13 Ibid. p.136.

14 Ibid., p.136.

15 Ibid., pp.136–37.

16 Ibid., p.136.

17 Ibid., p.137.

18 John Williams, 'Thomas, Lucy (*bap.* 1781, *d.* 1847)' in *Oxford Dictionary of National Biography* (Oxford: Oxford University Press, 2004) at https://doi.org/10.1093/ref:odnb/47974 [accessed 12 November.2018].

19 Robert Thomas Jenkins, 'LEWIS , Sir WILLIAM THOMAS (1837–1914)' (1959)' in *The Dictionary of Welsh Biography* at http://yba.llgc.org.uk/en/s-LEWI-THO-1837.html [accessed 28 September.2018].

20 Louvain Rees, 'A champion of female education and a pioneer on the scholarship front', *Wales Online* (1 March 2017) at https://www.walesonline.co.uk/lifestyle/nostalgia/champion-female-education-pioneer-scholarship-12628828 [accessed 24 September 2018].

21 Obituary of Mrs Higginson in *The Inquirer,* 1895, p. 69.

22 Elizabeth Crawford, *The Women's Suffrage Movement in Britain and Ireland: a Regional Survey* (London: Routledge, 2006), p.222; Angela V. John (ed.), *Our Mothers' Land: Chapters in Welsh Women's History, 1830–1939* (Cardiff: University of Wales Press, 1991), p.68; Obituary of Mrs Higginson in *The Inquirer,* 1895, p.69.

23 Obituary of Mrs Higginson in *The Inquirer,* 1895, p. 69.

24 Ibid.

25 Crawford, op.cit., p. 211.

26 Obituary of Emily Higginson in *The Christian Life,* 26th January 1895, p. 46; Obituary of Mrs Higginson in *The Inquirer,* 1895, p. 69.

27 Davies, op.cit., pp. 218–23.

28 Ibid.; Dr David Jenkins, 'Puddicombe, Anne Adalisa ('Allen Raine'; 1836–1908)' (1959) in *The Dictionary of Welsh Biography* at http://yba.llgc.org.uk/en/s-PUDD-ADA-1836.html [accessed 28 September.2018].

29 Obituary of 'Allen Raine' (Mrs Beynon Puddicombe) in *The Inquirer,* 27 June 1908, p. 403.

30 Davies, op.cit., pp.315–16.

31 Norah Wilson, Obituary of Dorothy Lloyd (January/February 1995) in Judy Hague (ed.), *A Century of the Unitarian Women's League 1908–2008: The British League of Unitarian and other Liberal Christian Women* (Sheffield: British League of Unitarian and Free Christian Women, 2008), p. 63.

32 Davies, *'They Thought For Themselves',* p. 88.

33 'British Unitarian Women Ministers' in Keith Gilley, 'Worship Material To Mark The Centenary Of The Induction Of Gertrude Von Petzold As England's First Woman Minister' (Worship Panel of the General Assembly of Unitarian & Free Christian Churches, 2004), p.6.

34 C. Harris, *The Use of Leisure in Bethnal Green* (London: Lindsey Press, 1927); Gilley, op.cit., p. 6.

35 Rev. J. Eric Jones (ed.), *Highland Place Unitarian Church: A Story of Resilience* (Aberdare: Highland Place Unitarian Church, 2011), p.64.

36 Ibid., p.64.

19 Unitarian women in Ireland

Derek McAuley

Introduction

Unitarian women in Ireland shared many of the experiences of their co-religionists in Great Britain. They were connected to networks which reached out to and from them across the Irish Sea. Yet they also had to confront the question of what it meant to be a Protestant in Ireland. The Unitarian community in Ireland (eventually consolidated in 1910 within the Non-Subscribing Presbyterian Church of Ireland) existed in a very different social and political environment. Ireland had a large majority Roman Catholic community whose rights were severely limited, and it was governed by a tiny Anglican Establishment. In the northern counties of Ulster and in scattered communities in other provinces were Presbyterian dissenters, mostly of Scottish origin, although a few owed their origin to the English Cromwellian plantations in the seventeenth century. It was within these communities in the eighteenth and nineteenth centuries that liberal 'New Light' thinking emerged, which rejected narrow conservative Calvinism, leading in time to the development of non-subscribing and Unitarian ideas. These theological liberals formed part of what is a substantial, essentially progressive Irish Presbyterian tradition.[1]

The nineteenth century was a period of economic development in the north of Ireland and, in common with Unitarians in the similarly industrialising north of England, a few families accumulated vast fortunes and great influence, moving towards more conservative political positions. This is reflected in the journey from support for the radical cause of the United Irishmen, who rebelled against British rule in 1798, to leading roles in Ulster Unionism by the descendants of Revd Thomas Drennan and related families with notable Unitarian women members (Table 1, overleaf).

The period during which Unitarian women in Ireland claimed their own space and an identity was one in which great ideological and constitutional

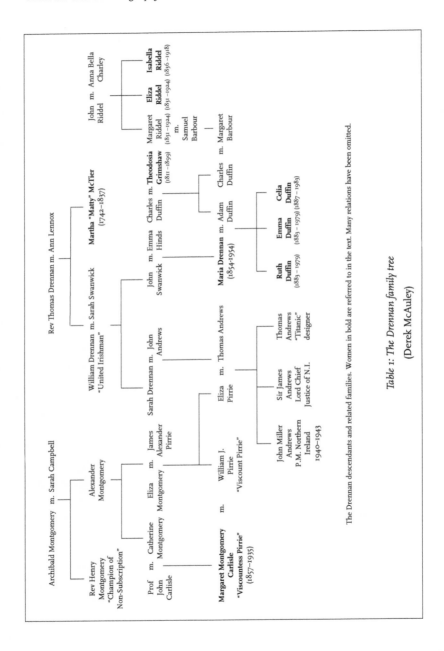

Table 1: *The Drennan family tree*
(Derek McAuley)

questions were contested. Ideas of national self-determination, of cultural and linguistic autonomy, and of Ireland's place within the world were central. As Ireland became starkly divided, leading ultimately to partition in 1921, Unitarian women in different ways sought to overcome sectarian boundaries and concentrate on what drew people together in common cause, seeking to reach across boundaries of religion, gender, culture, and politics.

The first group to be considered in this chapter, **Sarah Anne Rowan, Martha McTier,** and **Henrietta Mitchel Martin**, because of their associations with well-known husbands or brothers active in political life, have struggled to emerge as figures in their own right. The second group asserted themselves in the late nineteenth and early twentieth centuries. **Mary Anne Hutton, Rosamond Praeger, Dora Mellone,** and **Margaret Rachel Huxley** pursued their own, often radical, aspirations in different ways. Interestingly only the first of these married, and the three who were English born ended up living in Dublin after the partition of Ireland. The final group, except for **Ruby Purdy**, were part of the Non-Subscribing elite of Belfast. The **Duffin and Riddel sisters** and **Lady Pirrie** demonstrated the Unitarian concern for social welfare in a rapidly changing city. They were all committed to addressing issues of social injustice.

Sarah Anne Rowan (1764–1834)

Sarah Anne Rowan was the daughter of William Dawson, of Lisanisk, Co. Monaghan. In 1781 she married Archibald Hamilton Rowan. He was actively involved in Irish politics: in the 1780s in the Volunteer militia movement, and then the United Irishmen. In December 1792 he was imprisoned for distributing a call to arms.[2] He managed to escape to France, actively aided by his wife. Sarah has been described as a 'steadfast comrade'.[3] During his exile she worked to preserve his property and ensured that their children were educated. She was the most important advocate for his ultimate pardon. She believed that the Bible was the only valid guide of a Christian's faith, and that Unitarian Christianity was the Christianity of the Scriptures. As she wrote in a letter in 1799:

> *The more I have reflected on, and used my reason in matters of religion, the stronger has been my belief in Christianity. I hear Priestley has lately published 'a very absurd book' on religion; he has many enemies, however, and I think it more than probable that the book is misrepresented ... I would thank you to get it for me that I may, as I generally do, judge for myself.*[4]

Martha 'Matty' McTier (1742–1837)

Martha 'Matty' McTier was a sister of the well-known United Irishman William Drennan. Their father, Revd Thomas Drennan, was a Presbyterian 'New Light' minister. She married Samuel McTier, President of the First Belfast Society of United Irishmen. She corresponded with her brother for more than 40 years, and the Drennan–McTier letters provide important insights into a period of change. Mrs Maria Duffin and her daughter Ruth (see below) did much to preserve them, and they are deposited at the Public Records Office of Northern Ireland.

Martha was no mere recipient of her brother's correspondence. 'Twelve years older than her brother, she often assumed the role of a political adviser and exerted a considerable influence over his political writings.'[5] Martha also corresponded with Jane Greg, daughter of a wealthy Belfast merchant, an outspoken member of dissident women's societies, including the United Irishwomen. To protect her from arrest, Jane was sent to Manchester to live with her brother, Samuel Greg, and his wife Hannah, both of them prominent Unitarians.[6]

Martha's religious views were firmly aligned to 'New Light' Presbyterianism – 'calm, private and unprejudiced'. Yet she was no religious sceptic; nor spiritually apathetic. She condemned those, such as the Enlightenment philosopher David Hume and the radical political activist Tom Paine, who attacked religion or declared themselves atheists, and also the evangelical Christians for their doctrine and their self-righteous piety.[7]

Henrietta Mitchel Martin (1827–1913)

Henrietta Mitchel Martin was a daughter of Revd John Mitchel, minister at First (Non-Subscribing) Presbyterian Church, Newry, who had taken the oath of the United Irishmen as a boy. She was the youngest sister of John Mitchel (1815–1875), the Irish nationalist revolutionary who was a leading member of the Young Ireland movement, which promoted Irish independence. She too had been active in nationalist activities and wrote articles for the *United Irishman* newspaper. She married John Martin, a lifelong friend of her brother and fellow Young Irelander, in November 1868 at Rosslyn Hill Chapel, London.[8] From 1869 to 1870, they travelled in Canada and America, where they were warmly received in New York, Boston, and New Jersey. In 1871 John Martin was elected as a Member of Parliament for County Meath, arguing for home rule for Ireland.

In 1875 Henrietta accompanied her brother on his successful parliamentary election campaign, appearing at the hustings in Tipperary Town and Clonmel: an unusual act for a woman in Ireland at that time. After her husband's death in 1875, she took a break from nationalist politics when in the spring of 1876 she responded to a friend's call to assist an unidentified Unitarian minister with his work in Milan. She returned in May or June 1877.[9]

She travelled extensively to rally support for the Irish nationalist cause, and in 1903 she attended the Irish League Convention in Boston, USA, giving very public support to the Home Rule Movement.[10] She died in Dublin in July 1913 and, like her brother, was interred in the Unitarian Old Meeting House Green in Newry; the coffin was borne to the graveside by the 'John Mitchel' branch of the Irish National Foresters, a friendly society with a mass membership. John Redmond MP, leader of the Irish Parliamentary Party, sent a telegram of regret. The funeral service was conducted by Revd George J. Slipper, of Newry Non-Subscribing Presbyterian Church.[11] In reviewing Henrietta's life's work, I consider it somewhat unfair for Brigitte Anton to claim that all her activities were 'dedicated to her dead husband and his cause and were not done in her own right'.

Mary Anne (Margaret) Hutton (1862–1953)

Mary Anne Hutton, also known as Margaret, was born in Manchester, the daughter of Revd James Drummond and Frances Classon. James, however, was Dublin born. He moved to London as Principal of Manchester College in 1885.[12] On 27 March 1890 she married Arthur William Hutton at Rosslyn Hill Chapel, London. The Huttons were a wealthy Unitarian family in Dublin.[13] Formerly in the coachbuilding trade, theirs was the leading motor-car firm in Ireland.[14]

Mary studied Celtic literature at University College London. In 1909 she was the Margaret Stokes Memorial Lecturer and a member of the Senate of Queen's University of Belfast. Among her publications was a ground-breaking edition of *Tain Bo Cuailgbne* (*The Tain: An Irish Epic Told in English Verse*), the result of ten years of translation.[15] She was active in the Gaelic League, a social and cultural organisation formed in 1893 to promote the Irish language. In 1886 she had joined in organising the first Feis, a Gaelic arts and cultural festival to be held in Belfast, and she translated the programme into Irish.[16] Her large home on the middle-class Malone Road was 'a centre of cultural and artistic activity in Belfast', and she was part of a group of Protestant women who felt that the Irish language and culture were for all to celebrate.[17] She knew and corresponded with republican Patrick Pearse, one of the leaders of the 1916 Irish Rising in Dublin, and she visited and financially supported his school, St Enda's.[18] She converted to Catholicism in 1902 and moved to Dublin around 1910 after the death of her husband, no doubt finding Belfast uncongenial as political tensions rose.[19]

Rosamond Praeger (1867–1954)

Sophia Rosamond Praeger was a sculptor and illustrator. Her father, William Emil Praeger, was a Dutch migrant to Belfast.[20] Her mother was Marie Patterson, from a prominent non-subscribing Presbyterian family in Belfast.[21] Rosamond attended the School of Art, Belfast and the Slade School, London and also studied in Paris.[22] Her significance has not been widely recognised. John Hewitt's overview of the visual arts in Ulster

The sculptor Rosamond Praeger and angels carved for the Thomas Andrews Memorial Hall,
Comber, Co. Down
(The Inquirer 1 April 1922, p. 127)

concluded 'Of sculpture there is little to tell...', yet he commended Praeger's 'exceptionally popular' modelled busts, figures, or groups of children, in particular 'The Philosopher'.[23] When she died she was considered one of the most important Irish artists of her time, yet according to McBinn she is today, like so many women artists of her generation, 'a forgotten and marginalised figure'.[24] For Unitarians beyond Ireland she was a figure of note; she featured in two illustrated articles in *The Inquirer* at a time when photographs were rarely used.[25]

She completed many architectural works and memorials,[26] including the angels on the Thomas Andrews Memorial Hall, Comber, Co. Down.[27] Her Great War memorials have received increased recognition during the recent commemorations of the centenary of the ending of the First World War; most poignant is the memorial for Holywood Non-Subscribing Presbyterian Church, on which is inscribed the name of her younger brother, Egmont Apjohn Praeger.[28]

Praeger was an accomplished children's illustrator and she wrote and illustrated more than 25 books. She received many honours, including Presidency of the Royal Ulster Academy, an honorary doctorate from Queen's University, and an MBE in 1939.

Although she was described as a 'staunch unionist', she did work with cultural nationalists. She designed the sets of the very first show of *tableaux* produced in Belfast in 1898 for the Gaelic League by Alice Milligan, the most prominent northern Protestant nationalist. Mary Hutton (above) also took part.[29] Praeger also published illustrations in Sir Horace Plunkett's Celtic Revival journal *The Irish Homestead* and in the revolutionary journal *Shan Van Vocht* ('Poor Old Woman', a traditional name for Ireland). As late as 1943 she organised and exhibited her work at the Belfast Feis commemorating the fiftieth anniversary of the Gaelic League.[30]

McBinn shows that Praeger was committed to female emancipation, noting that she designed posters for suffrage groups in England and Ireland. She was also concerned about the high levels of poverty in Belfast and the effects on children; this may have inspired some of the sculptures for which she is best known,[31] and in her will she left a large sum to the National Society for the Prevention of Cruelty to Children.[32]

Dora Mellone (1873 –1950)

Dora Mellone was the daughter of Revd William Edward Mellone, who in 1896 was appointed to the ministry of First Presbyterian (Non Subscribing) Church, Warrenpoint, Co. Down. Her brother, Revd Sydney Herbert Mellone, was a prominent British Unitarian. Her sister-in-law was Catherine Drummond, cousin of Mary Hutton (see above). Andrew Hill refers to her briefly in his article on her brother, where he mentions her suffrage activities.[33]

Mellone is another woman whose role has been re-assessed. She was clearly a talented writer, public speaker, and organiser. She was Secretary of the Warrenpoint and Rostrevor Suffrage Society and of the Irishwomen's Suffrage Federation.[34] David Steers points out that between 1907 and 1918 she was the most prolific female contributor to the *Non-Subscribing Presbyterian* on a wide range of topics, including an important article entitled 'The Religious Aspect of Women's Suffrage'.[35] In it she drew on the ethics of Christ to claim that 'all should seek to realise themselves as individual human beings'.[36]

The Home Rule crisis from 1912 posed a major challenge to an already fractured suffrage movement. Mellone argued that it could transcend the traditional divisions in religion and politics by representing all shades of political opinion.[37] She also believed that militant suffragette action would fail, as Ireland faced civil war.[38] With the coming of the First World War most Unionist suffragists tended to suspend their activity, hoping to strengthen the claim for the vote.[39] Mellone was Secretary of the Suffrage Emergency Committee but argued strongly that militarism should not be allowed to 'swamp' the women's movement,[40] nor prevail at the expense of the rights of working women.[41] In the 1920s she was living in Blackrock, south of Dublin, and she spoke at the 'Towards a Better Ireland' Conference in Dublin in 1926, which was an attempt on the part of the Protestant community to assert their role.[42]

Mellone became a regular columnist for *The Inquirer*, with some eighteen articles and a letter published between 1927 and 1932. The most intriguing and lengthy series is unusual: writing partly in colloquial Ulster-Scots under the title 'Mrs McFetridge', she commented from a liberal non-subscribing perspective on controversial issues affecting the Northern Ireland Protestant community, such as the heresy trial of the Presbyterian minister and theologian Revd James Davey in 1927.[43]

Margaret Rachel Huxley (1854–1940)

Margaret Huxley is celebrated as a nurse and promoter of nurse training[44] who achieved international recognition 'for her pioneering work on behalf of nurses and nursing standards'.[45] Born in Croydon, Surrey, she pursued a career in nursing despite family opposition. After training she took up a post in Dublin in 1882 and was then appointed matron and lady superintendent with responsibility for nurse training at Sir Patrick Dun's Hospital. She led the establishment of the Dublin Metropolitan Technical School for Nurses in 1894. She was heavily involved in promoting the profession of nursing, as a founder member of several British, Irish, and international nurses' organisations. She was a member of the first General Nursing Council for Ireland from 1920 to 1923.

In 1911 Huxley joined Dublin Unitarian Church. She took a special interest in public health and the notoriously poor housing in Dublin. In 1927 the congregation decided to take action and, with a substantial personal donation from her, they established what became the 'Margaret Huxley Public Utility Society', providing several houses in the appropriately named 'Huxley Crescent'.[46]

More recently she has been identified by Patricia Murphy as one of 'the forgotten heroines of the Easter Rising', subsequently rendered invisible in the official narrative. She was among nursing and medical staff who provided life-saving aid to both rebels and soldiers.[47] She rejected publicity and honours, but did accept an honorary MA degree from Dublin University in 1928.[48] She is commemorated as 'A great woman' by a window in Dublin Unitarian Church with the words 'Courage, Efficiency, Kindness'.[49]

Emma Sylvia Duffin (1883–1979)

Emma Sylvia Duffin was a daughter of Adam and Maria Duffin. Adam was a successful businessman and a member of the first Senate of Northern Ireland in 1921, reflecting decades of intense political activity.[50] Maria was the granddaughter of William Drennan and great-niece of Martha

McTier (above) and she was one of the founders of the Belfast Charity Organisation, which in 1919 became the Belfast Council for Social Welfare.

Emma was educated by a governess and then at Cheltenham Ladies' College. She attended Belfast Art College and worked as a book and card illustrator. She illustrated the children's novels of her sister Ruth (see below) and volumes of poetry written by Ruth and another sister, Celia.

During World War One she enlisted, with two of her sisters, in the Voluntary Aid Detachment, serving in Egypt and France. Her diaries, in which she described her harrowing experiences, have now attracted attention.[51] In World War Two she re-enlisted and was Commandant of the VAD Unit at Stranmillis Military Hospital in Belfast, making a personal contribution to supporting the survivors of the Belfast blitz of 1941.[52]

She was an active member of the Belfast Council for Social Welfare Committee and served as Honorary Secretary from 1933 until 1953, being the 'moving spirit of the Council'.[53] Her work reflects the dominant role of the Protestant community in the development of voluntary social services in Northern Ireland.[54]

Ruth Duffin (1877–1968)

Ruth Duffin was the eldest daughter of Adam and Maria. In 1914 she was appointed Warden of Riddel Hall, south Belfast, built though the benefaction of the Riddel sisters (see below). She remained there for thirty years, being awarded an Honorary MA by the University in 1943.[55] Gillian McClelland points out that Ruth's grandmother, Theodosia (*née* Grimshaw), had been a committee member of the Belfast Ladies Institute, which sought to promote education for women.[56] In advising her students she was a strong advocate of freedom of conscience, reflecting her Unitarian background.[57]

She published, with her sister Celia, two books of poetry and several children's books.[58] She also contributed to national publications such as *The Manchester Guardian.*[59] She maintained her literary connections all her life and was a close friend of Elizabeth Yeats, sister of W.B.[60]

The Riddel sisters: Eliza (1831–1924) and Isabella (1836–1918)

The Riddel sisters were quiet philanthropists, most notably benefactors of Riddel Hall at the Queen's University of Belfast, having inherited an enormous sum of money from their brother. Their donation of £25,000 in 1912 provided a residence for 65 'female Protestant students' (the religious restriction was not unusual at that time, though subsequently controversial). They contributed a further £50,000 in donations and legacies. The minister of First Presbyterian Church, Belfast, to which they belonged, was to be a permanent member of the Hall's Committee.[61] McClelland regards them as good representatives of their religious beliefs, 'characterised by a warm concern for all manner of human beings'.[62] The Riddel Memorial Plaque, which was unveiled in 1926, was the work of Rosamond Praeger (see above).[63] Eliza was honoured as a member of the Senate of Queen's University.[64]

The sisters also gave generous support to Unitarian denominational causes, including gifting an organ to their congregation and supporting the Sustentation Fund of the Non-Subscribing Presbyterian Church, the Belfast Domestic Mission, and the Home Missionary College in Manchester.[65]

Margaret Montgomery Pirrie (1857–1935)

Margaret was the daughter of John Carlisle, Head Master of the English Department of the Royal Belfast Academical Institution (RBAI) and former Inspector of National Schools. Her mother was Catherine, a niece of Revd Henry Montgomery, the great champion of religious non-subscription. She married her cousin William James Pirrie in 1879. Her husband was a leading businessman and between 1895 and 1924 he was chairman of Harland and Wolff, the Belfast shipbuilders. He also served as Lord Mayor of Belfast between 1896 and 1898. He was ennobled as Baron Pirrie in 1906 and made Viscount Pirrie in 1921.[66] Politically he supported the Liberal policy of Home Rule.[67] In 1921 he was elected to the Senate of the Parliament of Northern Ireland.

Margaret has been recognised as making an important contribution to his rise to high position and was a very popular Lady Mayoress; indeed, 'she was admired and loved by all, her personality was magnetic'.[68] In her own right, however, she was the first woman Honorary Burgess and the first woman Justice of the Peace in Belfast. Following her husband's death in 1924, she became President of Harland and Wolff; this was no mere sinecure and she acted fully in the role. In recognition of this status she was made the first lady honorary member of the Belfast Chamber of Commerce. She was elected President of RBAI in 1931.[69]

Belfast's Royal Victoria Hospital was one of Margaret's abiding interests. In the 1890s she played the leading role in a major public appeal, and she was President of the Hospital from 1914 until her death.[70] She also took an interest in the Mater Infirmorum Hospital in north Belfast, erected by the Roman Catholic community.[71] Her obituary in *The Inquirer* indicates that, although primarily living in London in later life, she retained her membership of both First Presbyterian Church and All Souls, Belfast.[72]

Ruby Purdy (1914–2009)

Ruby Matilda Eileen Heatherington was born in east Belfast, daughter of George Heatherington, from a Church of Ireland background. She was educated at Belmont School. She and her father and eldest brother often attended public meetings of the Independent Labour Party in the Labour Hall in York Street, Belfast. After her brother heard Unitarian sermons preached by the Revd A.L. Agnew, the family decided to attend his radical York Street Non-Subscribing Presbyterian Church. She took part in the Sunday fellowship, where she was exposed to the views of a range of speakers, and it was there that she gained a political education, participating in debates and mock parliaments in the Church Hall.[73] Agnew was a strong supporter of the Labour cause; in 1925 he had published an article entitled 'Why I Am A Socialist'.[74] Ruby was married in 1935 to David Purdy, who became a prominent member of the Northern Ireland Labour Party.[75] She was involved in helping anti-fascist refugees from the Spanish Civil War in the 1930s. She and her family were rendered homeless in the Belfast Blitz. She was active in supporting David Bleakley's successful election campaigns for the Labour Party, which in the 1950s was strongly influenced by Christian Socialist ideas, committed to the Union, and opposed to sectarianism.[76]

In later life she was an active member of the East Belfast Historical Society and in various committee activities at All Souls Church, Elwood Avenue, where the York Street congregation had decanted after its destruction in the Belfast Blitz.[77]

Endnotes

1 Roger Courtney, *Dissenting Voices: Rediscovering the Irish Progressive Presbyterian Tradition* (Belfast, Ulster Historical Foundation, 2013).

2 Liam Chambers, 'Rowan, Archibald Hamilton (1751–1834)', *Oxford Dictionary of National Biography* [accessed 28 October 2018].

3 Fergus Whelan, 'The United Irishman who cheated both noose and guillotine', *Irish Times*, 7 September 2015; www.irishtimes.com/culture/books/the-united-irishman-who-cheated-both-noose-and-guillotine-1.2343305 [accessed 28 October 2018].

4 Quoted in Robert Spears, *Record of Unitarian Worthies* (London, E.T. Whitefield, 1876), p.48.

5 Catriona Kennedy, '"Womanish epistles?" Martha McTier, female epistolarity and late eighteenth-century Irish radicalism', *Women's History Review*, 13.4 (2004).

6 Jenny Uglow, *In These Times: Living in Britain Through Napoleon's Wars 1793–1813* (London, Faber and Faber, 2014), p.230.

7 Jonathan Jeffrey Wright, *The 'Natural Leaders' and their World: Politics, Culture and Society in Belfast c.1801–1832* (Liverpool, Liverpool University Press, 2012), pp.204–14.

8 Brigitte Anton, 'Northern voices: Ulsterwomen in the Young Ireland Movement', in *Coming into the Light*, Janice Holmes and Diane Urquhart (Belfast, Institute of Irish Studies, 1994), pp.66–92.

9 Ibid., p.71. I have been unable to find further information about this intriguing venture.

10 Ibid., pp.70–71.

11 *Loughorne Times*, 3 September 2010, reproducing unidentified press article [now offline].

12 A.S. Peake, revised by R.K. Webb, 'Drummond, James, 1835–1918)', *Oxford Dictionary of National Biography* [accessed 28 October 2018].

13 Rory Delany, 'One memorial plaque', *Oscail* magazine, April 2006, http://oscailtmagazine.com/Unitarian%20Magazine/06April.html [accessed 24 October 2018].

14 Jim Cooke, 'Ireland's Premier Coachbuilder: The Story of the Coachbuilding Firm of John Hutton & Sons Dublin' (Dublin, n. pub, n.d.), p.31.

15 Kate Newman, 'Mary A. Hutton (1862–1953)', *Dictionary of Ulster Biography* www.newulsterbiography. co.uk [accessed 28 October 2018].

16 D.A J. Macpherson, *Women and the Irish Nation: Gender, Culture and Irish Identity, 1890–1914* (Basingstoke, Palgrave Macmillan, 2012), pp. 91, 104.

17 Diarmaid O Doibhlin, 'Womenfolk of the Glens of Antrim and the Irish language', in *Feis Na Ngleann: a Century of Gaelic Culture in the Antrim Glens*, by Eamon Phoenix (Belfast, Ulster Historical Foundation, 2005).

18 Flann Campbell, *The Dissenting Voice: Protestant Democracy in Ulster from Plantation to Partition* (Belfast, The Blackstaff Press, 1991), pp.365, 369.

19 She was not the only Northern Irish Unitarian to take this step. George Hare Patterson, lay preacher and then Missionary in charge of the Domestic Mission in Belfast in 1896, also converted ('George Hare Patterson' in 'Catholic Converts and Conversion' by Dave Armstrong (n.p., Lulu Press, 2013).

20 'Sophia Rosamond Praeger HRHA', *Mapping the Practice and Profession of Sculpture in Britain and Ireland 1851–1951*, University of Glasgow History of Art and HATII, online database 2011 http://sculpture.gla.ac.uk/view/person. php?id=msib3_1204633850 [accessed 07 October 2018].

21 Joseph McBinn, 'A populous solitude: the life and art of Sophia Rosamond Praeger, 1867–1954', *Women's History Review*, 18.4 (2009), pp.577–96 and 580–82.

22 Kate Newman, 'Sophia Rosamond Praeger (1867–1954): Sculptor', *Dictionary of Ulster Biography*, www. newulsterbiography.co.uk [accessed 31 January 2017].

23 John Hewitt, 'Painting and sculpture in Ulster', in *Ancestral Voices: The Selected Prose of John Hewitt*, ed. by Tom Clyde (Belfast, The Blackstaff Press, 1987), p.105 (originally published 1951).

24 McBinn, op.cit., p.580.

25 *The Inquirer*, No. 4161 (1 April 1922), p.197; and No. 4243 (18 June 1927), p.394.

26 *Mapping the Practice and Profession of Sculpture in Britain and Ireland 1851–1951* (see note 20).

27 Kate Newman, op.cit. Andrews, a non-subscribing Presbyterian, was Managing Director of the Harland and Wolff Shipyard, and was lost in the sinking of the Titanic.

28 *Non-Subscribing Presbyterian*, No 1316 (November 2016), pp.14–15.

29 Catherine Morris, 'Alice Milligan: republican tableaux and the Revival', *Field Day Review*, 6 (2010), pp.133–65 (p.151). *Tableaux vivants* were a hybrid of theatre and pictorial art also known as 'living pictures' and '*poses plastiques*', representing scenes from Irish life and history.

30 Roger Blaney, 'The Praeger family of Holywood', *Familia 1999: Ulster Genealogical Review*, 15, pp.91–100.

31 McBinn, op.cit., pp.580–87.

32 'Rosamond Praeger: the artist who loved children', in 'People in our Congregations' (*The Non-Subscribing Presbyterian Church of Ireland*, 2000), pp.6–9.

33 Andrew M. Hill, 'Too soon forgotten: Sydney Herbert Mellone 1869–1956', in *Unitarian to the Core: Unitarian College Manchester, 1854–2004*, ed. by Len Smith (Lancaster, Carnegie Publishing, 2004), p.106.

34 Diane Urquhart, 'An articulate and definite cry for political freedom: the Ulster suffrage movement', *Women's History Review*,11:2 (2002), pp.273–92.

35 David Steers, 'The Non-Subscribing Presbyterian Church in the 20th century, Part Five', *Non-Subscribing Presbyterian* (no. 1252, March 2011), pp. 4–6.

36 Quoted in Courtney, op.cit., p.293.

37 Diane Urquhart, op.cit., p.278.

38 In 'Votes for Women' (19 September 1913), quoted in 'Newry and Mourne in the First World War: an education resource', www.bagenalscastle.com/documents/Key%20Stage%203%20education%20resource.pdf [accessed 14 October 2018].

39 Mary Cullen, 'A history of her own', *Irish Times* (17 October 2012) www.irishtimes.com/culture/heritage/century/century-women-and-the-vote/a-history-of-her-story-1.553415 [accessed 11 October 2018].

40 Speech by Lyn Carvill on International Women's Day 2016, 'Women Reclaim 1916 Agenda'.

41 Senia Paseta, 'New issues and old: women and politics in Ireland, 1914–1918', *Women's History Review*, 27:3 (2018), pp.432–49. See also Senia Paseta, 'Women and war in Ireland, 1914–18' in *History Ireland* (July/August 2014), Vol. 22, www.historyireland.com/volume-22/women-war-ireland-1914-18/ [accessed 14 October 2018].

42 Roy Johnson, 'The "TABI" Conference, 1926', www.rjtechne.org/century130703/1920s/tabi26.htm [accessed 17 October 2018).

43 *Inquirer* No. 4435 (2 July 1927).

44 Susan McGann, 'Huxley, Margaret Rachel (1854–1940), nurse and promoter of nurse training', *Oxford Dictionary of National Biography* [accessed 28 October 2018].

45 Rory Delany, 'Memorials to a great woman', *Oscailt*, December 2008, www.oscailtmagazine.com/unitarian%20magazine/Great%20Woman.html [accessed 24 February 2017].

46 Ibid.

47 Patricia Murphy, 'The forgotten heroines of the Easter Rising', *Irish Times*, 28 January 2016, www.irishtimes.com/culture/books/the-forgotten-heroines-of-the-easter-rising-1.2513777 [accessed 24 February 2017).

48 'Margaret Huxley honoured', *Inquirer* No. 4489 (14 July 1928), p.363.

49 Dublin Unitarians, *The Dublin Unitarian Church Building* (Dublin, 2013).

50 Patrick Buckland (ed.), *Irish Unionism* (Belfast; Northern Ireland Public Record Office, 1973) documents his activities in opposing Irish Home Rule.

51 Trevor Parkhill, '"Their sister in both senses", The memoirs of Emma Duffin, VAD nurse in the First World War', *Faith and Freedom*, 67.1 (2014), pp.20–34; Laura Kelly, 'The healers', review of *The First World War Diaries of Emma Duffin: Belfast Voluntary Aid Detachment Nurse* by Trevor Parkhill, *Irish Literary Supplement*, 35.2 (2016), p.19.

52 Trevor Parkhill, 'Emma Duffin (1883–1979)', *Dictionary of Ulster Biography* www.newulsterbiography.co.uk [accessed 21 October 2018].

53 Ibid.

54 Denis P. Barritt and Charles F. Carter, *The Northern Ireland Problem*, 2nd edn (London, Oxford University Press, 1972), pp.117–19.

55 Obituary, *Inquirer*, no. 6574 (6 July 1968), p. 3.

56 Gillian McClelland, *Pioneering Women: Riddel Hall and Queen's University Belfast* (Belfast, Ulster Historical Foundation, 2005), p.13.

57 Ibid., p. 100.

58 Parkhill, op.cit., note 8; and Billy Mills, *Ruth Duffin Irish Woman Poet* (2016) https://ellipticalmovements.wordpress.com/2016/05/22/ruth-duffin-irish-woman-poet/ [accessed 21 October 2018).

59 Obituary, *Inquirer*.

60 McClelland, op.cit., p.79.

61 Ibid., pp.26–36.

62 Ibid., pp.25–26.

63 Ibid., pp. 96 and 173.

64 Richard Froggart, 'Eliza Riddel (1831–1924): Philanthropist', *Dictionary of Ulster Biography* www.newulsterbiography.co.uk [accessed 21 October 2018].

65 'Two generous and caring ladies' in 'People in Our Congregations' (n.p., *The Non-Subscribing Presbyterian Church of Ireland*, 2000), pp.6–9.

66 H. Jefferson, *Viscount Pirrie of Belfast* (Belfast, William Mullan & Sons, n.d.).

67 Patricia Jalland, 'Irish home-rule finance: a neglected dimension of the Irish Question, 1910–14' in *Reactions to Irish Nationalism, 1865–1914*, ed. by Alan O. Day (London, The Hambledon Press, 1987), pp.298–304.

68 Jefferson, op.cit., p.85.

69 Ibid., p.91.

70 'Margaret Montgomery Carlisle (1857–1935): philanthropist' in *Celebrating Belfast Women: A City Guide through Women's Eyes* (Belfast, Women's Resource and Development Agency, 2011).

71 Jefferson, op.cit., pp.85–6.

72 Obituary, *Inquirer*, no. 4852 (29 June 1935), p.321.

73 Courtney, op.cit., pp.348–9.

74 Ibid., pp.324–5.

75 David Bleakley, *Faulkner: Conflict and Consent in Irish Politics* (London and Oxford, Mowbrays, 1974), p.37.

76 Aaron Edwards, *A History of the Northern Ireland Labour Party* (Manchester, Manchester University Press, 2009), p.59.

77 Courtney, op.cit., p.349.

References

1 Manuscripts and unpublished works

Barr, Margaret (1931) 'The Social Consequences of the Feminist Movement', typescript notes, MS MOSA 1, Harris Manchester College Oxford.

Beard, Annie, Manchester High School for Girls, record for Annie Beard, 1879–1886, archives of Manchester High School for Girls.

British and Foreign Unitarian Association, Register of Members, from 1915; bound volume maintained by the Secretary of the B&FUA at Essex Hall, London.

Brockdish Parish Registers, Norfolk Record Office.

Doughty, John (1837) Last Will and Testament, proved 5 April 1837, Public Record Office (PROB 11/1/1876).

Fox, George (1910) 'Sketch of my Ministry at Mossley from March 8th 1857 till December 7th 1865 (1910)', in the Unitarian College Collection, John Rylands University Library, Manchester.

Herford family trees and related material, in the Herford MSS, Harris Manchester College Oxford.

Hill, Andrew (2005) 'The American Invader or what Dorothea Lynde Dix did for Scotland', sermon preached at St Mark's Church, Edinburgh, on 31 July.

Hyde Chapel archives (1905) Presentation Album to Rev Enfield Dowson.

London Borough of Hackney Archives Department, New Gravel Pit Chapel D/E/237 GRA Financial Records 1742–1889, Sunday School accounts 1790–1811.

Manchester College, Oxford (1902) Annual Reports for 1892–3, Harris Manchester College.

Mellone, Dora (2016) Speech by Lyn Carvill on International Women's Day 2016, 'Women Reclaim 1916 Agenda'.

Peart, Ann (2006) 'Forgotten Prophets: The Lives of Unitarian Women 1760-1904' unpublished doctoral thesis, University of Newcastle, 2006 https://theses.ncl.ac.uk/dspace/bitstream/10443/245/1/peart05.pdf .

Peart, Ann (2010) 'Links Through Time and Space: Connections between British and Transylvanian Women of the Past Hundred Years', unpublished presentation at the centenary meeting of the Transylvanian Unitarian Women's League, Kolozsvar, October 2010.

von Petzold, Gertrude (1897) Reference from St Andrews University, illegible signature, 26 September 1897, HMCO MS MNC. MISC. 12/iii. Harris Manchester College Oxford.

von Petzold Gertrude, report, HMCO MS MNC MISC. 85, appendix 3, Harris Manchester College Oxford.

Reed, Cliff (1996) 'The Continuing Mission: The Story of Bedfield Unitarian Chapel, Suffolk', an address given at the Centenary Service, 17 November 1996, unpublished.

Tarrant, Dorothy (1967) 'Recollections' talk, given to the London Unitarian Club, copy in Ruston MS at Dr Williams's Library.

Unitarian Church, Stockport, 'Minutes of the Ladies' Auxiliary Society (1883–1892)', Unitarian College Collection, John Rylands Library, Manchester.

Woodhouse, Annie Beard, Beard Family Papers, Unitarian College Collection, John Rylands Library, Manchester.

2 *Published works*

Aikin, Lucy (1810) *Epistles on Women, Exemplifying Their Character and Conditions in Various Ages and Nations*, London: Joseph Johnson.

Alcott, Louisa May (1872) *Shawl Straps*, Boston USA: Roberts Bros.

Allen, Bernard (1948) *Down the Stream of Life*, London: Lindsey Press.

Allen (Mrs Bernard) (Rose) (n.d., c. 1936) *Helen Brooke Herford and the Women's League*, London: British League of Unitarian and Other Christian Women.

Alliance of Unitarian Women, 'Unitarian Universalist Women's Federation', www.uuwf.org/who-we-are (accessed 27 November 2018).

Anonymous (1908) *Souvenir of Bi-Centenary Hyde Chapel*, Hyde: Cartwright and Rattray.

Anton, Brigitte (1994) 'Northern voices: Ulsterwomen in the Young Ireland Movement', in Janice Holmes and Diane Urquhart (eds), *Coming into the Light*, Belfast: Institute of Irish Studies, 66–92.

Armstrong, Dave (2013) *Catholic Converts and Conversion*, n.p.: Lulu Press.

Banks, Olive (1985) *The Biographical Dictionary of British Feminists Volume One 1800–1930*, Brighton: Wheatsheaf Books.

Barbauld, Anna Laetitia (1826) *The Works of Anna Laetitia Barbauld with a Memoir by Lucy Aikin*, 2 vols. London: Longman, Hurst Rees, Orme, Brown and Green.

Barr, Margaret (1937) *The Great Unity*, London: Lindsey Press.

Barr, A. Margaret (1970) 'How I Became a Unitarian', in Y. Surrendra Paul (ed.) *Margaret Barr: A Universal Soul*, Udaipur, India: Unitarian Inter-faith Fellowship of India (1975).

Barr, Margaret (ed. Roy Smith) (1974) *A Dream Come True: The Story of Kharang*, London: Lindsey Press.

Barritt Denis P. and Charles F. Carter (1972) *The Northern Ireland Problem*, 2nd edn, London: Oxford University Press.

Bartle, George (1994) *An Old Radical and his Brood, Sir John Bowring and his Family*, London: Janus.

Bedford, Jane (1998) 'Margaret Ashton: Manchester's "First Lady"', *Manchester Regional History Review* 12 (4): 3–17.

Begley, Anthony (2006) 'Helen Allingham, the artist, and her Ballyshannon connections', *Annual Journal of the County Donegal Historical Society* 58.

Bernet, Claus (2007) 'Gertrude von Petzold (1876–1952): Quaker and first woman minister', *Quaker Studies* 12 (1): 129–33.

Billington, Louis and Rosamund Billington (1987) ' " A burning zeal for righteousness": women in the British anti-slavery movement, 1820–1860', in Jane Rendall (ed.) *Equal or Different: Women's Politics 1800–1914*, Oxford: Basil Blackwell.

Blain, Virginia (2004) 'Adams, Sarah Flower', *Oxford Dictionary of National Biography*, www.oxforddnb.com (accessed 9 August 2018).

Blaney, Roger (1999) 'The Praeger family of Holywood', *Familia 1999: Ulster Genealogical Review* 15: 91–100.

Bleakley, David (1974) *Faulkner: Conflict and Consent in Irish Politics*, London and Oxford: Mowbrays.

Bolam, C. G., J. Goring, H.L. Short, and R. Thomas (1968) *The English Presbyterians: From Elizabethan Puritanism to Modern Unitarianism*, London: George Allen & Unwin.

Boyle, R.D. and T. Boyle (2001) *A Century Scored: Cavendish School, A History of the Early Years 1902–1945*, privately printed.

Le Breton, Anna Letitia (ed.) (1894) *Correspondence of William Ellery Channing, D.D. and Lucy Aikin, from 1826 to 1842*, London: Williams and Norgate.

Le Breton, Philip Hemery (1864) 'Memoir of Miss Aikin', in Philip Hemery le Breton (ed.) *Memoirs, Miscellanies and Letters of the Late Lucy Aikin*, London: Longman, Green, Longman, Roberts & Green.

Broadrick, A.A. (1908) 'Message from Mrs Broadrick', *The Christian Life* 293.

Brooks, Marilyn L. (1995) 'Mary Hays: finding a "voice" in dissent', *Enlightenment and Dissent* 14: 3-24.

Brooks, Marilyn L. (ed.) (2000) *Memoirs of Emma Courtney* by Mary Hays, Ontario: Broadview Press.

Brooks, Marilyn L. (2009) 'Mary Hays', in *Oxford Dictionary of National Biography*, www.oxforddnb.com (accessed June 2018).

Buckland, Patrick (ed.) (1973) *Irish Unionism*, Belfast: Northern Ireland Public Record Office.

Burns, Mary (2004) 'Rosalind Lee', in Judy Hague (ed.) (2008).

Camden New Journal (2016) 'Watercolour pioneer, Helen Allingham', 16 June.

Campbell, Flann (1991) *The Dissenting Voice: Protestant Democracy in Ulster from Plantation to Partition*, Belfast: The Blackstaff Press.

Cappe, Catharine (1812) 'Memoir of Mrs. Lindsey', *Monthly Repository* 7: 109–18.

Cappe, Catharine (1822) *Memoirs of the Life of the Late Mrs. Catharine Cappe Written by Herself*, London: Longman, Hurst, Rees, Orme and Brown.

Carpenter, J. Estlin (1879) *The Life and Work of Mary Carpenter*, London: Macmillan.

Carpenter, Mary (1847) *Morning and Evening Meditations for Every Day in a Month*, Boston (USA): Wm. Crosby and H.P. Nichols.

Chambers, Liam (2004) 'Rowan, Archibald Hamilton', in *Oxford Dictionary of National Biography*, www.oxforddnb.com (accessed 28 October 2018).

Chapple, J.A.V. and Arthur Pollard (eds) (1997) *The Letters of Mrs Gaskell*, Manchester: Mandolin.

Chapple, John and Alan Shelston (eds) (2000) *Further Letters of Mrs Gaskell*, Manchester: Manchester University Press.

Chapple, J.A.V. and Anita Wilson (eds) 1996) *Private Voices: The Diaries of Elizabeth Gaskell and Sophia Holland*, Keele: Keele University Press.

The Christian Life, June 6 1908, p. 299.

Church of England Database Person ID 118631, 'Jeremiah Harrison'.

Collingwood, Judy (2004) 'Rye, Maria Susan', in *Oxford Dictionary of National Biography*, www.oxforddnb.com (accessed 28 October 2018).

Cooke, Jim (n.d.) 'Ireland's Premier Coachbuilder: The Story of the Coachbuilding Firm of John Hutton & Sons Dublin', Dublin: n. pub.

Courtney, Roger (2013) *Dissenting Voices: Rediscovering the Irish Progressive Presbyterian Tradition*, Belfast: Ulster Historical Foundation.

Crawford, Elizabeth (2001) *The Women's Suffrage Movement: A Reference Guide 1866–1928*, London: Routledge.

Crawford, Elizabeth (2006) *The Women's Suffrage Movement in Britain and Ireland: A Regional Survey*, Abingdon: Routledge.

Croft, Joy (ed.) (1984) *Growing Together: The Report of the Unitarian Working Party on Feminist Theology*, London: General Assembly of Unitarian and Free Christian Churches.

Cullen, Mary (2012) 'A history of her own', *Irish Times* (17 October) www.irishtimes.com/culture/heritage/century/century-women-and-the-vote/a-history-of-her-story-1.553415 (accessed 11 October 2018).

Davidoff, Leonore and Catherine Hall (1987) *Family Fortunes. Men and Women of the English Middle Class 1780–1850*, London: Routledge.

Davies, D. Elwyn (1980) *Y Smotiau Duon: Braslun o Hanes y Traddodiad Rhyddfrydol ac Undodiaeth*, Llandysul: Gwasg Gomer; published in English as D. Elwyn Davies, *'They Thought For Themselves': A Brief Look at the History of Unitarianism in Wales and the Tradition of Liberal Religion*, Llandysul: Gwasg Gomer (1982).

Davies, D. Elwyn (1999) *Cewri'r Ffydd: Bywgraffiadur y Mudiad Undodaidd yng Nghymru* (Giants of the Faith: A Biography of the Unitarian Movement in Wales), Llandysul: Gwasg Gomer.

Davis, V.D. (1932) *A History of Manchester College from its Foundation in Manchester to its Establishment in Oxford*, London: George Allen & Unwin.

Delany, Rory (2006) 'One memorial plaque', *Oscail* magazine, April http://oscailtmagazine.com/Unitarian%20Magazine/06April.html (accessed 24 October 2018).

Delany, Rory (2008) 'Memorials to a great woman', *Oscailt*, December, www.oscailtmagazine.com/unitarian%20magazine/Great%20Woman.html (accessed 24 February 2017).

Dennis, Barbara (2004) 'Swanwick, Anna', in *Oxford Dictionary of National Biography*, www.oxforddnb.com.

The Dictionary of Welsh Biography (Aberystwyth: The National Library of Wales, 2007) at http://yba.llgc.org.uk/en/index.html (accessed 24 September 2018).

Dingsdale, Ann, 'Kensington Society', *Oxford Dictionary of National Biography*, www.oxforddnb.com (accessed 9 August 2018).

Ditchfield, G.M. (ed.) (2007, 2012) *The Letters of Theophilus Lindsey (1723–1808)* 1.1747–1778; 2. 1789–1808, Woodbridge: The Boydell Press.

Ditchfield, G.M. (2010) 'Hannah Lindsey and her circle: the female element in early English Unitarianism', *Enlightenment and Dissent* 26: 54–79.

Doibhlin, Diarmaid O. (2005) 'Womenfolk of the Glens of Antrim and the Irish language', in Eamon Phoenix, *Feis Na Ngleann: A Century of Gaelic Culture in the Antrim Glens*, Belfast: Ulster Historical Foundation.

Dublin Unitarians (2013) *The Dublin Unitarian Church Building*, Dublin.

Edwards, Aaron (2009) *A History of the Northern Ireland Labour Party*, Manchester: Manchester University Press.

Elferdink, Claudia (2014) 'Margaret Brackenbury Crook', *Dictionary of Unitarian and Universalist Biography*, http://uudb.org/ (accessed 1 December 2018).

Englishwoman's Review, January 1869, pp.148–50; July 1870, pp.226–7.

Englishwoman's Review, April 1870, pp.102–7.

English Woman's Journal (1858–1864), Nineteenth Century Serials Edition (NCSE), www.ncse.ac.uk/headnotes/ewj. html (accessed 2 October 2018).

Froggart, Richard, 'Eliza Riddel (1831–1924): Philanthropist', *Dictionary of Ulster Biography*, www.newulsterbiography.co.uk (accessed 21 October 2018).

General Assembly of Unitarian and Free Christian Churches (1971–2) *Directory*.

Gilley, Keith (1984) 'Women and the Unitarian ministry', in Joy Croft (ed.) (1984).

Gilley, Keith (1997) 'Gertrude von Petzold – the pioneer woman minister', *Transactions of the Unitarian Historical Society* 21 (3): 157–72.

Gilley, Keith (2004) 'Worship Material To Mark The Centenary Of The Induction Of Gertrude von Petzold As England's First Woman Minister', London: Worship Panel of the General Assembly of Unitarian & Free Christian Churches.

Gladstone, Florence M. (1922) *Aubrey House, Kensington 1698–1920*, London: A.L. Humphreys.

Gleadle, Kathryn (1995) *The Early Feminists. Radical Unitarians and the Emergence of the Women's Rights Movement, 1831–51*, London: Martin's Press.

Gleadle, Kathryn (2001) *British Women in the Nineteenth Century*, Basingstoke: Palgrave.

Gleadle, Kathryn (2004) 'Flower, Eliza', in *Oxford Dictionary of National Biography*, www.oxforddnb.com (accessed 8 August 2018).

Gordon, Alexander, revised by R,K.Webb (2004) 'Yates, James', in *Oxford Dictionary of National Biography*, www.oxforddnb. com (accessed 6 November 2018).

Gordon, Lyndall (2005) *Mary Wollstonecraft: A New Genus*, London: Little, Brown.

Hague, Judy (ed.) (2008) *A Century of the Unitarian Women's League 1908–2008*, Sheffield: British League of Unitarian and Free Christian Women.

Hague, Judy and Graham Hague (1986) *The Unitarian Heritage: An Architectural Survey of Chapels and Churches in the Unitarian Tradition in the British Isles*, Sheffield: privately published.

Haight, G.S. (1954–5, 1978) *The Letters of George Eliot*, 9 vols., New Haven Connecticut: Yale University Press.

Hamilton, Susan (ed.) (1995) *'Criminals, Idiots, Women and Minors': Victorian Writing by Women on Women*, Peterborough, Canada: Broadview Press.

Handley, Graham (2005) *An Elizabeth Gaskell Chronology*, Basingstoke: Palgrave Macmillan.

Hardwick, Lorna (2004) 'Tarrant, Dorothy', in *Oxford Dictionary of National Biography*, www.oxforddnb.com.

Harris, C. (1927) *The Use of Leisure in Bethnal Green*, London: Lindsey Press.

Hayek, F.A. (ed.) (1951) *John Stuart Mill and Harriet Taylor: Their Correspondence and Subsequent Marriage*, London: Routledge and Kegan Paul.

Hewitt, John (ed. Tom Clyde) (1987) 'Painting and sculpture in Ulster', in *Ancestral Voices: The Selected Prose of John Hewitt*, Belfast: The Blackstaff Press (originally published 1951).

Hill, Andrew M. (1988) 'Channing and British Unitarianism: sowing the seeds', *Transactions of the Unitarian Historical Society* 19 (2): 71–7.

Hill, Andrew M. (2004) 'Too soon forgotten: Sydney Herbert Mellone 1869–1956', in Leonard Smith (ed.) *Unitarian to the Core: Unitarian College Manchester, 1854–2004*, Lancaster: Carnegie Publishing.

Hill, Andrew M. (2013) 'Newcome Cappe at York', *Transactions of the Unitarian Historical Society* 25: 3: 151–76.

Hill, Andrew M. (forthcoming) 'A pattern of York feminism: Catharine Cappe as spinster, wife and widow', *Transactions of the Unitarian Historical Society*.

Hill, Florence (1908) 'Central Postal Mission and Unitarian Workers' Union', *The Christian Life*, June 6: 299.

Hill, Florence (1913) 'The Unitarian Postal Mission', *The Christian Life*, May 10: 233.

Hirsch, Pam (1998) *Barbara Leigh Smith Bodichon: Feminist, Artist and Rebel*, London: Chatto & Windus.

Hirsch, Pam (2007) 'Bodichon, Barbara Leigh Smith', *Oxford Dictionary of National Biography*, www.oxforddnb.com (accessed 9 August 2018).

Hitchings, Caroline, F. (1985) *Universalist and Unitarian Women Ministers*, Boston, USA: Unitarian Universalist Historical Society.

Hodges, Peter (ed.) (2017) *Kinver Edge and the Rock Houses: Centenary Guide 2017*, National Trust.

Hoecker-Drysdale, Susan (2002) 'HM and the rise of sociology', in *A Harriet Martineau Miscellany*, The Martineau Society.

Holt, Raymond (1938) *The Unitarian Contribution to Social Progress in England*, London: Lindsey Press.

Hunter, Fred (2005) 'Meteyard, Eliza', *Oxford Dictionary of National Biography*, www.oxforddnb.com (accessed 10 October 2018).

The Inquirer (1842), p. 15 ('Marriages').

The Inquirer (1874) 'Notting Hill Free Public Library' (3 October): 649–50.

The Inquirer (1915) 'Hospitals for the Belgian wounded' (9 January): 17 and 20.

The Inquirer (1917) 'Opening of Lawrence House' (9 June): 272–3.

The Inquirer (1928) 'Margaret Huxley honoured', 4489 (14 July): 363.

Jalland, Patricia (1987) 'Irish home-rule finance: a neglected dimension of the Irish Question, 1910–14' in Alan O. Day (ed.) *Reactions to Irish Nationalism, 1865–1914*, London: The Hambledon Press.

James, Felicity (2012) 'Lucy Aikin and the legacies of dissent' in James and Inkster (eds) (2012).

James, Felicity, and Ian Inkster (eds.) (2012) *Religious Dissent and the Aikin–Barbauld Circle, 1740–1860*, Cambridge: Cambridge University Press. Also at *Dissenting Academies Online*.

Jefferson, H. (n.d.) *Viscount Pirrie of Belfast*, Belfast: William Mullan & Sons.

Jenkins, David (1959) 'Puddicombe, Anne Adalisa ("Allen Raine"; 1836–1908)', *The Dictionary of Welsh Biography*, http://yba. llgc.org.uk/en/s-PUDD-ADA-1836.html (accessed 28 September 2018).

Jenkins, Geraint H., Ffion Mair Jones, and David Ceri Jones (eds) (2007) *The Correspondence of Iolo Morganwg*, Vol. 3, 1810–1826, Cardiff: University of Wales Press.

Jenkins, Robert Thomas (1959) 'Lewis, Sir William Thomas', *The Dictionary of Welsh Biography*, http://yba.llgc.org.uk/ en/s-LEWI-THO-1837.html (accessed 28 September 2018).

John, Angela V. (ed.) (1991) *Our Mothers' Land: Chapters in Welsh Women's History, 1830–1939*, Cardiff: University of Wales Press.

Johnson, Roy 'The "TABI" Conference, 1926', www.rjtechne. org/century130703/1920s/tabi26.htm (accessed 17 October 2018).

Jones, J. Eric (ed.) (2011) *Highland Place Unitarian Church: A Story of Resilience*, Aberdare: Highland Place Unitarian Church.

Jones, Mollie (2004) 'Rosalind Lee', in Judy Hague (ed.) (2008).

Keach, William (1998) 'Barbauld, romanticism and the survival of dissent' in Anne Janowitz (ed.) *Romanticism and Gender*, Cambridge: D.S. Brewer.

Kell, E. (1844) 'Memoir of Mary Hays: with some unpublished letters addressed to her by Robert Robinson, of Cambridge, and others', *Christian Reformer* 129: 813–14.

Kelly, Laura (2016) 'The healers', review of *The First World War Diaries of Emma Duffin: Belfast Voluntary Aid Detachment Nurse* by Trevor Parkhill, *Irish Literary Supplement* 35 (2): 19.

Kennedy, Catriona (2004) '"Womanish epistles?" Martha McTier, female epistolarity and late eighteenth-century Irish radicalism', *Women's History Review* 13 (4).

Kielty, John (ed.) (1954) *Year Book of the General Assembly*, London: Unitarian and Free Christian Churches.

Knight, S.H.K. (1973) Obituary for Dorothy Tarrant, *The Inquirer*, 29 September.

Lacey, Candida Ann (ed.) (1987) *Barbara Leigh Smith and the Langham Place Group*, London: Routledge & Kegan Paul.

Laurie, Winifred (1975) 'Annie Margaret Barr' in Y. Surrendra Paul (ed.) *Margaret Barr: A Universal Soul*, Udaipur, India: Unitarian Inter-faith Fellowship of India (1975).

Lee, Rosalind (1939) 'Refugees in Central Europe', in Judy Hague (ed.) (2008).

Levy, Michelle (2012) '"The different genius of woman": Lucy Aikin's historiography' in James and Inkster (eds.) (2012).

Lewis, Tom (1947) *The History of the Hen Dŷ Cwrdd, Cefn Coed y Cymmer*, Llandysul: J. D. Lewis & Sons, Gomerian Press.

Long, Arthur (1984) 'Unitarian women ministers', in Joy Croft (ed.) (1984).

McBinn, Joseph (2009) 'A populous solitude: the life and art of Sophia Rosamond Praeger, 1867–1954', *Women's History Review* 18 (4): 577–96, 580–82.

McCarthy, William (2008) *Anna Letitia Barbauld: Voice of the Enlightenment*, Baltimore: John Hopkins University Press.

McCarthy, William and Elizabeth Kraft (eds) (1994) *The Poems of Anna Letitia Barbauld*, Athens USA and London: University of Georgia Press.

McClelland, Gillian (2005) *Pioneering Women: Riddel Hall and Queen's University Belfast*, Belfast: Ulster Historical Foundation.

McGann, Susan (2004) 'Huxley, Margaret Rachel (1854–1940), nurse and promoter of nurse training', *Oxford Dictionary of National*, www.oxforddnb.com (accessed 28 October 2018).

McLachlan, H. (1939) 'Annie Beard Woodhouse' (obituary), *The Inquirer*: 554.

McLachlan, H. John (1973) 'Margaret Barr – a vision and a hope', *The Inquirer*, 1 September: 1–3.

McLachlan, John (1991) *The Wine of Life: A Testament of Vital Encounter*, Sheffield: John McLachlan.

Macpherson, D.A.J. (2012) *Women and the Irish Nation: Gender, Culture and Irish Identity, 1890–1914*, Basingstoke: Palgrave Macmillan.

Malleson, W.T. (1908) 'Clementia Taylor' (obituary), *Englishwoman's Review*, 15 July.

The Manchester Guardian, 'Death of Mrs Gaskell', 14 November 1865.

Manton, Jo (1976) *Mary Carpenter and the Children of the Streets*, London: Heinemann.

'Margaret Montgomery Carlisle (1857–1935): philanthropist' in *Celebrating Belfast Women: A City Guide through Women's Eyes* Belfast: Women's Resource and Development Agency.

Martineau, Harriet (1838, 1962) *Society in America*, ed. Seymour Martin Lipset, New York: Anchor Books, Doubleday.

Martineau, Harriet (1877, 1983) *Autobiography* (originally published 1877), London: Virago.

Mellone, Dora (1913) 'Votes for Women' (19 September 1913), quoted in 'Newry and Mourne in the First World War: an education resource', www.bagenalscastle.com/documents/Key%20Stage%203%20education%20resource.pdf (accessed 14 October 2018).

Middleton, Thomas (1908) *A History of Hyde Chapel*, Manchester: Cartwright and Rattray.

Middleton, Thomas (1932) *The History of Hyde and Its Neighbourhood*, Hyde: Higham Press.

Midgley, Clare (1992) *Women Against Slavery: The British Campaigns 1780–1870*, London: Routledge.

Miles, Alfred H. (1905) 'Critical and biographical essay; Sarah Flower Adams (1805–1848)' in *The Sacred Poets of the Nineteenth Century*, www.bartleby. com/294/124.html (accessed 15 October 2018).

Mills, Billy (2016) *Ruth Duffin Irish Woman Poet*, https://ellipticalmovements. wordpress.com/2016/05/22/ruth-duffin-irish-woman-poet/ (accessed 21 October 2018).

Mitchell, Marjory G. (1958) *History of the British League of Unitarian and Other Christian Women*, London: British League of Unitarian and Other Christian Women.

Mitchell, Sally (2004) *Frances Power Cobbe: Victorian Feminist, Journalist, Reformer*, Charlottesville and London: University of Virginia Press.

Morris, Catherine (2010) 'Alice Milligan: republican tableaux and the Revival', *Field Day Review* 6: 133–65.

Murphy, Patricia (2016) 'The forgotten heroines of the Easter Rising', *Irish Times*, 28 January, www.irishtimes.com/culture/books/the-forgotten-heroines-of-the-easter-rising-1.2513777 (accessed 24 February 2017).

Murray, Janet (1982) *Strong-Minded Women and Other Lost Voices from Nineteenth Century England*, New York: Pantheon.

Newman, Kate, 'Mary A. Hutton (1862–1953)', *Dictionary of Ulster Biography*, www. newulsterbiography.co.uk (accessed 28 October 2018).

Newman, Kate, 'Sophia Rosamond Praeger (1867–1954): Sculptor', *Dictionary of Ulster Biography*, www. newulsterbiography.co.uk (accessed 31 January 2017).

Northcroft, D.M. (1929) *Women Free Church Ministers*, London: Edgar G. Dunstan & Co.

O'Brien, Padraig (1989) *Warrington Academy 1757–86, Its Predecessors and Successors*, Wigan: Owl Books.

Page, Anthony (1998) 'The Enlightenment and a second reformation: the religion and philosophy of John Jebb (1736–86)', *Enlightenment and Dissent* 17: 48–82.

Parkhill, Trevor (2014) '"Their sister in both senses": the memoirs of Emma Duffin, VAD nurse in the First World War', *Faith and Freedom* 67 (1): 20–34.

Parkhill, Trevor, 'Emma Duffin (1883–1979)', *Dictionary of Ulster Biography* www. newulsterbiography.co.uk (accessed 21 October 2018).

Pašeta, Senia (2014) 'Women and war in Ireland, 1914–18' in *History Ireland* 22, www.historyireland.com/volume-22/women-war-ireland-1914-18/ (accessed 14 October 2018).

Pašeta, Senia (2018) 'New issues and old: women and politics in Ireland, 1914–1918', *Women's History Review* 27 (3): 432–49.

Peake, A.S., revised by R.K.Webb (2004) 'Drummond, James, 1835–1918)', *Oxford Dictionary of National Biography*, www.oxforddnb.com (accessed 28 October 2018).

Peart, Ann (1999) 'Forgotten prophets: Unitarian women and religion', in George Chryssides (ed.) *Unitarian Perspectives on Contemporary Religious Thought*, London: Lindsey Press.

Peart, Ann (2008) '"Deconsidered by Men": women and the British Unitarian movement before 1904', *Transactions of the Unitarian Historical Society* 24 (2): 61–80.

Peart, Ann (2010) 'Elizabeth Gaskell Worship Pack', London: General Assembly of Unitarian and Free Christian Churches.

Plant, Helen (2003) *Unitarianism, Philanthropy and Feminism in York, 1782–1821: The Career of Catharine Cappe*, York: University of York Borthwick Paper 103.

Poovey, Mary (1989) *Uneven Developments: The Ideological Work of Gender in Mid-Victorian England*, London: Virago.

'Praeger, Rosamond' (1922, 1927), *The Inquirer*, 4161: 197; 4243: 394.

'Praeger, Rosamond' (2016) *Non-Subscribing Presbyterian*, 1316: 14–15.

'Rosamond Praeger: the artist who loved children' (2000), in 'People in Our Congregations', *The Non-Subscribing Presbyterian of Ireland*, pp.6–9.

'Sophia Rosamond Praeger HRHA', *Mapping the Practice and Profession of Sculpture in Britain and Ireland 1851–1951*, University of Glasgow History of Art and HATII, online database 2011 http://sculpture.gla.ac.uk/view/person.php?id=msib3_1204633850 (accessed 07 October 2018).

Prochaska, Frank (2004) 'Carpenter, Mary', in *Oxford Dictionary of National Biography*, www.oxforddnb.com (accessed 4 November 2018).

Radcliffe, S.K. (1955) *The Story of South Place*, London: Watts & Co.

Rees, Louvain (2017) 'A champion of female education and a pioneer on the scholarship front', *Wales Online*, 1 March, www.walesonline.co.uk/lifestyle/nostalgia/champion-female-education-pioneer-scholarship-12628828 (accessed 24 September 2018).

Rees, Thomas (1818) 'Mary Rees Bevan' (obituary), *The Monthly Repository of Theology and General Literature* 13: 143–4.

'Reid, Elisabeth Jesser', *Oxford Dictionary of National Biography*, www.oxforddnb.com (accessed 8 September 2018).

Rendall, Jane (1989) 'Friendship and politics: Barbara Leigh Smith Bodichon (1827–91) and Bessie Rayner Parkes (1829–1925)' in Susan Mendus and Jane Rendall (eds), *Sexuality and Subordination*, London: Routledge.

Rendall, Jane (2005) 'Langham Place Group', *Oxford Dictionary of National Biography*, www.oxforddnb.com (accessed 9 August 2018).

Reynolds, Jaime (2015–6) 'Madame Mayor: the first wave of Liberal women in local government leadership 1918–1939', *Journal of Liberal History* 89: 6–19.

Robson, Ann P. (2004) 'Mill (née Hardy; other married name Taylor), Harriet', *Oxford Dictionary of National Biography*, www.oxforddnb.com (accessed 9 August 2018).

Rodgers, Betsy (1958) *Georgian Chronicle: Mrs Barbauld and her Family*, London: Methuen & Co.

Ronan, Alison (2014) 'A Small Vital Flame'. *Anti-War Women in NW England 1914–1918*, Saarbrucken: Scholar's Press.

Ronan, Alison (2015) *Unpopular Resistance; The Rebel Networks of Men and Women in Opposition to the First World War in Manchester and Salford 1914–1918*, Manchester: North West Labour History Society.

Ronan, Alison (n.d.) 'Hanging the Pacifist' (leaflet).

Ross, Marlon B. (1994) 'Configurations of feminine reform: the woman writer and the tradition of dissent', in Carol Shiner Wilson and Joel Haefner (eds) *Revisioning Romanticism: British Women Writers 1776–1837*, Philadelphia: University of Pennsylvania Press.

Rowe, Mortimer (1959) *The Story of Essex Hall*, London: Lindsey Press.

Rowntree, Ruth (2004) *'Religious Devills' of Hampstead. Individually Respected, Collectively Reviled*, Oxford: Harris Manchester College.

Ruston, Alan (1980) *Unitarianism and Early Presbyterianism in Hackney*, privately published.

Ruston, Alan (2012) 'British Unitarianism in the 20th century: a survey', *Transactions of the Unitarian Historical Society* 25(2): 707–83.

Ruston, Alan *Obituaries of Unitarian Ministers 1900–2004, Index and Synopsis*, Unitarian Historical Society website, www.unitarianhistory.org.uk (accessed 24 November 2018).

Sanders, Valerie (2002) 'James and Harriet: brother and sister', *Transactions of the Unitarian Historical Society* 22 (4): 321–8.

Sargant, Norman C. (1987) *Mary Carpenter in India*, Bristol: A.J. Sargant.

Scott, Dorothy (1980) *The Halfway House to Infidelity: A History of the Melbourne Unitarian Church 1853–1973*, Melbourne, Australia: Unitarian Fellowship of Australia and Melbourne, Unitarian Peace Memorial Church.

Seaburg, Alan (2002),'Caroline Soule', *Dictionary of Unitarian & Universalist Biography* (accessed 24 November 2018).

Seditious Meetings Act 1795, Wikipedia, https://en.wikipedia.org/wiki/Seditious_Meetings_Act_1795 (accessed 31 October 2018).

Shattock, Joan (2014) 'Parkes [married name Belloc], Elizabeth Rayner [Bessie]', *Oxford Dictionary of National Biography*, www.oxforddnb.com (accessed 5 November 2018).

Shelston, Alan (2010) *Brief Lives: Elizabeth Gaskell*, London: Hesperus Press.

Short, L. Baker (1963) *Pioneers of Scottish Unitarianism*, privately printed.

Simon, Lady, of Wythenshawe (1949) *Margaret Ashton and Her Times*, The Margaret Ashton Memorial Lecture for 1948, Manchester: Manchester University Press.

Smith, Leonard (2006) *The Unitarians: A Short History*, Arnside: Lensden Publishing.

Spears, Robert (1876) *Record of Unitarian Worthies*, London: E.T. Whitefield.

Spears, Robert (1906) *Memorable Unitarians*, London: British and Foreign Unitarian Association.

Steers, David (2011) 'The Non-Subscribing Presbyterian Church in the 20th century, Part Five', *Non-Subscribing Presbyterian* 1252: 4–6.

Stephenson, H.W. (1931) *Unitarian Hymn-Writers*, London: Lindsey Press.

Stevenson, Margaret (1959) 'Rosalind Lee', *The Inquirer* 346.

Strachey, Ray (1928, 1978) *The Cause: A Short History of the Women's Movement in Great Britain*, London: Virago.

Tagart, M. Lucy (1903) *The Hungarian and Transylvanian Unitarians*, London: Unitarian Christian Publishing Office.

Tarrant, Dorothy (1950) 'Unitarians and Bedford College', *Transactions of the Unitarian Historical Society* 9 (4): 201–6.

Tarrant, Dorothy (1963) 'What Unitarians Believe', London: General Assembly of Unitarian and Free Christian Churches; unitarian.org.uk/documents.

Taylor, Ina (1990) *Helen Allingham's England*, Caxton Editions, 2000, first published 1990.

Taylor, Ina (2004) 'Allingham, Helen', *Oxford Dictionary of National Biography*, www.oxforddnb.com.

Taylor, Kate (1993) 'Helen Allingham', *National Unitarian Fellowship Newsletter* 286, January/February.

Thomas, Gwyneth (1975) 'Annie Margaret Barr' in Y. Surrendra Paul (ed.), *Margaret Barr: A Universal Soul*, Udaipur, India: Unitarian Inter-faith Fellowship of India.

Thomas, Jack (2004) 'Rosalind Lee', in Judy Hague (ed.) (2008).

Todd, Janet (2000) *Mary Wollstonecraft: A Revolutionary Life*, London: Weidenfeld & Nicolson.

Tolles, E.B. (ed.) (1952) *Slavery and the 'Woman Question'. Lucretia Mott's Diary of her Visit to Great Britain to Attend the World's Anti-Slavery Convention of 1840*, London: Friends' Historical Society.

Tuke, Margaret J. (1939) *A History of Bedford College for Women 1849–1937*, Oxford: Oxford University Press.

'Two generous and caring ladies' (Eliza and Isabella Riddel) in 'People in Our Congregations' n.p., *The Non-Subscribing Presbyterian of Ireland* (2000).

Uglow, Jenny (1993) *Elizabeth Gaskell: A Habit of Stories*, London: Faber and Faber.

Uglow, Jenny (2014) *In These Times: Living in Britain Through Napoleon's Wars 1793–1813*, London: Faber and Faber.

Urquhart, Diane (2002) 'An articulate and definite cry for political freedom: the Ulster suffrage movement', *Women's History Review* 11 (2): 273–92.

Walker, Gina Luria (2014) 'The invention of female biography', *Enlightenment and Dissent* 29: 79–121.

Walker, Gina Luria (2018) *Mary Hays (1759–1843) The Growth of a Woman's Mind*, London: Routledge (first published in 2006 by Ashgate).

Walton, Geri, *English Author Lucy Aikin (Mary Godolphin)*, www.geriwalton.com/english-suthor-lucy-aikin-mary-godolphin (accessed 4 August 2018).

Watts, Ruth (2000) 'Mary Carpenter: educator of the children of the "perishing and dangerous classes"', in Mary Hilton and Pam Hirsch (eds), *Practical Visionaries: Women, Education and Social Progress 1790–1930*, Harlow: Pearson Education.

Watts, **Ruth** (2002) 'Rational religion and feminism: the challenge of Unitarianism in the nineteenth century' in Susan Morgan (ed.) *Women, Religion and Feminism in Britain, 1750–1900,* London: Palgrave MacMillan.

Watts, **Ruth** (2007) *Women in Science; A Social and Political History,* London: Routledge.

Webb, **R.K.** (1960) *Harriet Martineau: A Radical Victorian,* London: Heinemann..

Webb, **R.K.** (1988) 'The Gaskells as Unitarians', in Joanne Shattock (ed.), *Dickens and Other Victorians; Essays in Honour of Philip Collins,* London: Macmillan.

Webb, **R.K.** (2004) 'Martineau, Harriet', *Oxford Dictionary of National Biography,* www.oxforddnb.com (accessed 9 August 2018).

Webb, **R,K.** (2009) 'Fox, William Johnson', *Oxford Dictionary of National Biography,* www.oxforddnb.com (accessed 1 October 2018).

Webb, **R.K.** (2009) 'Smith (Thomas) Southwood', *Oxford Dictionary of National Biography,* www.oxforddnb.com (accessed 4 October 2018).

Welch, **Robert** (2004) 'Allingham, William', *Oxford Dictionary of National Biography,* www.oxforddnb.com.

Wheatley, **Vera** (1957) *The Life and Work of Harriet Martineau,* London: Secker and Warburg.

Whelan, **Fergus** (2015) 'The United Irishman who cheated both noose and guillotine', *Irish Times,* 7 September 2015; www.irishtimes.com/culture/books/the-united-irishman-who-cheated-both-noose-and-guillotine-1.2343305 (accessed 28 October 2018).

Wicker, **Colin H.** (1983) 'Unitarians in Dundee: Williamson Memorial Unitarian Christian Church' (stencils from typescript).

Wikipedia, 'George Allanson-Winn, 1st Baron Headley, https://en.wikipedia.org/wiki/George_Allanson-Winn,_1st_Baron_Headley.

Wikisource, 'Adams, Sarah Flower', https://en.wikisource.org/wiki/Adams,_Sarah_Flower_(DNB00) (accessed 16 October 2018),

Willard, **Frances E.** (1887) 'Frances Power Cobbe', *The Inquirer* 1887: 634.

Williams, **John** (2004) 'Thomas, Lucy', *Oxford Dictionary of National Biography,* www.oxforddnb.com (accessed 12 November 2018).

Wilson, **Norah** (1995) Obituary of Dorothy Lloyd in Judy Hague (ed.) (2008).

Wood, **H.T.**, revised by Ralph Harrington (2015) 'Adams, William Bridges', *Oxford Dictionary of National Biography* (accessed 16 October 2018).

Woodhouse, **Annie Beard** (1930) *A Visit to the Unitarians of the Khasi Hills, Assam, India,* London: General Assembly of Unitarian & Free Christian Churches.

Wright, **Jonathan Jeffrey** (2012) *The 'Natural Leaders' and their World: Politics, Culture and Society in Belfast c.1801–1832,* Liverpool: Liverpool University Press.

Wykes, **David** (1988) 'Dissenting academy or Unitarian seminary? Manchester College at York (1803–1840)', *Transactions of the Unitarian Historical Society* 19: 113–29.

Yates, **Gayle Graham** (ed.) (1985) *Harriet Martineau on Women*, New Brunswick: Rutgers University Press.

Yeldham, **Charlotte** (1997) *Margaret Gillies RWS, Unitarian Painter of Mind and Emotion 1803–1887*, Lampeter: Edwin Mellen Press.

Yeldham, **Charlotte** (2004) 'Gillies, Margaret', *Oxford Dictionary of National Biography*, www.oxforddnb.com (accessed 4 October 2018).

3 Obituaries (unattributed)

(**Mrs Bernard Allen [Rose Allen]**) *The Inquirer*, 3 August 1946.

(**Allingham, Helen**) *The Times*, 30 September 1926.

(**Allingham, Helen**) *The Inquirer*, 2 October 1926: 619.

(**Ashton, Margaret**) *The Inquirer*, 23 October 1937: 521.

(**Ashton, Margaret**) *The Manchester Guardian*, 16 October 1937.

(**Broadrick, Mrs T.B.**) *The Christian Life*, 1925: 245.

(**Carpenter Mary**) *The Christian Life*, 1877: 399–400.

(**Carpenter, Mary**) *The Inquirer*, 1877: 552.

(**Carpenter, Mary**) *The Christian Life*, 1878: 128.

(**Duffin, Ruth**) *The Inquirer*, 6 July 1968: 3.

(**Higginson, Emily**) *The Inquirer*, 1895: 69.

(**Higginson, Emily**) *The Christian Life*, 26 January 1895: 46.

(**Jones, Mrs R.J.**) *The Inquirer*, 1899: 167.

(**Martin, Henrietta Mitchel**) *Loughorne Times*, 3 September 2010, reproducing unidentified press article (now offline).

(**Mellone, Dora**) *The Inquirer*, 2 July 1927.

(**Mewhort, Grace**) *The Inquirer*, 18 January 1975: 4.

(**Phillips, Helen**) *The Inquirer*, 1961: 192.

(**Pirrie, Margaret Montgomery**) *The Inquirer*, 29 June 1953: 321.

('**Allen Raine**' [Mrs Beynon Puddicombe]) *The Inquirer*, 27 June 1908: 403.

(**Rees, Mary**) *The Cambrian*, 21 November 1829: 3.

(**Rees, Mary**) *The Christian Reformer, or, New Evangelical Miscellany*, 1829: 15: 528–9.

(**Tagart, Edward**) *The Inquirer*, 1858: 684.

(**Tagart, Helen**) *The Inquirer* 1871: 193.

(**Tagart, M. Lucy**) *The Inquirer*, 1925: 359.

(**Taylor, Clementia**) *The Inquirer*, 18 April 1908: 245–6.

Index